CHAMPIONS

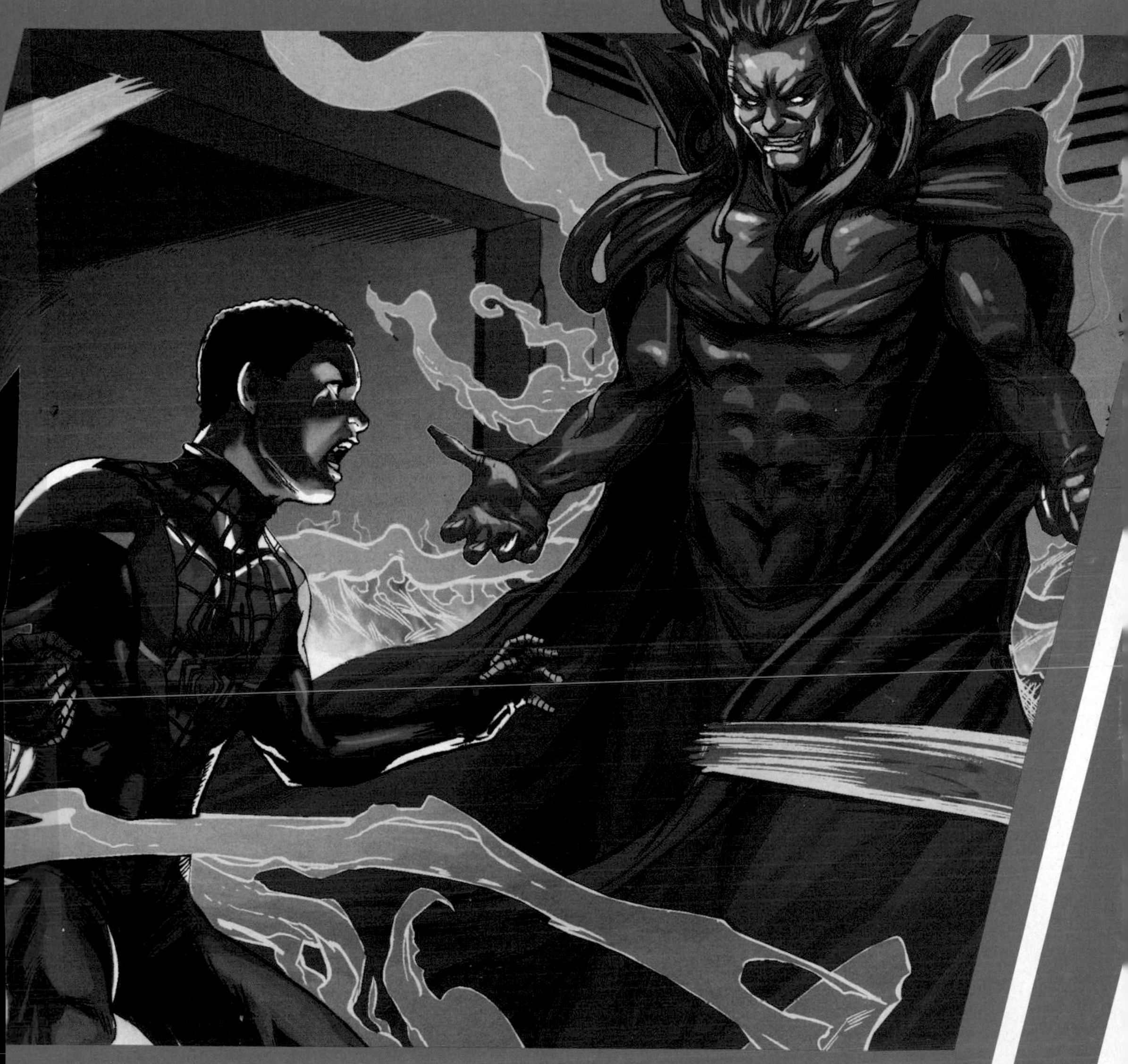

BEAT THE DEVIL

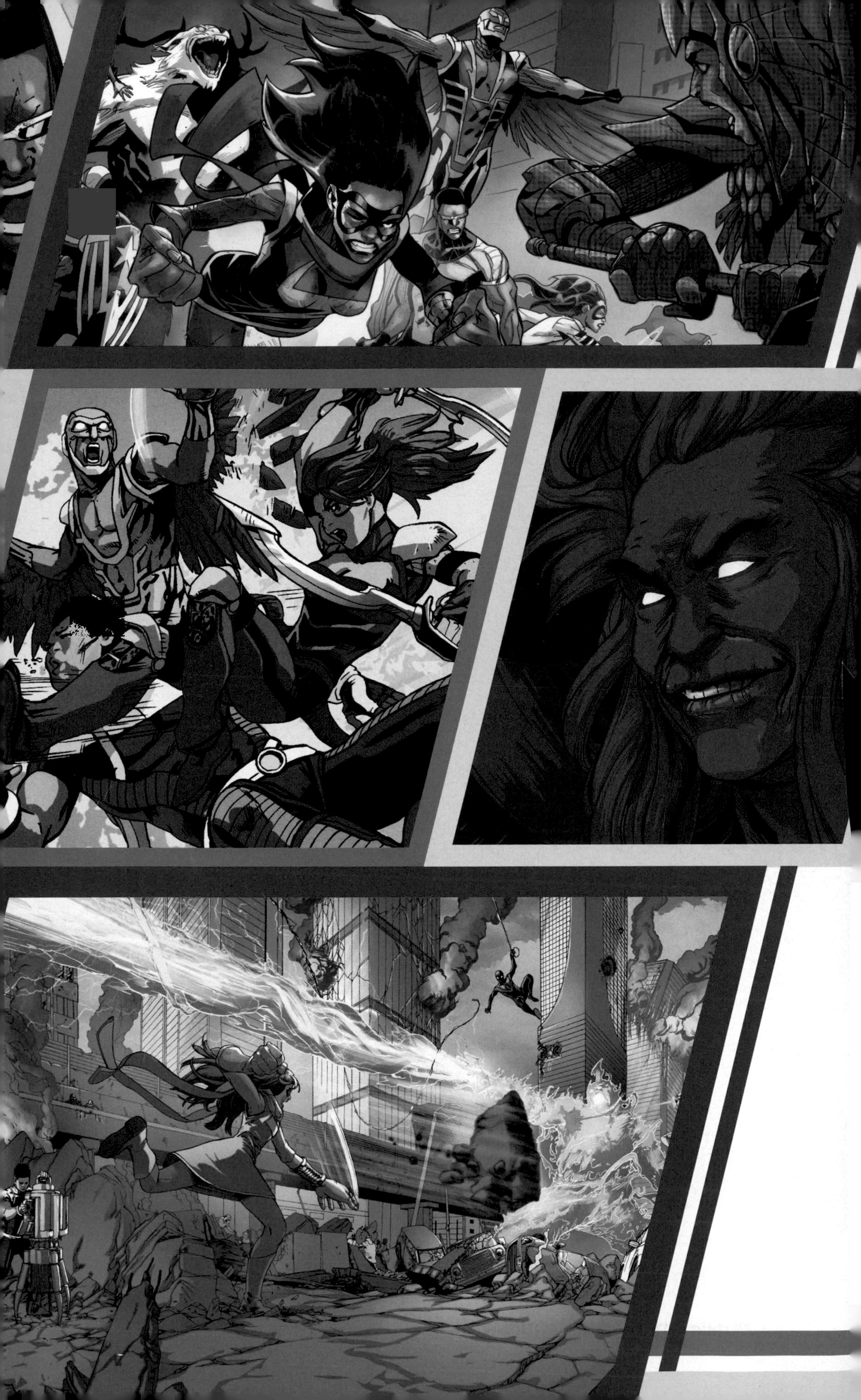

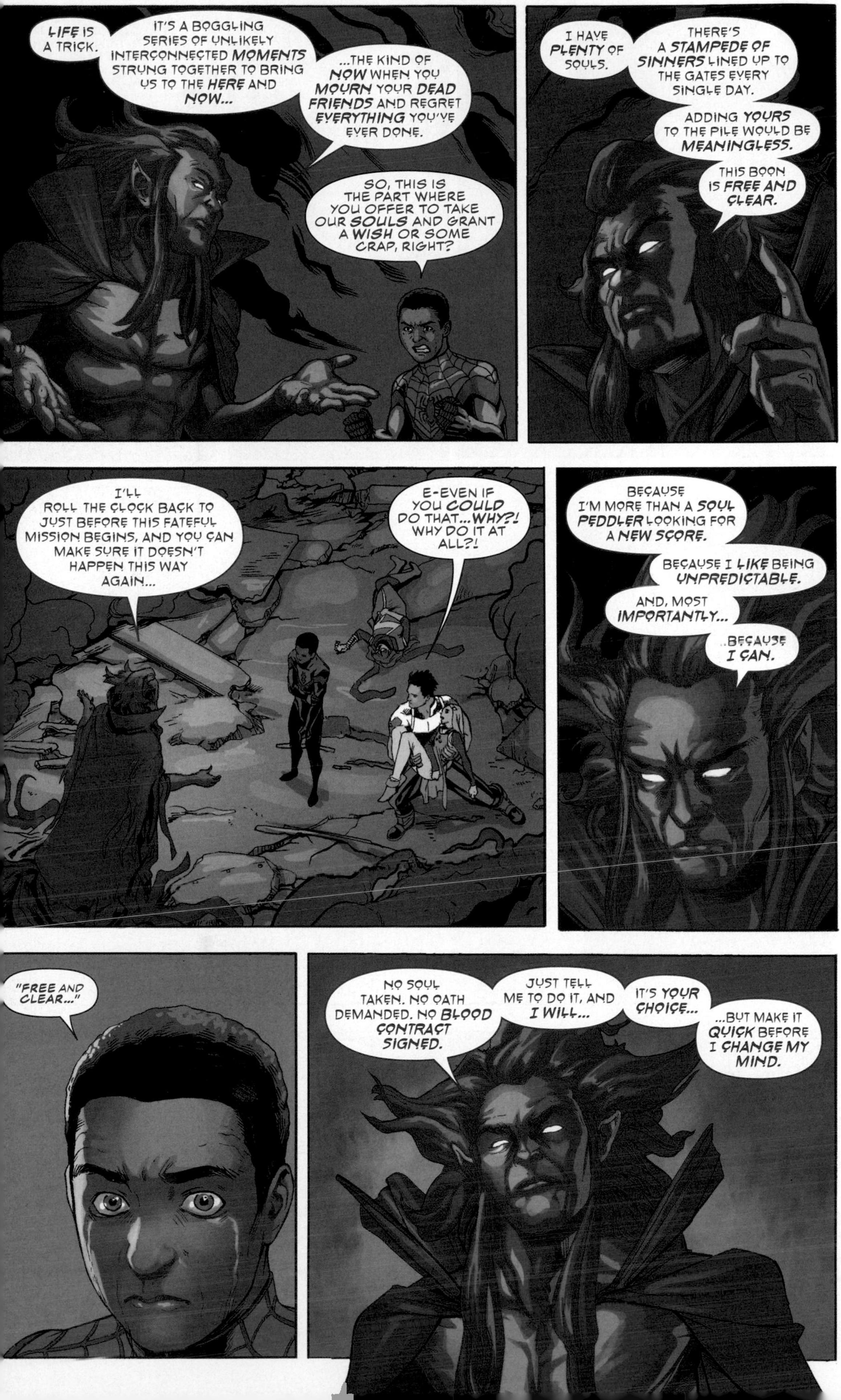
LIFE IS A TRICK.
IT'S A BOGGLING SERIES OF UNLIKELY INTERCONNECTED MOMENTS STRUNG TOGETHER TO BRING US TO THE HERE AND NOW...
...THE KIND OF NOW WHEN YOU MOURN YOUR DEAD FRIENDS AND REGRET EVERYTHING YOU'VE EVER DONE.
SO, THIS IS THE PART WHERE YOU OFFER TO TAKE OUR SOULS AND GRANT A WISH OR SOME CRAP, RIGHT?
I HAVE PLENTY OF SOULS.
THERE'S A STAMPEDE OF SINNERS LINED UP TO THE GATES EVERY SINGLE DAY.
ADDING YOURS TO THE PILE WOULD BE MEANINGLESS.
THIS BOON IS FREE AND CLEAR.
I'LL ROLL THE CLOCK BACK TO JUST BEFORE THIS FATEFUL MISSION BEGINS, AND YOU CAN MAKE SURE IT DOESN'T HAPPEN THIS WAY AGAIN...
E-EVEN IF YOU COULD DO THAT...WHY?! WHY DO IT AT ALL?!
BECAUSE I'M MORE THAN A SOUL PEDDLER LOOKING FOR A NEW SCORE.
BECAUSE I LIKE BEING UNPREDICTABLE.
AND, MOST IMPORTANTLY...
...BECAUSE I CAN.
"FREE AND CLEAR..."
NO SOUL TAKEN. NO OATH DEMANDED. NO BLOOD CONTRACT SIGNED.
JUST TELL ME TO DO IT, AND I WILL...
IT'S YOUR CHOICE...
...BUT MAKE IT QUICK BEFORE I CHANGE MY MIND.

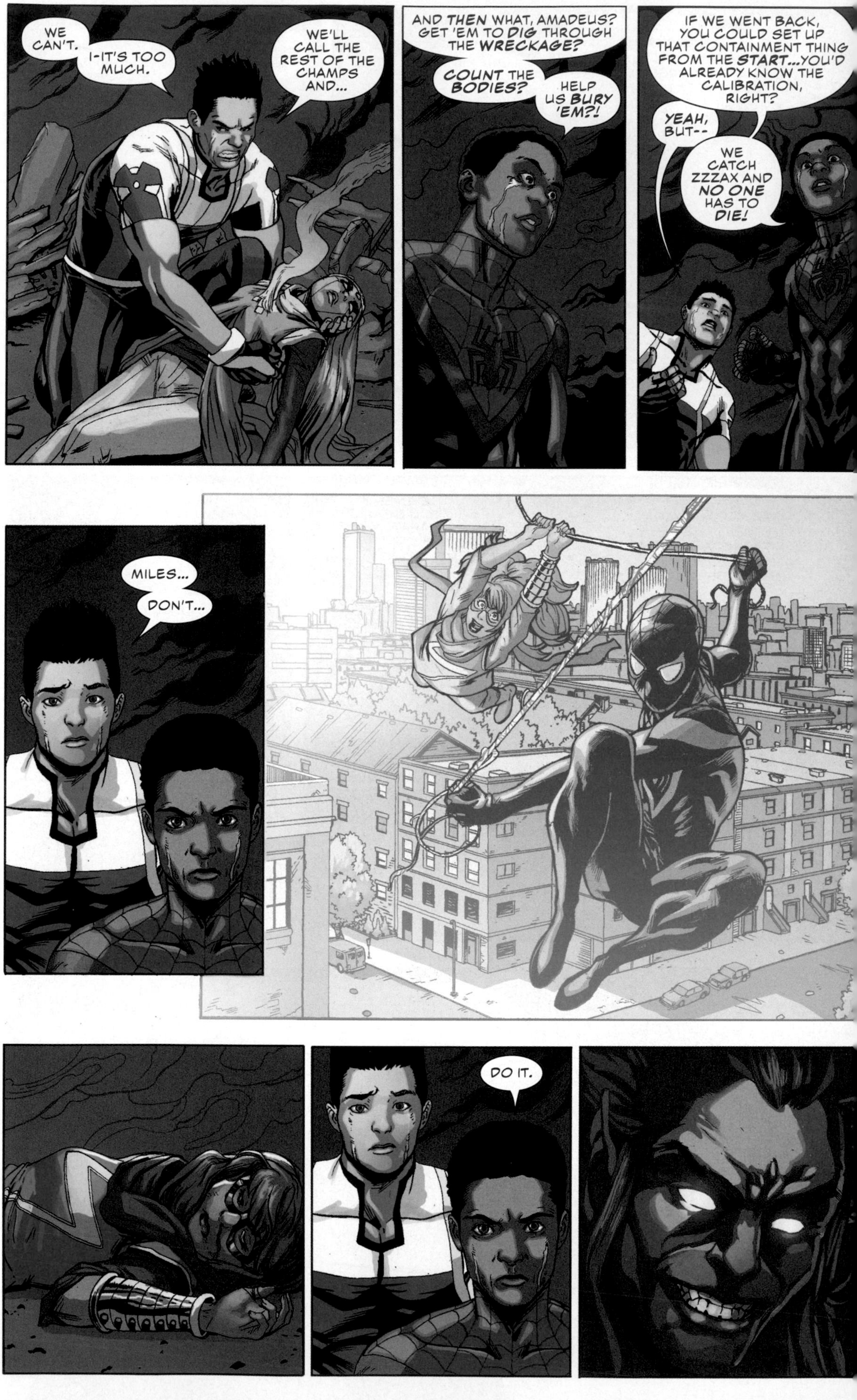
WE CAN'T.
I-IT'S TOO MUCH.
WE'LL CALL THE REST OF THE CHAMPS AND...
AND THEN WHAT, AMADEUS? GET 'EM TO DIG THROUGH THE WRECKAGE?
COUNT THE BODIES?
HELP US BURY 'EM?!
IF WE WENT BACK, YOU COULD SET UP THAT CONTAINMENT THING FROM THE START...YOU'D ALREADY KNOW THE CALIBRATION, RIGHT?
YEAH, BUT--
WE CATCH ZZZAX AND NO ONE HAS TO DIE!
MILES...
DON'T...
DO IT.

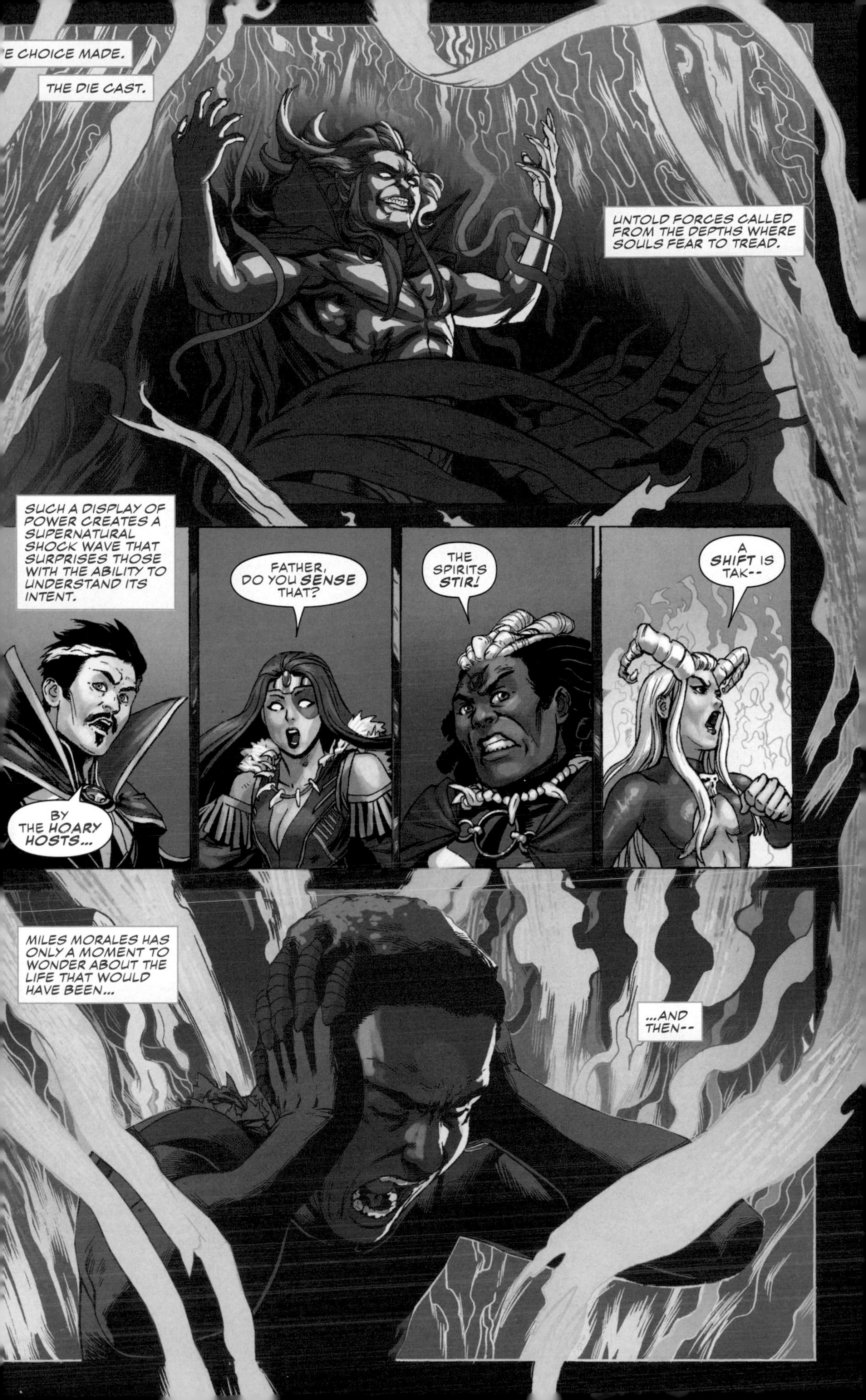
E CHOICE MADE.
THE DIE CAST.
UNTOLD FORCES CALLED FROM THE DEPTHS WHERE SOULS FEAR TO TREAD.
SUCH A DISPLAY OF POWER CREATES A SUPERNATURAL SHOCK WAVE THAT SURPRISES THOSE WITH THE ABILITY TO UNDERSTAND ITS INTENT.
BY THE HOARY HOSTS...
FATHER, DO YOU SENSE THAT?
THE SPIRITS STIR!
A SHIFT IS TAK--
MILES MORALES HAS ONLY A MOMENT TO WONDER ABOUT THE LIFE THAT WOULD HAVE BEEN...
...AND THEN--

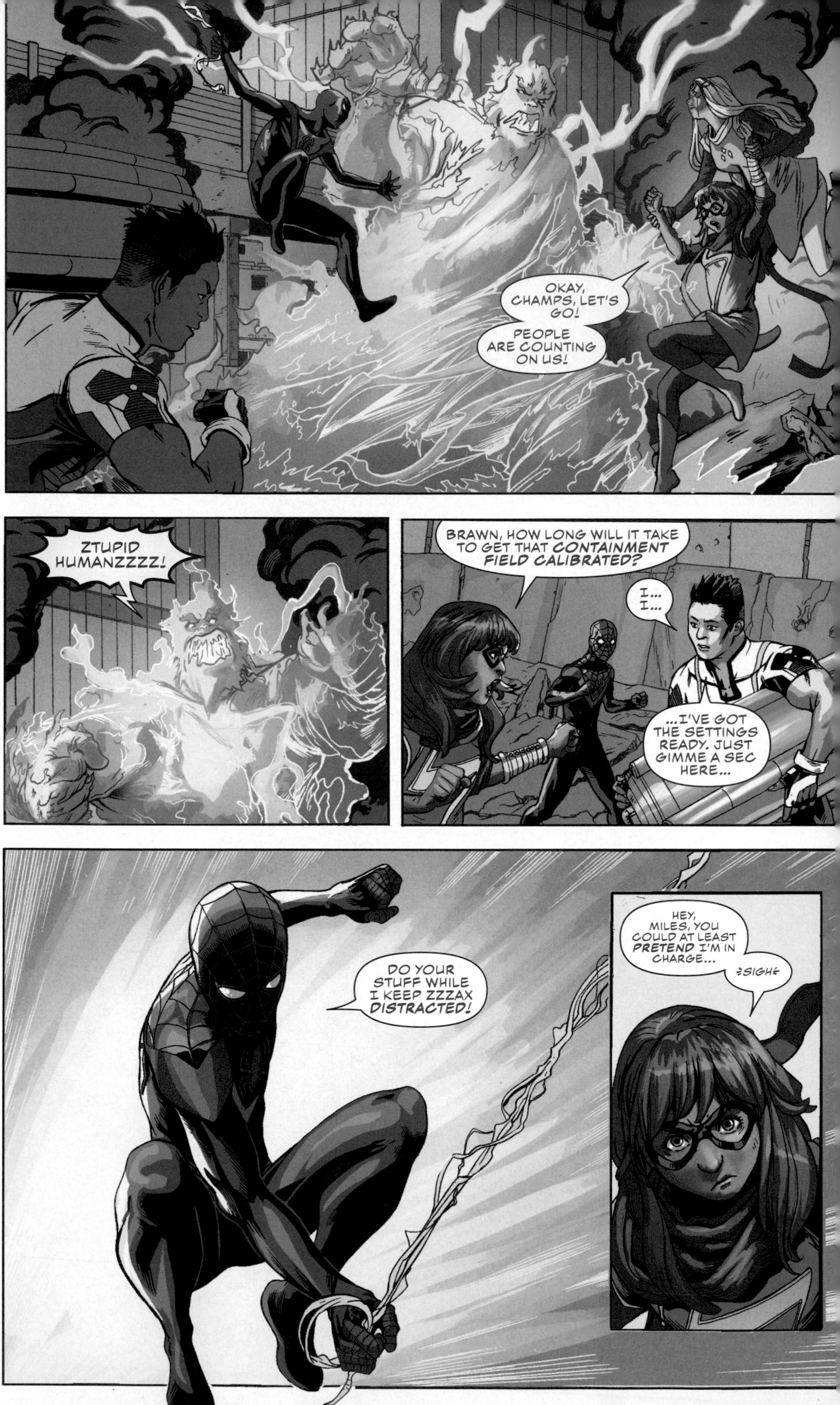
OKAY, CHAMPS, LET'S GO!
PEOPLE ARE COUNTING ON US!
ZTUPID HUMANZZZZ!
BRAWN, HOW LONG WILL IT TAKE TO GET THAT **CONTAINMENT FIELD CALIBRATED?**
I... I...
...I'VE GOT THE SETTINGS READY. JUST GIMME A SEC HERE...
DO YOUR STUFF WHILE I KEEP ZZZAX **DISTRACTED!**
HEY, MILES, YOU COULD AT LEAST **PRETEND** I'M IN CHARGE...
SIGH

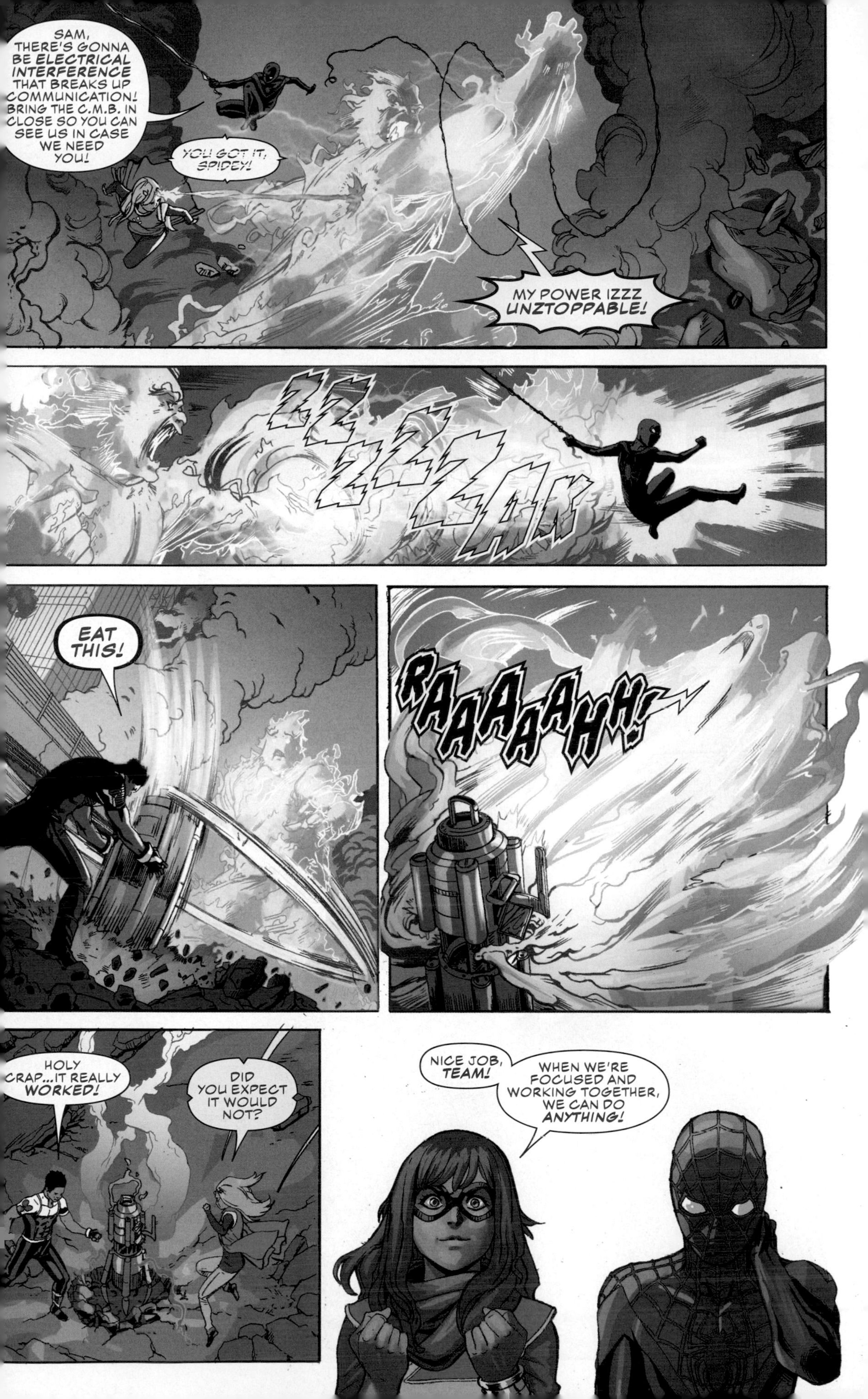
SAM, THERE'S GONNA BE ELECTRICAL INTERFERENCE THAT BREAKS UP COMMUNICATION! BRING THE C.M.B. IN CLOSE SO YOU CAN SEE US IN CASE WE NEED YOU!
YOU GOT IT, SPIDEY!
MY POWER IZZZ UNZTOPPABLE!
ZZZZAK
EAT THIS!
RAAAAAHH!
HOLY CRAP...IT REALLY WORKED!
DID YOU EXPECT IT WOULD NOT?
NICE JOB, TEAM!
WHEN WE'RE FOCUSED AND WORKING TOGETHER, WE CAN DO ANYTHING!

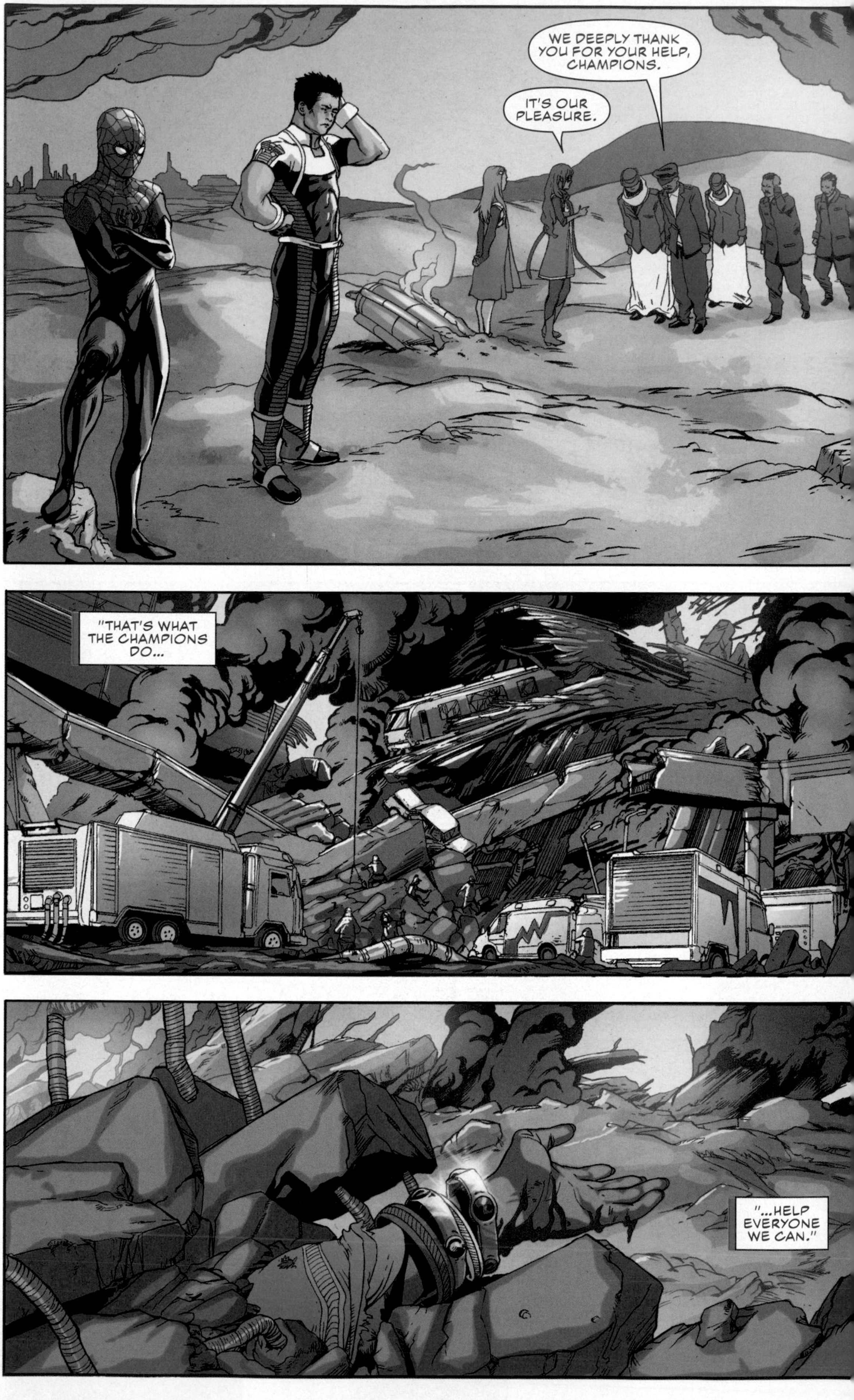
WE DEEPLY THANK YOU FOR YOUR HELP, CHAMPIONS.
IT'S OUR PLEASURE.
"THAT'S WHAT THE CHAMPIONS DO...
"...HELP EVERYONE WE CAN."

3

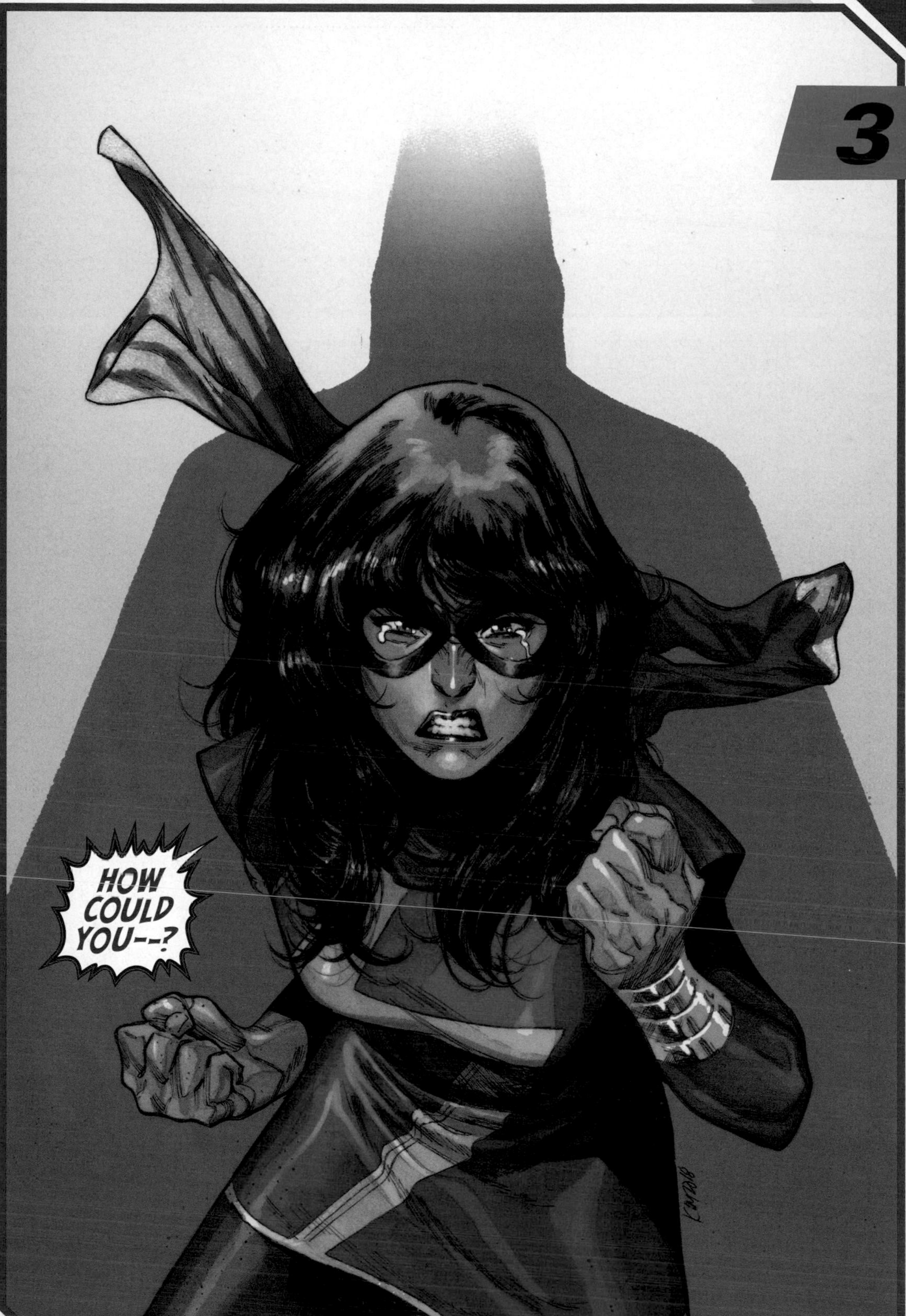
HOW COULD YOU--?

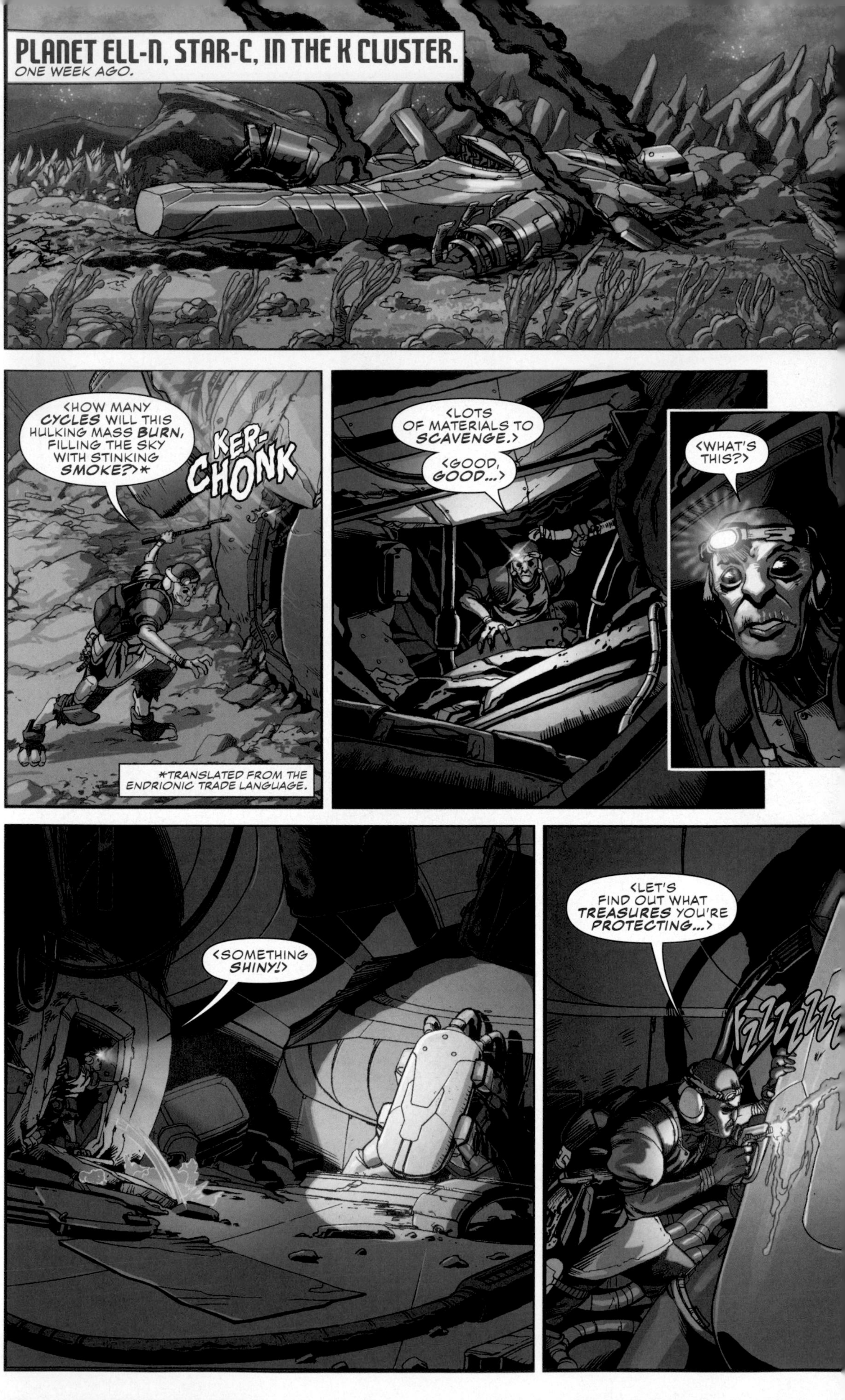
PLANET ELL-N, STAR-C, IN THE K CLUSTER.
ONE WEEK AGO.
<HOW MANY CYCLES WILL THIS HULKING MASS BURN, FILLING THE SKY WITH STINKING SMOKE?>*
KER-CHONK
*TRANSLATED FROM THE ENDRIONIC TRADE LANGUAGE.
<LOTS OF MATERIALS TO SCAVENGE.>
<GOOD, GOOD...>
<WHAT'S THIS?>
<SOMETHING SHINY!>
<LET'S FIND OUT WHAT TREASURES YOU'RE PROTECTING...>
FZZZZZZZ

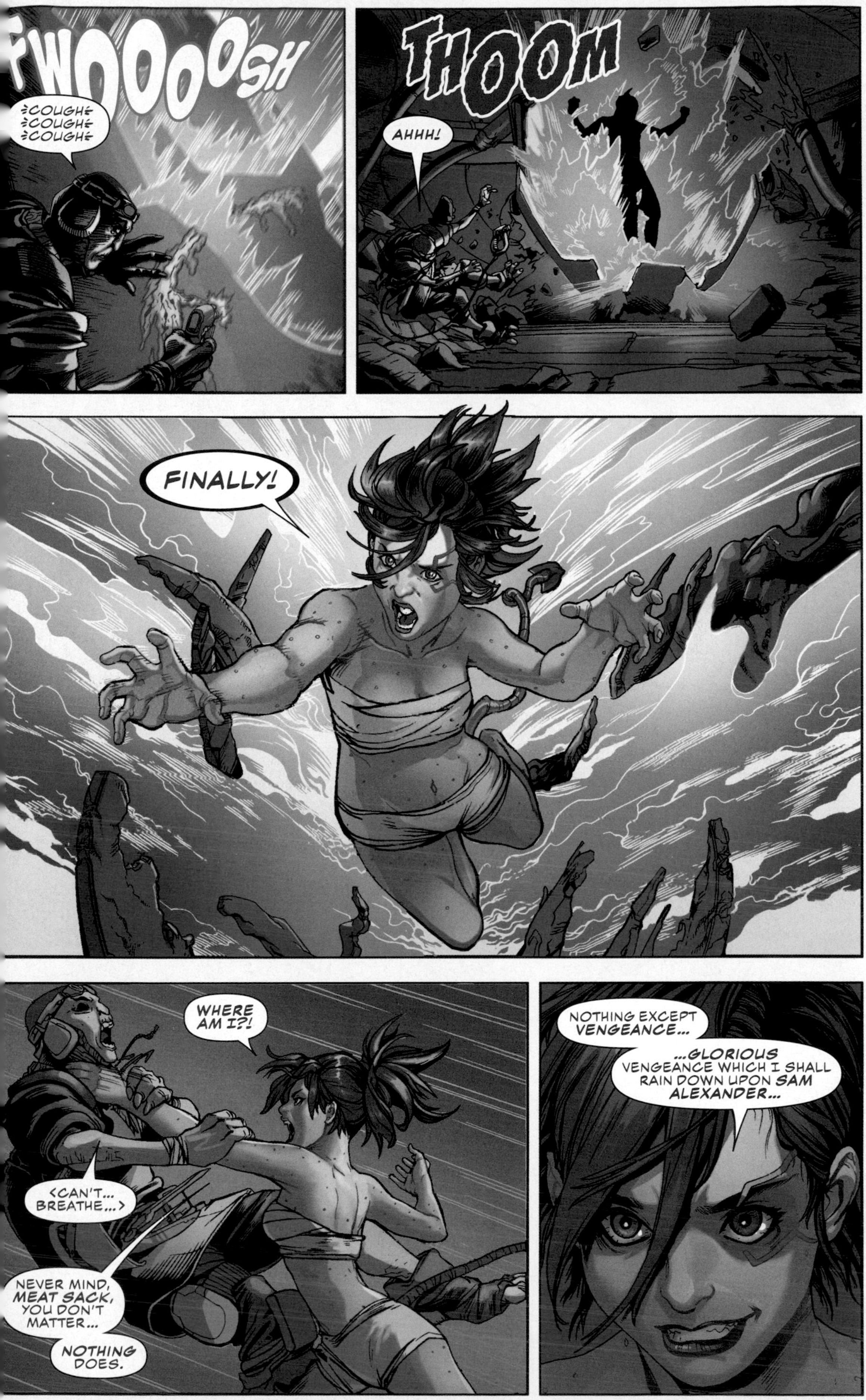
FWOOOOOSH
COUGH
COUGH
COUGH
THOOM
AHHH!
FINALLY!
WHERE AM I?!
<CAN'T... BREATHE...>
NEVER MIND, MEAT SACK, YOU DON'T MATTER...
NOTHING DOES.
NOTHING EXCEPT VENGEANCE...
...GLORIOUS VENGEANCE WHICH I SHALL RAIN DOWN UPON SAM ALEXANDER...

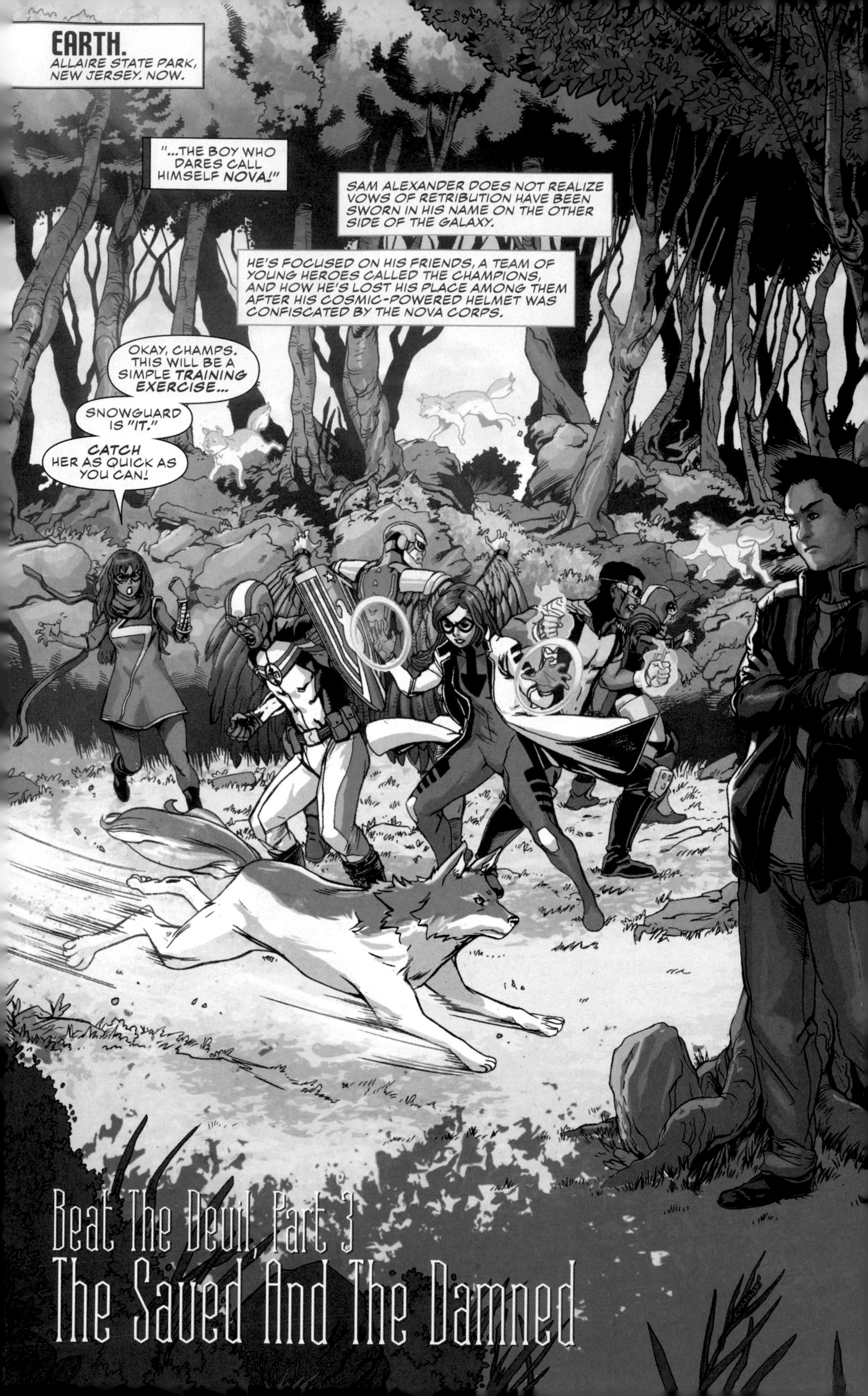
EARTH.
ALLAIRE STATE PARK, NEW JERSEY. NOW.
"...THE BOY WHO DARES CALL HIMSELF NOVA!"
SAM ALEXANDER DOES NOT REALIZE VOWS OF RETRIBUTION HAVE BEEN SWORN IN HIS NAME ON THE OTHER SIDE OF THE GALAXY.
HE'S FOCUSED ON HIS FRIENDS, A TEAM OF YOUNG HEROES CALLED THE CHAMPIONS, AND HOW HE'S LOST HIS PLACE AMONG THEM AFTER HIS COSMIC-POWERED HELMET WAS CONFISCATED BY THE NOVA CORPS.
OKAY, CHAMPS. THIS WILL BE A SIMPLE TRAINING EXERCISE...
SNOWGUARD IS "IT."
CATCH HER AS QUICK AS YOU CAN!
Beat The Devil, Part 3
The Saved And The Damned

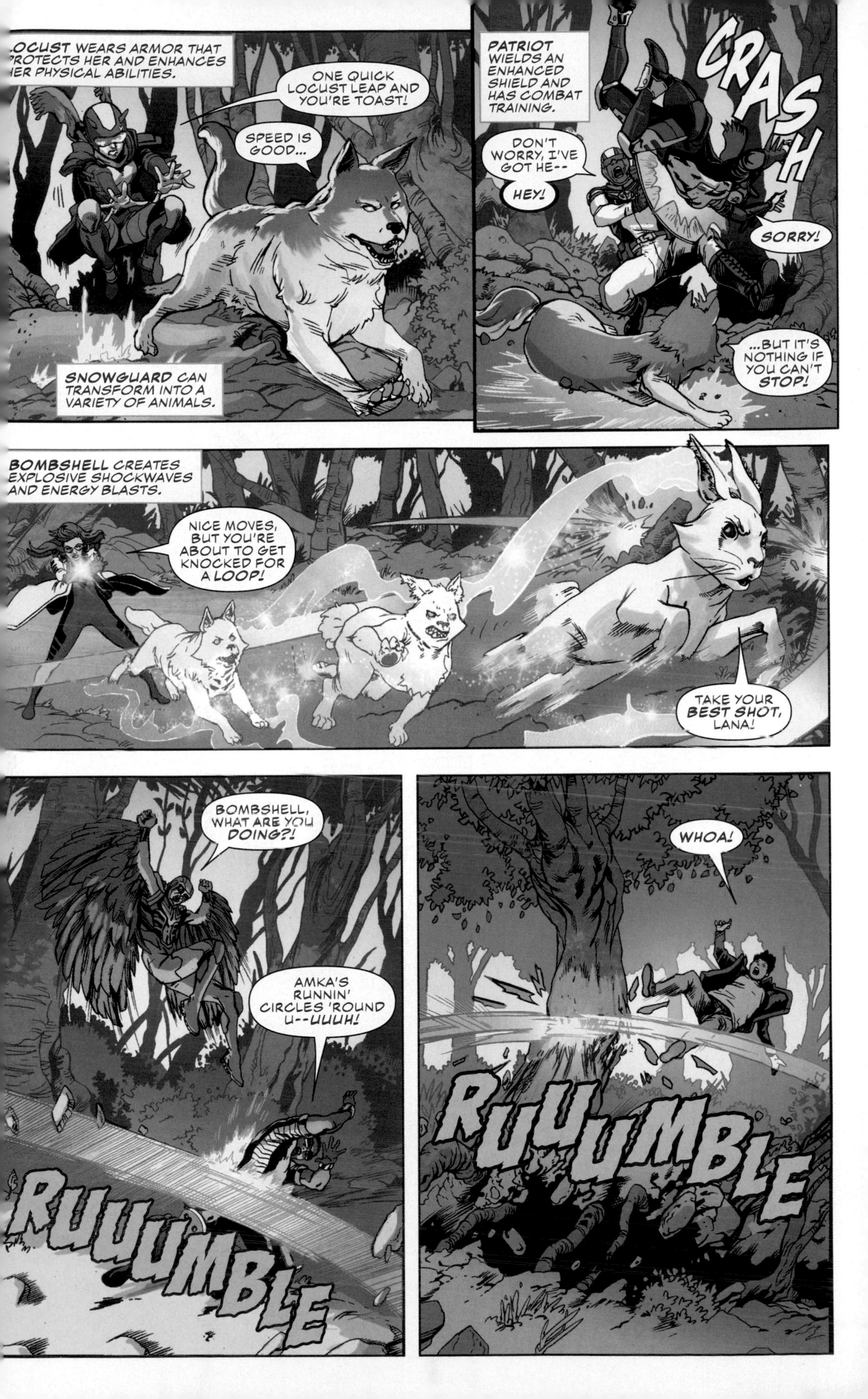
LOCUST WEARS ARMOR THAT PROTECTS HER AND ENHANCES HER PHYSICAL ABILITIES.
ONE QUICK LOCUST LEAP AND YOU'RE TOAST!
SPEED IS GOOD...
SNOWGUARD CAN TRANSFORM INTO A VARIETY OF ANIMALS.
PATRIOT WIELDS AN ENHANCED SHIELD AND HAS COMBAT TRAINING.
CRASH
DON'T WORRY, I'VE GOT HE--
HEY!
SORRY!
...BUT IT'S NOTHING IF YOU CAN'T STOP!
BOMBSHELL CREATES EXPLOSIVE SHOCKWAVES AND ENERGY BLASTS.
NICE MOVES, BUT YOU'RE ABOUT TO GET KNOCKED FOR A LOOP!
TAKE YOUR BEST SHOT, LANA!
BOMBSHELL, WHAT ARE YOU DOING?!
AMKA'S RUNNIN' CIRCLES 'ROUND U--UUUH!
RUUUMBLE
WHOA!
RUUUMBLE

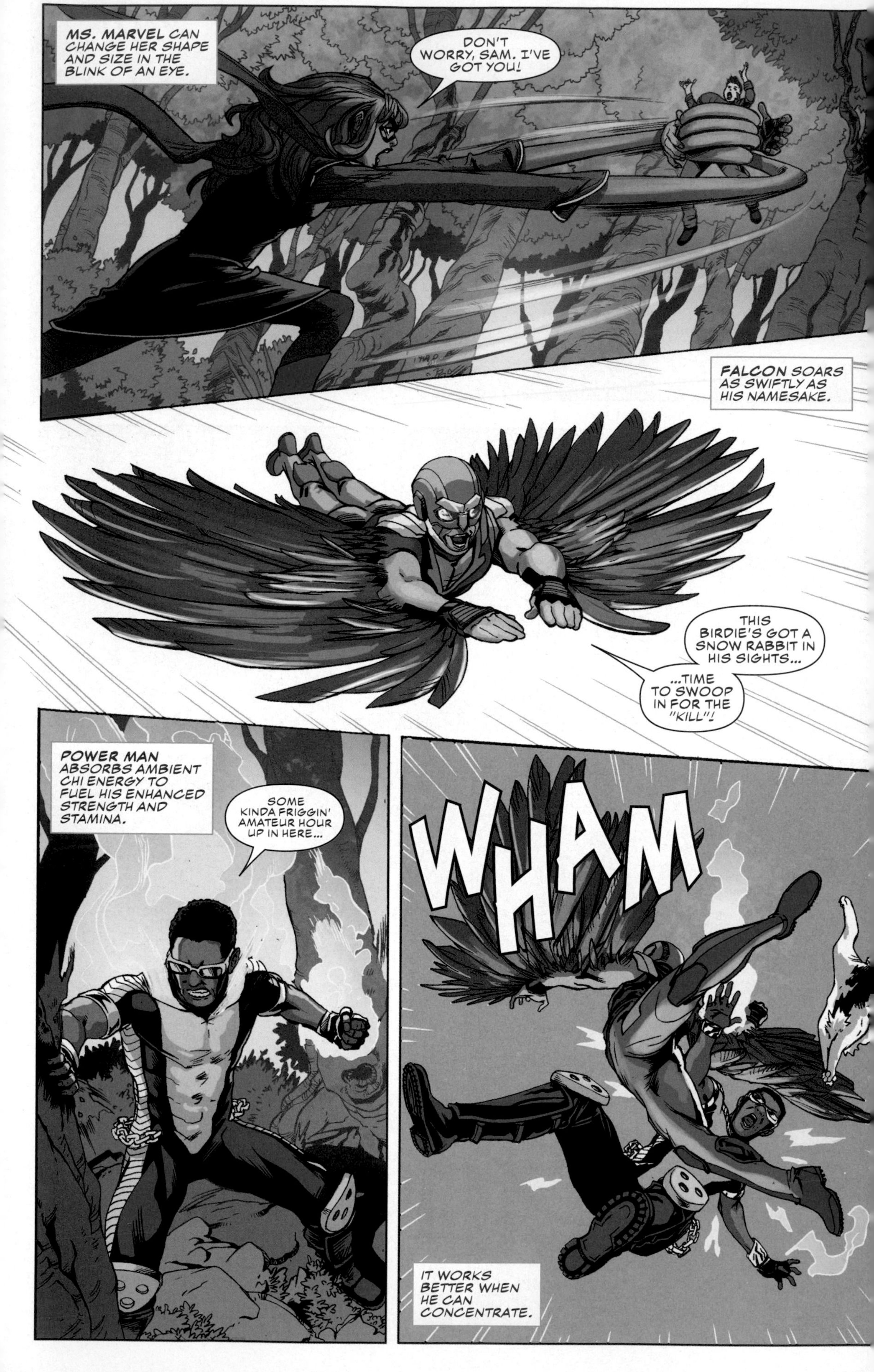
MS. MARVEL CAN CHANGE HER SHAPE AND SIZE IN THE BLINK OF AN EYE.
DON'T WORRY, SAM. I'VE GOT YOU!
FALCON SOARS AS SWIFTLY AS HIS NAMESAKE.
THIS BIRDIE'S GOT A SNOW RABBIT IN HIS SIGHTS...
...TIME TO SWOOP IN FOR THE "KILL"!
POWER MAN ABSORBS AMBIENT CHI ENERGY TO FUEL HIS ENHANCED STRENGTH AND STAMINA.
SOME KINDA FRIGGIN' AMATEUR HOUR UP IN HERE...
WHAM
IT WORKS BETTER WHEN HE CAN CONCENTRATE.

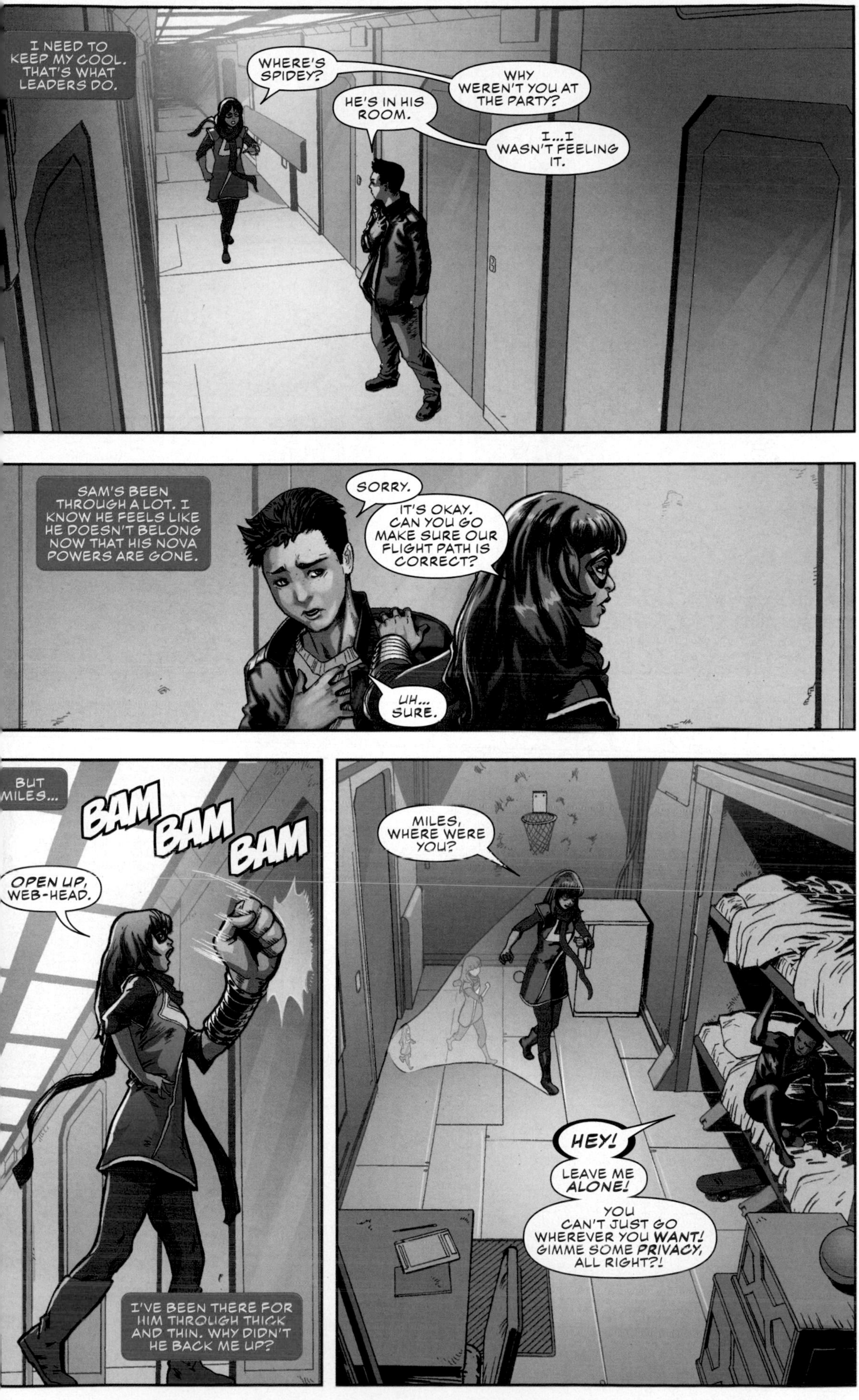
I NEED TO KEEP MY COOL. THAT'S WHAT LEADERS DO.
WHERE'S SPIDEY?
WHY WEREN'T YOU AT THE PARTY?
HE'S IN HIS ROOM.
I...I WASN'T FEELING IT.
SAM'S BEEN THROUGH A LOT. I KNOW HE FEELS LIKE HE DOESN'T BELONG NOW THAT HIS NOVA POWERS ARE GONE.
SORRY.
IT'S OKAY. CAN YOU GO MAKE SURE OUR FLIGHT PATH IS CORRECT?
UH... SURE.
BUT MILES...
BAM BAM BAM
OPEN UP, WEB-HEAD.
I'VE BEEN THERE FOR HIM THROUGH THICK AND THIN. WHY DIDN'T HE BACK ME UP?
MILES, WHERE WERE YOU?
HEY!
LEAVE ME ALONE!
YOU CAN'T JUST GO WHEREVER YOU WANT! GIMME SOME PRIVACY, ALL RIGHT?!

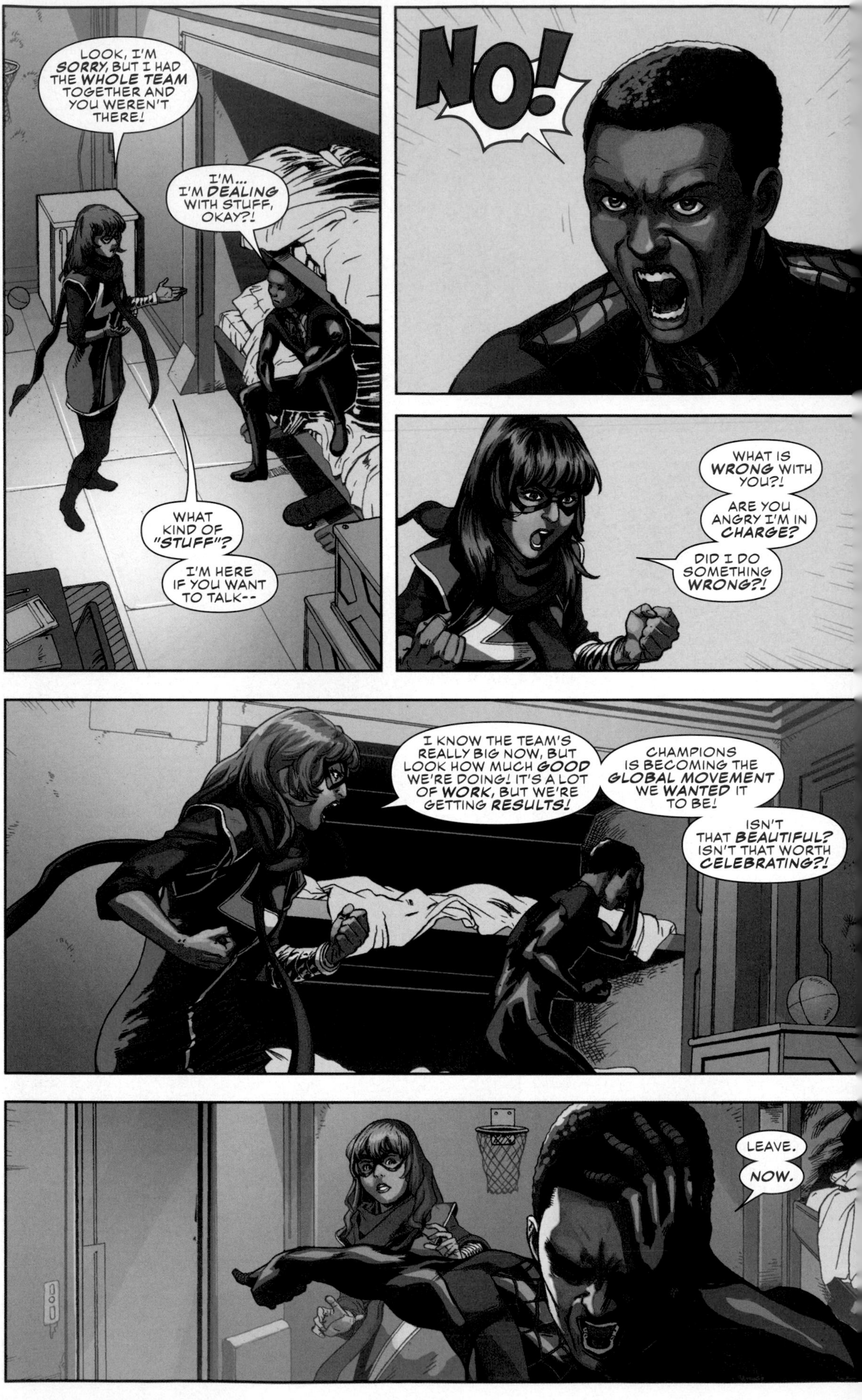
LOOK, I'M SORRY, BUT I HAD THE WHOLE TEAM TOGETHER AND YOU WEREN'T THERE!
I'M... I'M DEALING WITH STUFF, OKAY?!
WHAT KIND OF "STUFF"?
I'M HERE IF YOU WANT TO TALK--
NO!
WHAT IS WRONG WITH YOU?!
ARE YOU ANGRY I'M IN CHARGE?
DID I DO SOMETHING WRONG?!
I KNOW THE TEAM'S REALLY BIG NOW, BUT LOOK HOW MUCH GOOD WE'RE DOING! IT'S A LOT OF WORK, BUT WE'RE GETTING RESULTS!
CHAMPIONS IS BECOMING THE GLOBAL MOVEMENT WE WANTED IT TO BE!
ISN'T THAT BEAUTIFUL? ISN'T THAT WORTH CELEBRATING?!
LEAVE.
NOW.

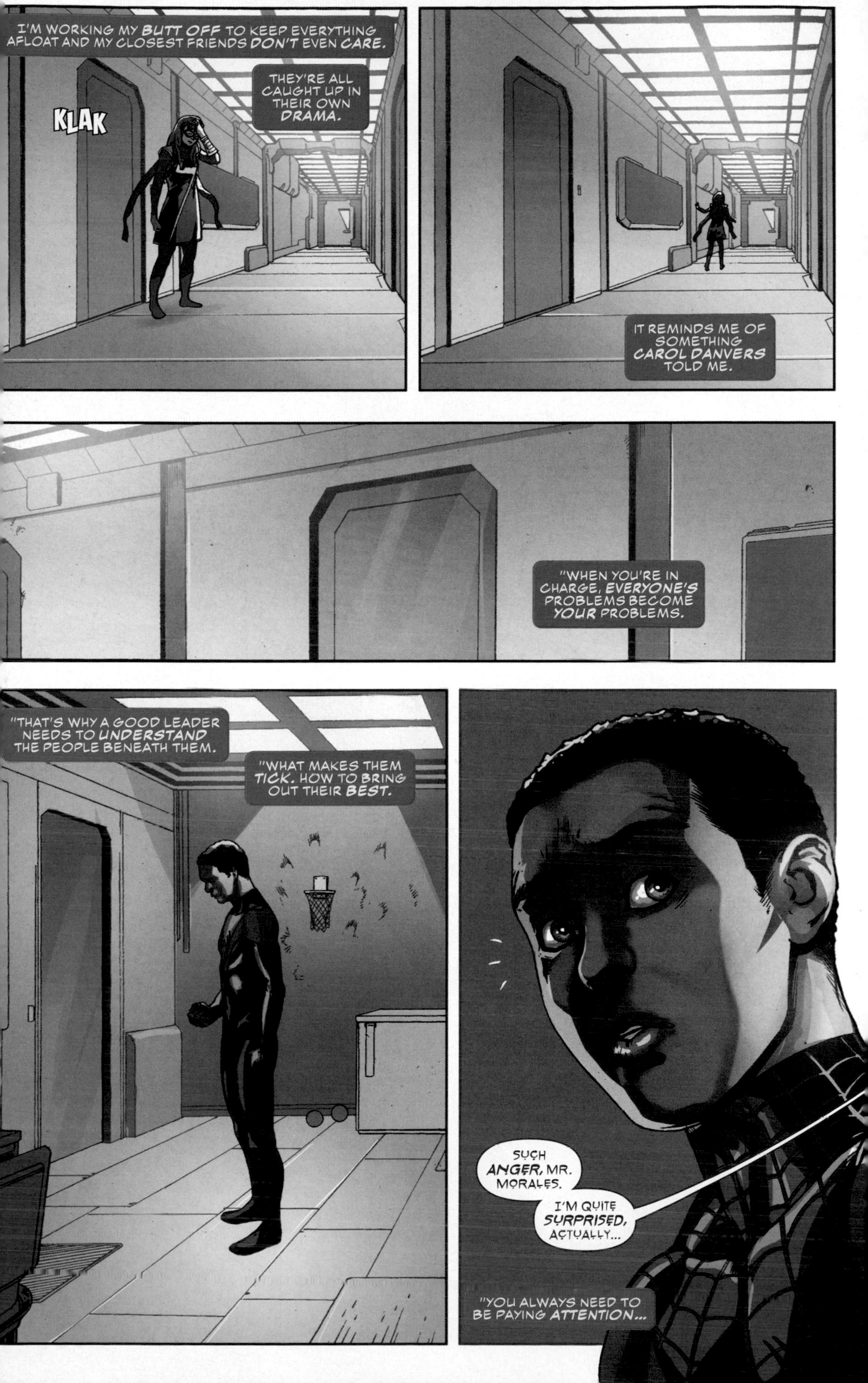
I'M WORKING MY BUTT OFF TO KEEP EVERYTHING AFLOAT AND MY CLOSEST FRIENDS DON'T EVEN CARE.
KLAK
THEY'RE ALL CAUGHT UP IN THEIR OWN DRAMA.
IT REMINDS ME OF SOMETHING CAROL DANVERS TOLD ME.
"WHEN YOU'RE IN CHARGE, EVERYONE'S PROBLEMS BECOME YOUR PROBLEMS.
"THAT'S WHY A GOOD LEADER NEEDS TO UNDERSTAND THE PEOPLE BENEATH THEM.
"WHAT MAKES THEM TICK. HOW TO BRING OUT THEIR BEST.
SUCH ANGER, MR. MORALES.
I'M QUITE SURPRISED, ACTUALLY...
"YOU ALWAYS NEED TO BE PAYING ATTENTION...

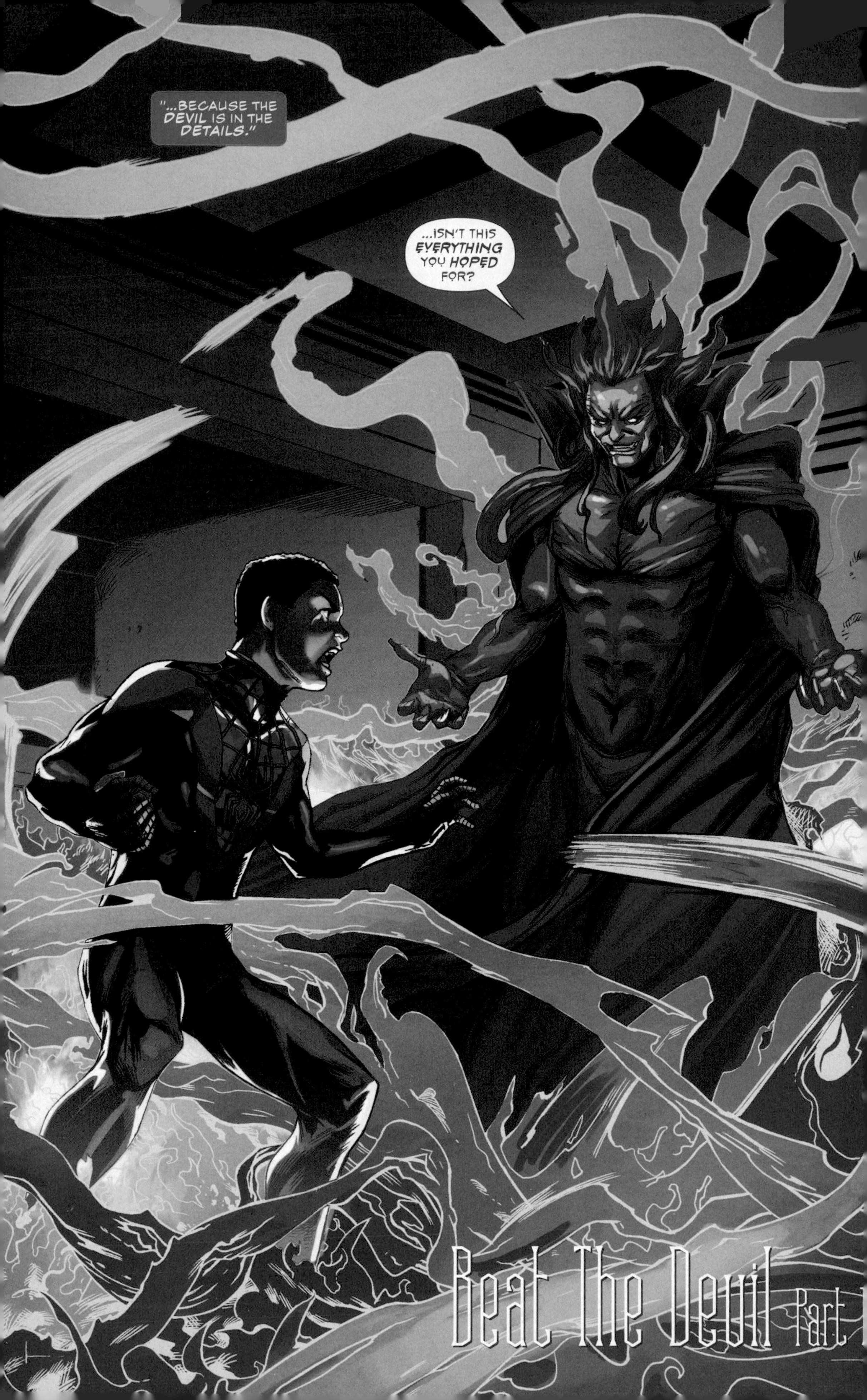
"...BECAUSE THE DEVIL IS IN THE DETAILS."
...ISN'T THIS EVERYTHING YOU HOPED FOR?
Beat The Devil Part 1

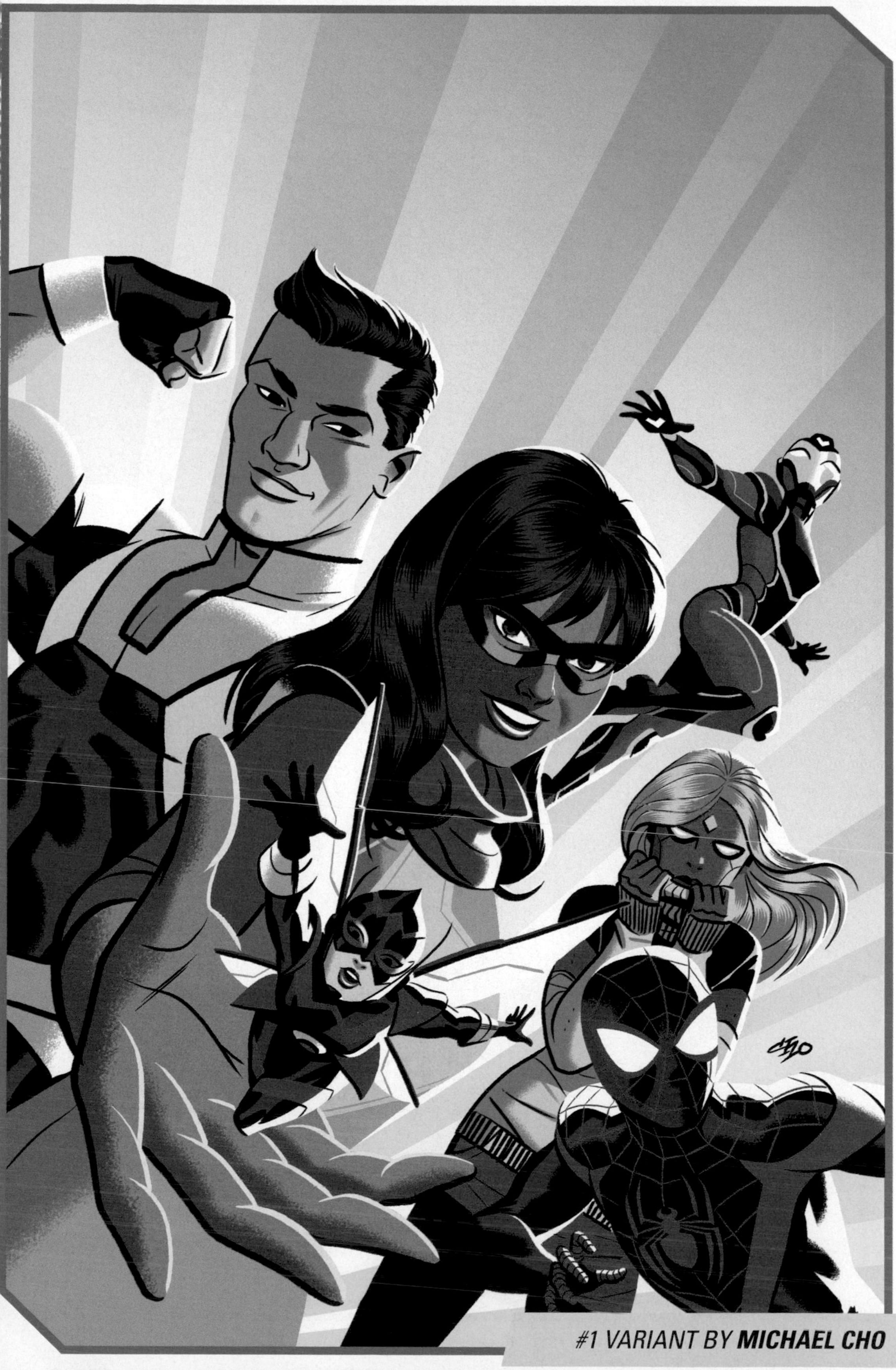

#1 VARIANT BY **MICHAEL CHO**

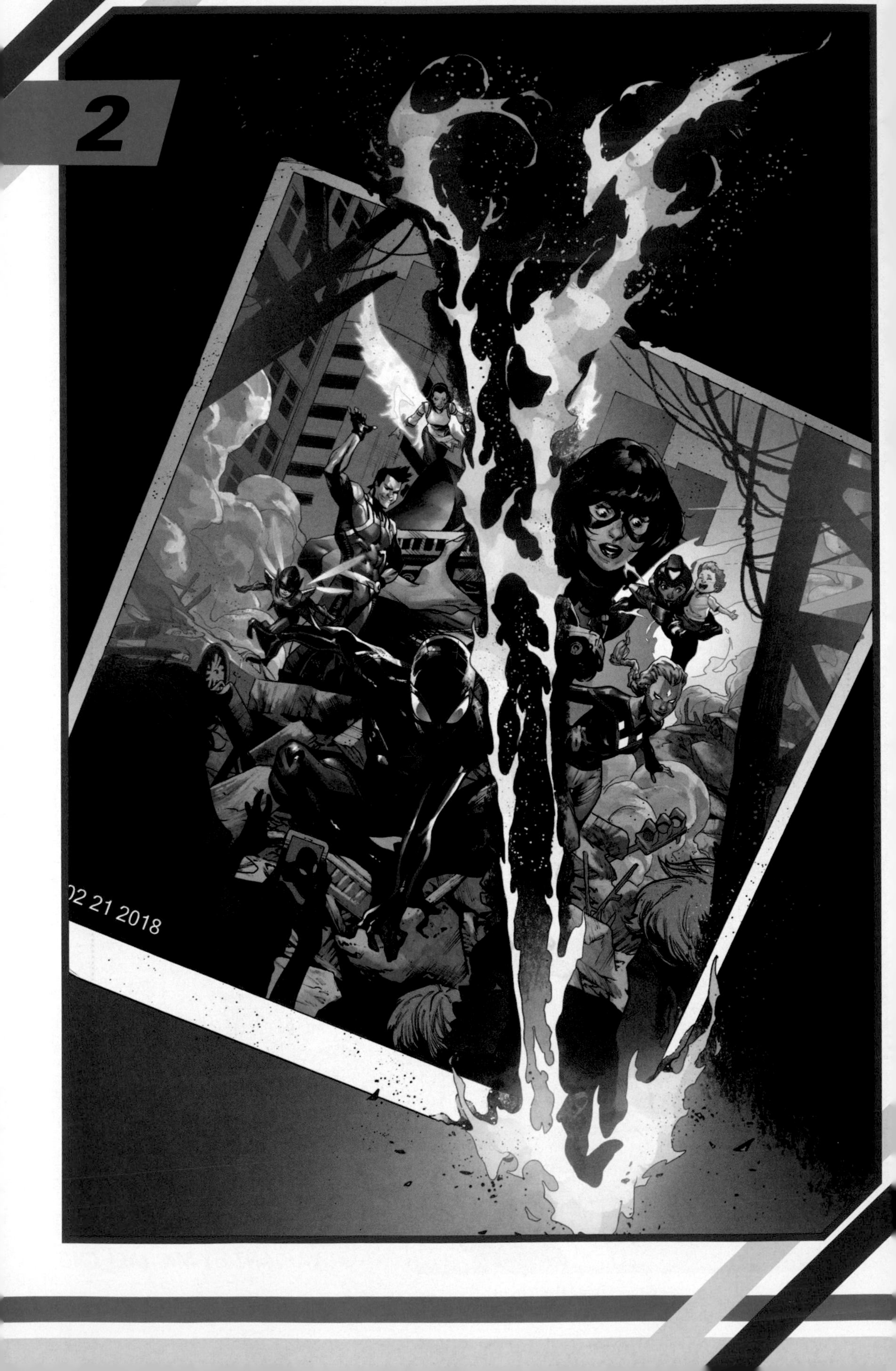
2
02 21 2018

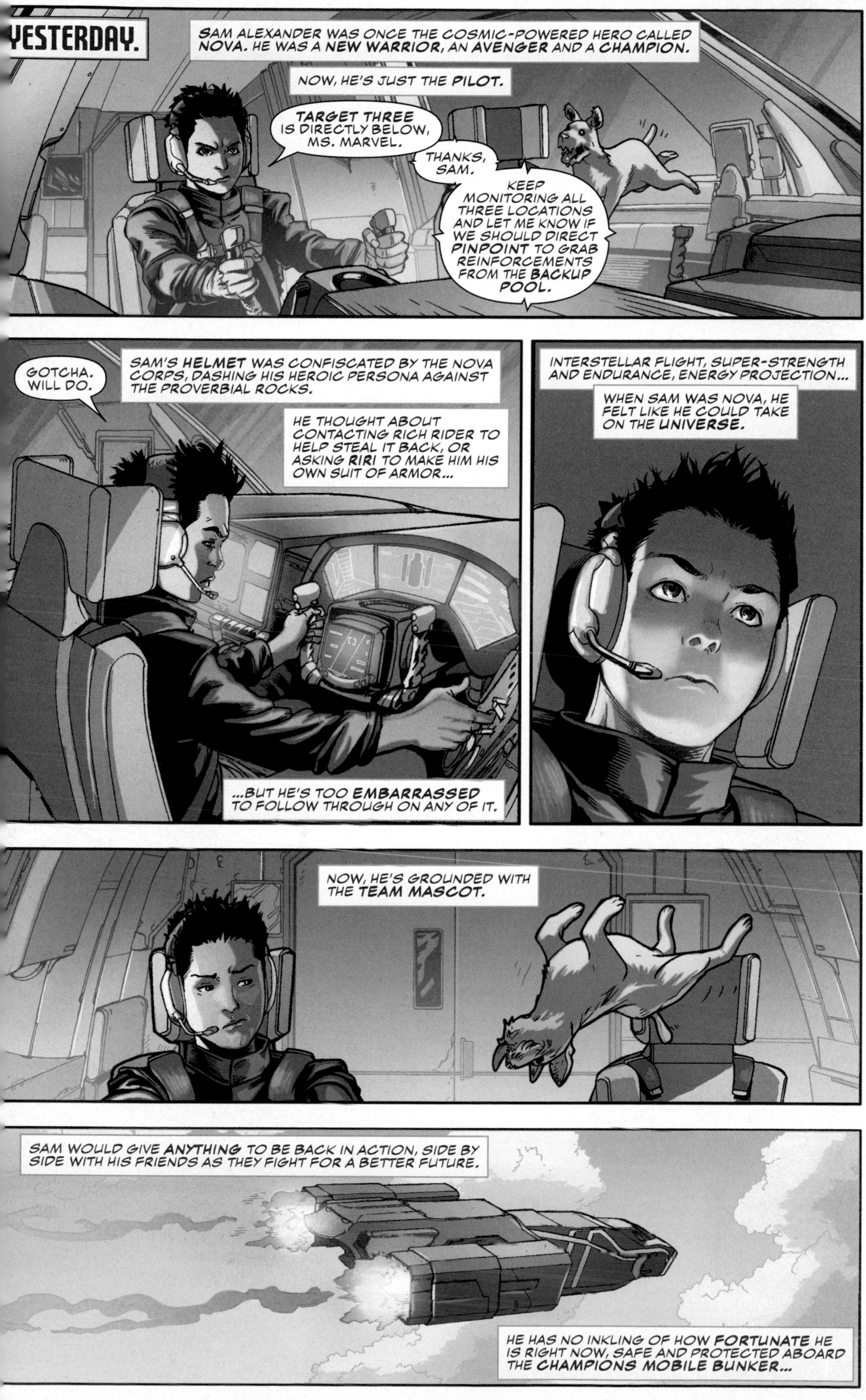
YESTERDAY.
SAM ALEXANDER WAS ONCE THE COSMIC-POWERED HERO CALLED NOVA. HE WAS A NEW WARRIOR, AN AVENGER AND A CHAMPION.
NOW, HE'S JUST THE PILOT.
TARGET THREE IS DIRECTLY BELOW, MS. MARVEL.
THANKS, SAM.
KEEP MONITORING ALL THREE LOCATIONS AND LET ME KNOW IF WE SHOULD DIRECT PINPOINT TO GRAB REINFORCEMENTS FROM THE BACKUP POOL.
GOTCHA. WILL DO.
SAM'S HELMET WAS CONFISCATED BY THE NOVA CORPS, DASHING HIS HEROIC PERSONA AGAINST THE PROVERBIAL ROCKS.
HE THOUGHT ABOUT CONTACTING RICH RIDER TO HELP STEAL IT BACK, OR ASKING RIRI TO MAKE HIM HIS OWN SUIT OF ARMOR...
...BUT HE'S TOO EMBARRASSED TO FOLLOW THROUGH ON ANY OF IT.
INTERSTELLAR FLIGHT, SUPER-STRENGTH AND ENDURANCE, ENERGY PROJECTION...
WHEN SAM WAS NOVA, HE FELT LIKE HE COULD TAKE ON THE UNIVERSE.
NOW, HE'S GROUNDED WITH THE TEAM MASCOT.
SAM WOULD GIVE ANYTHING TO BE BACK IN ACTION, SIDE BY SIDE WITH HIS FRIENDS AS THEY FIGHT FOR A BETTER FUTURE.
HE HAS NO INKLING OF HOW FORTUNATE HE IS RIGHT NOW, SAFE AND PROTECTED ABOARD THE CHAMPIONS MOBILE BUNKER...

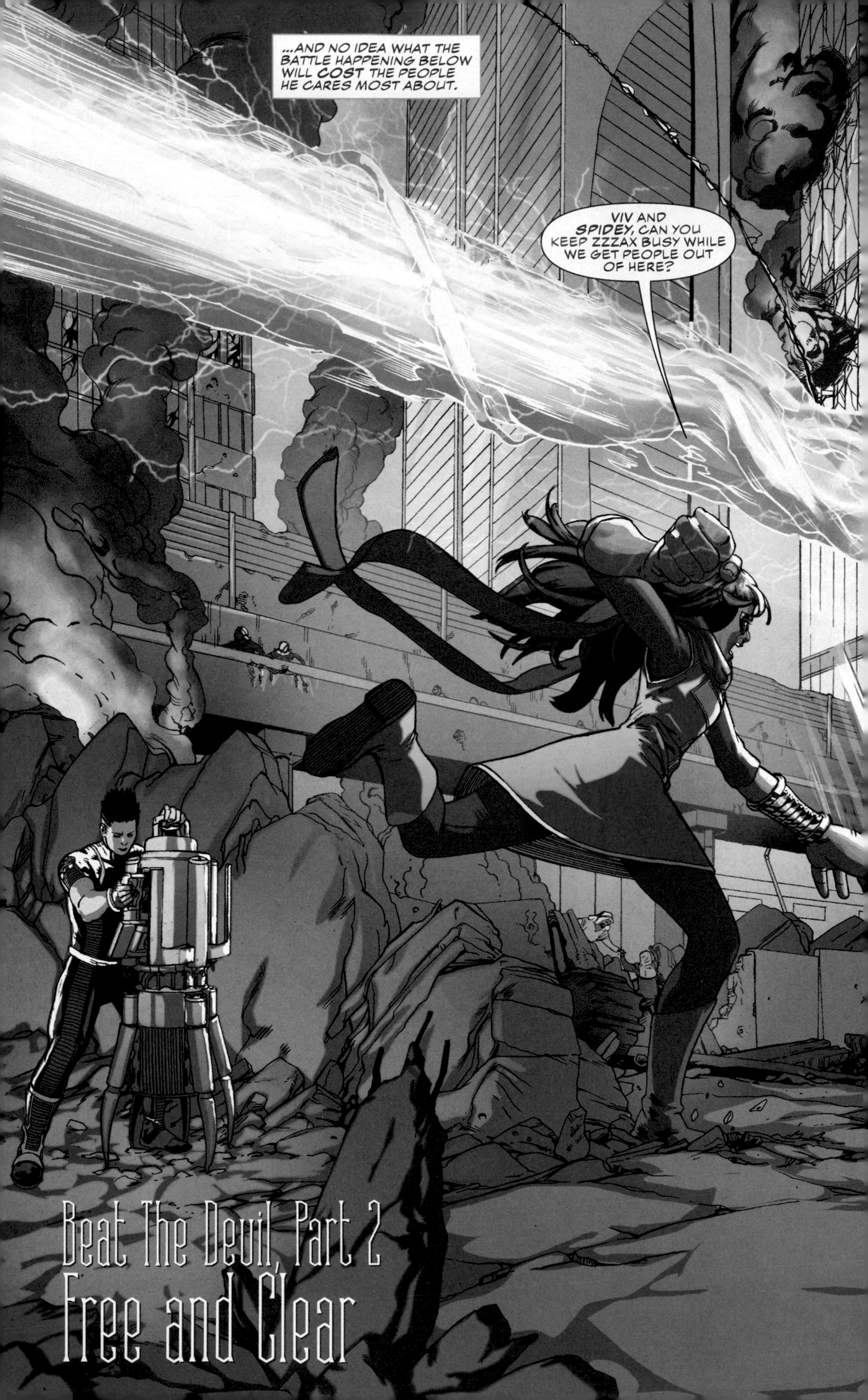
...AND NO IDEA WHAT THE BATTLE HAPPENING BELOW WILL COST THE PEOPLE HE CARES MOST ABOUT.
VIV AND SPIDEY, CAN YOU KEEP ZZZAX BUSY WHILE WE GET PEOPLE OUT OF HERE?
Beat The Devil, Part 2
Free and Clear

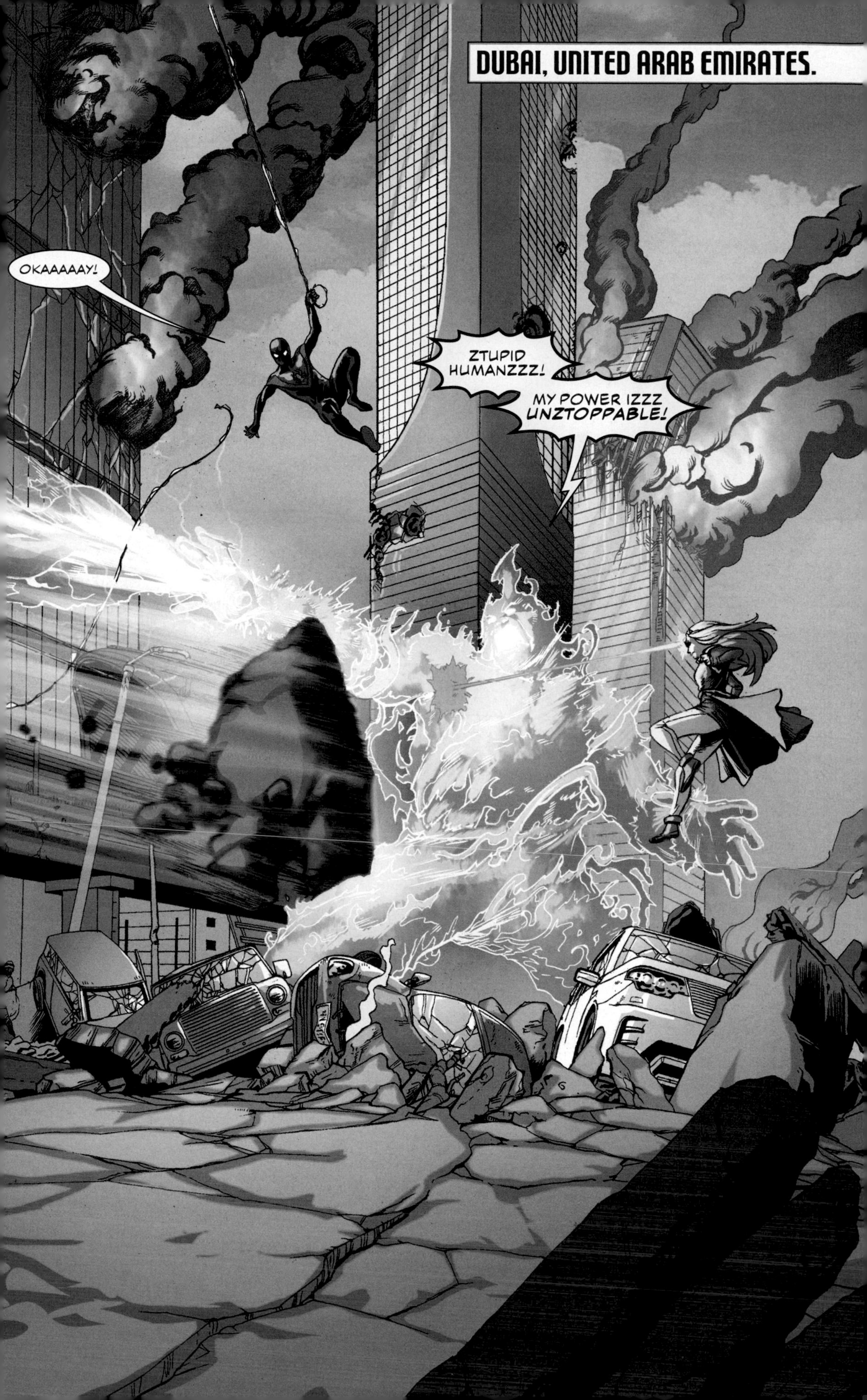
DUBAI, UNITED ARAB EMIRATES.
OKAAAAAY!
ZTUPID HUMANZZZ!
MY POWER IZZZ UNZTOPPABLE!

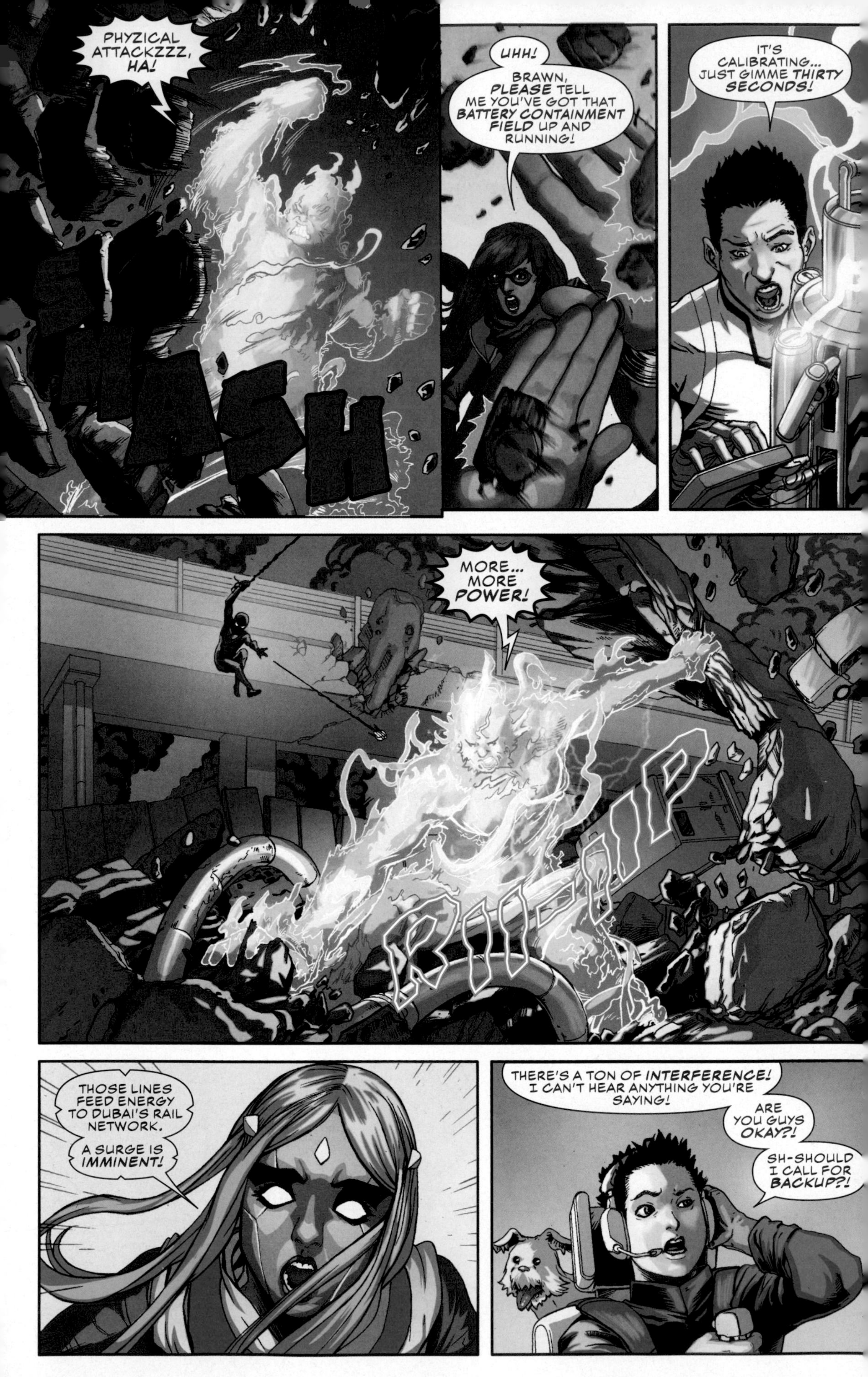
PHYZICAL ATTACKZZZ, HA!
SMASH
UHH!
BRAWN, PLEASE TELL ME YOU'VE GOT THAT BATTERY CONTAINMENT FIELD UP AND RUNNING!
IT'S CALIBRATING... JUST GIMME THIRTY SECONDS!
MORE... MORE POWER!
RIIIIP
THOSE LINES FEED ENERGY TO DUBAI'S RAIL NETWORK.
A SURGE IS IMMINENT!
THERE'S A TON OF INTERFERENCE! I CAN'T HEAR ANYTHING YOU'RE SAYING!
ARE YOU GUYS OKAY?!
SH-SHOULD I CALL FOR BACKUP?!

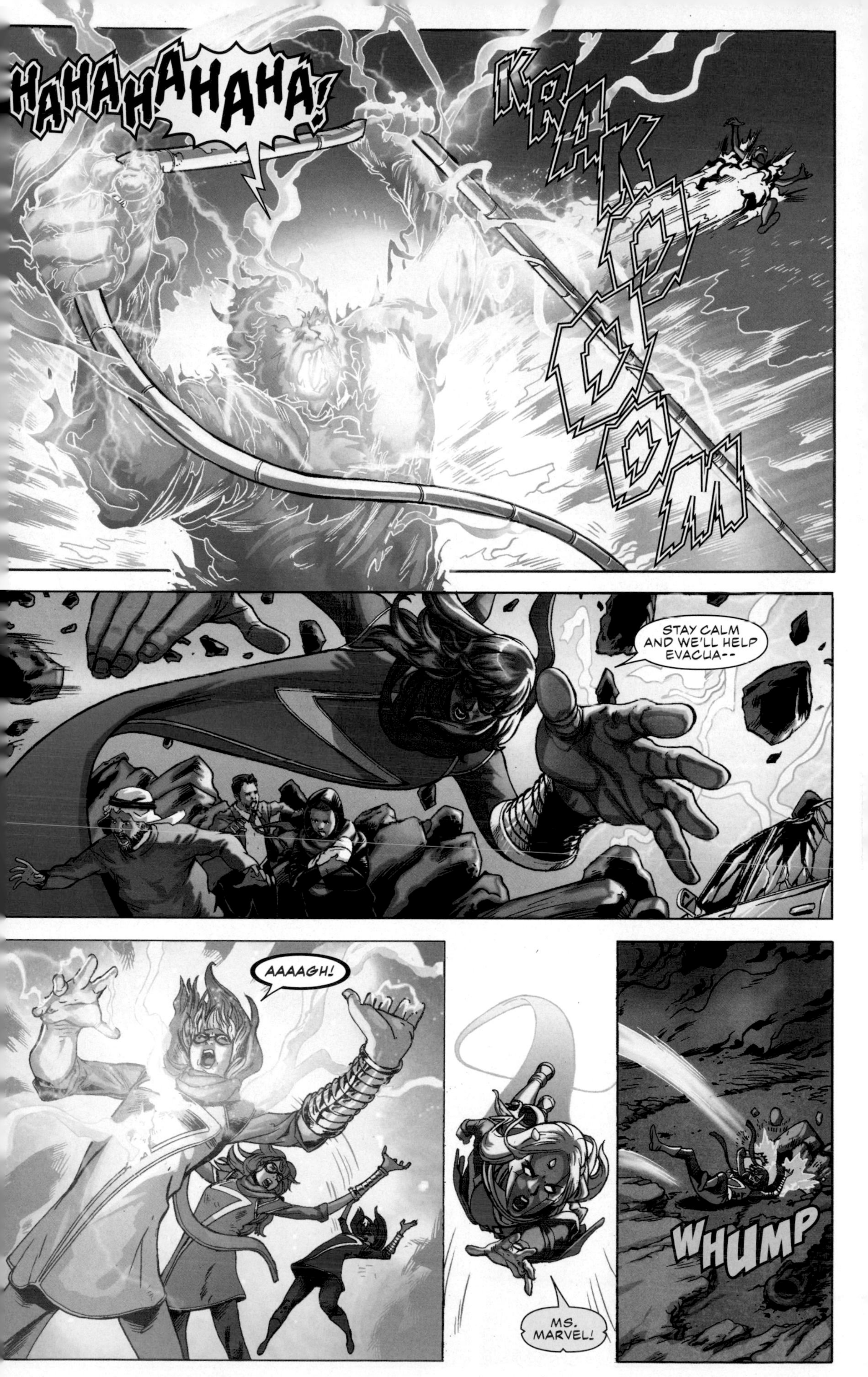
HAHAHAHAHAHA!
KRAKOOOM
STAY CALM AND WE'LL HELP EVACUA--
AAAAGH!
MS. MARVEL!
WHUMP

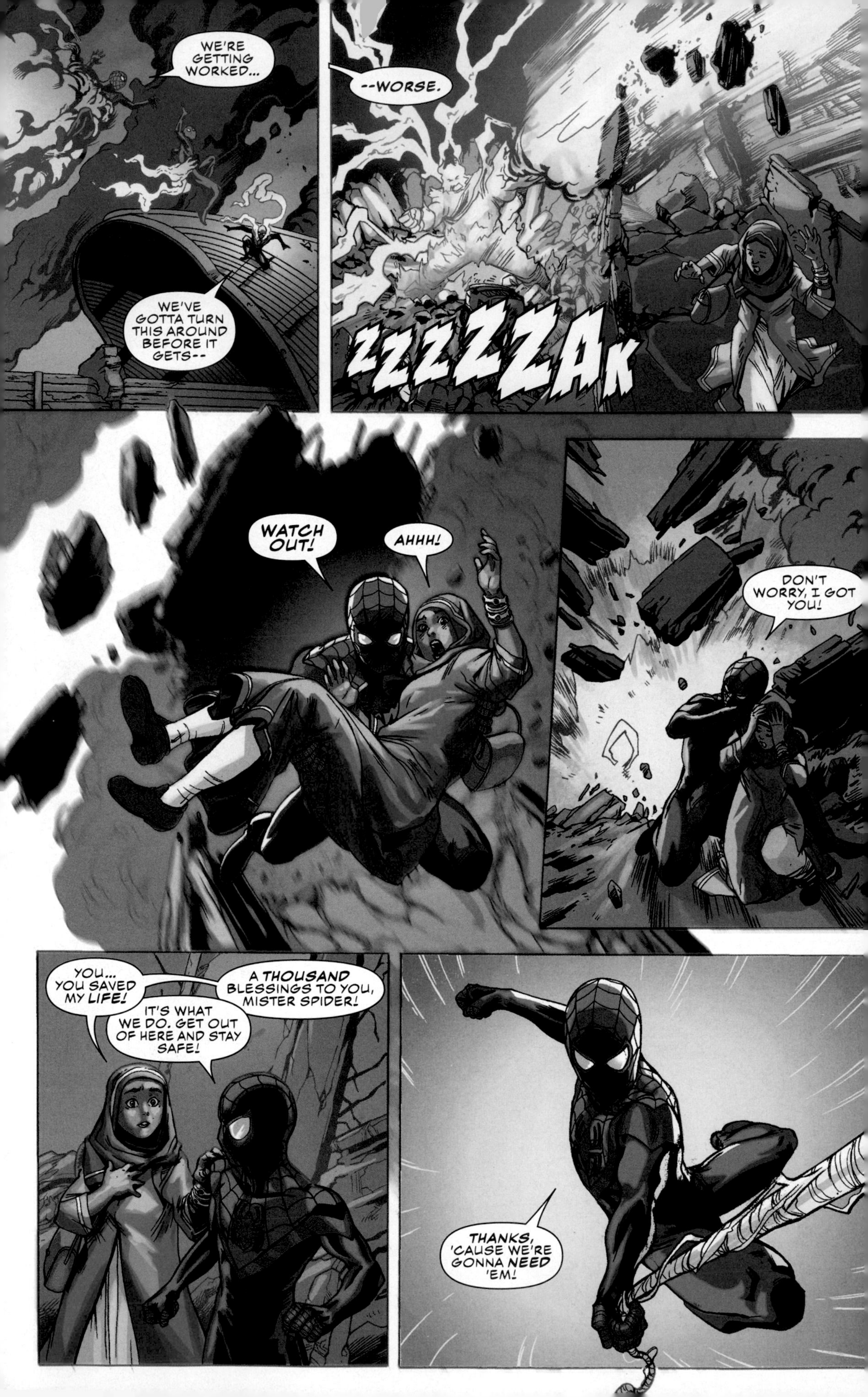
WE'RE GETTING WORKED...
WE'VE GOTTA TURN THIS AROUND BEFORE IT GETS--
--WORSE.
ZZZZZZAK
WATCH OUT!
AHHH!
DON'T WORRY, I GOT YOU!
YOU... YOU SAVED MY LIFE!
A THOUSAND BLESSINGS TO YOU, MISTER SPIDER!
IT'S WHAT WE DO. GET OUT OF HERE AND STAY SAFE!
THANKS, 'CAUSE WE'RE GONNA NEED 'EM!

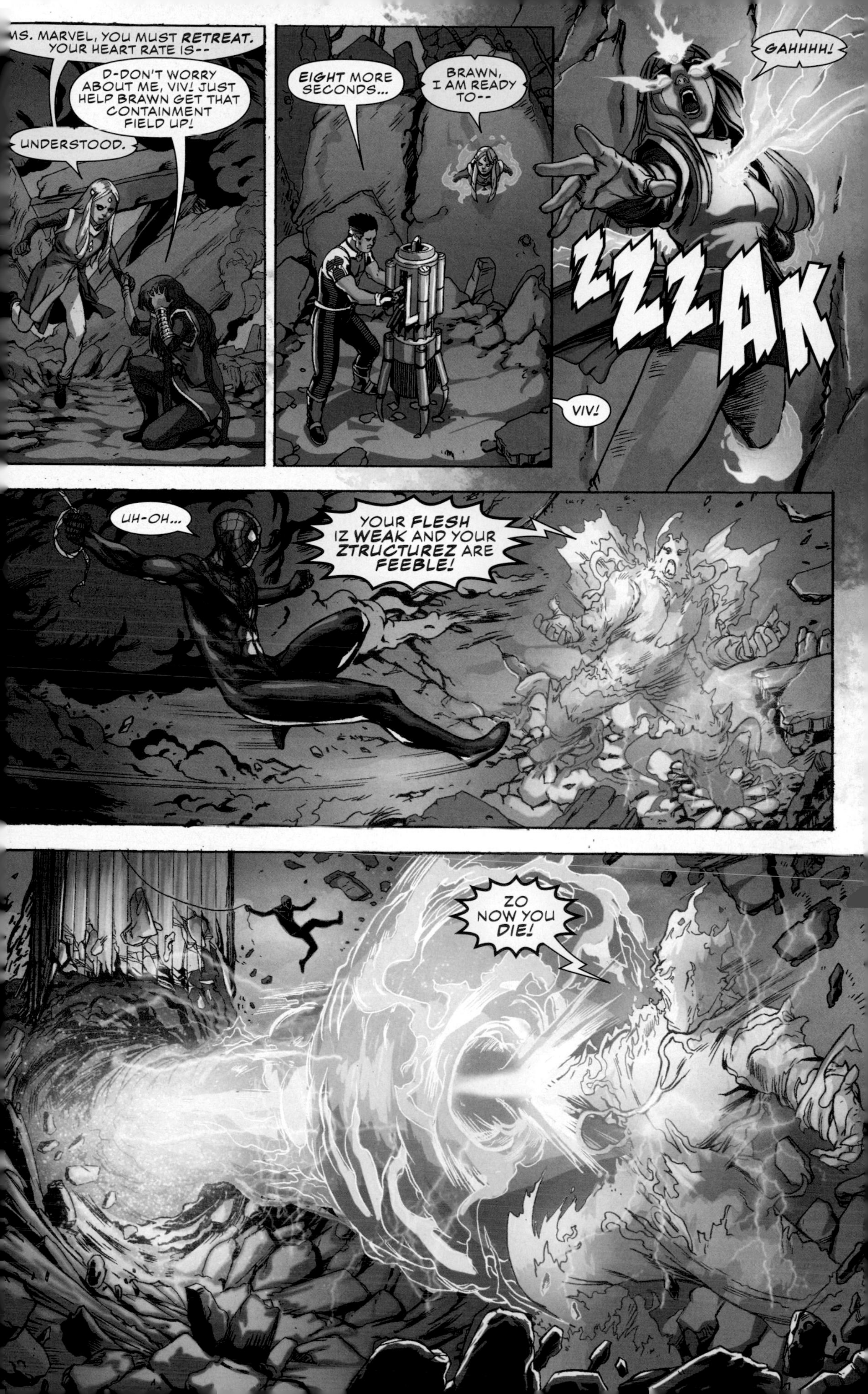
MS. MARVEL, YOU MUST RETREAT. YOUR HEART RATE IS--
D-DON'T WORRY ABOUT ME, VIV! JUST HELP BRAWN GET THAT CONTAINMENT FIELD UP!
UNDERSTOOD.
EIGHT MORE SECONDS...
BRAWN, I AM READY TO--
GAHHHH!
ZZZAK
VIV!
UH-OH...
YOUR FLESH IZ WEAK AND YOUR ZTRUCTUREZ ARE FEEBLE!
ZO NOW YOU DIE!

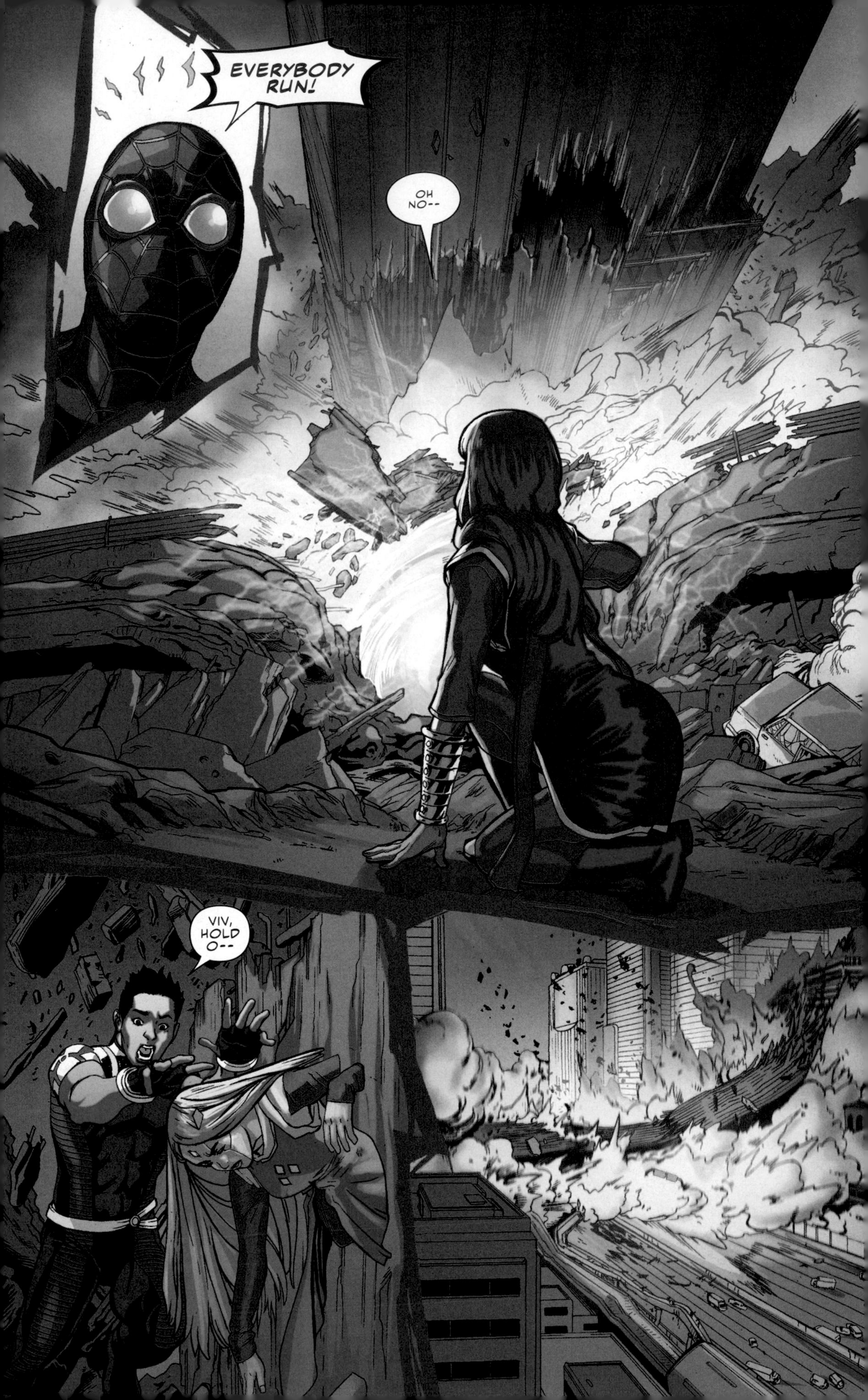
EVERYBODY RUN!
OH NO--
VIV, HOLD O--

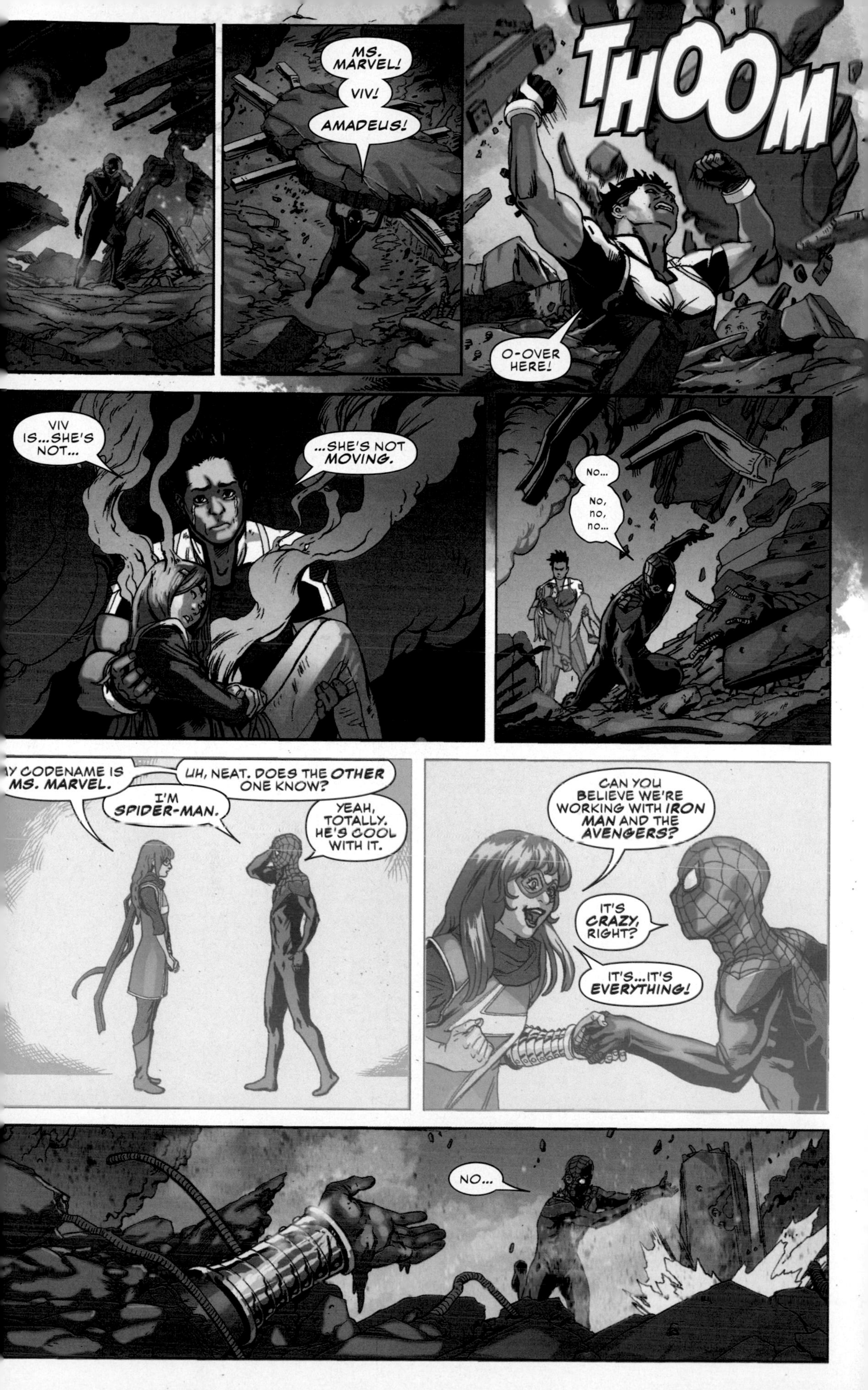
MS. MARVEL!
VIV!
AMADEUS!
THOOM
O-OVER HERE!
VIV IS...SHE'S NOT...
...SHE'S NOT MOVING.
NO...
NO, NO, NO...
Y CODENAME IS MS. MARVEL.
I'M SPIDER-MAN.
UH, NEAT. DOES THE OTHER ONE KNOW?
YEAH, TOTALLY. HE'S COOL WITH IT.
CAN YOU BELIEVE WE'RE WORKING WITH IRON MAN AND THE AVENGERS?
IT'S CRAZY, RIGHT?
IT'S...IT'S EVERYTHING!
NO...

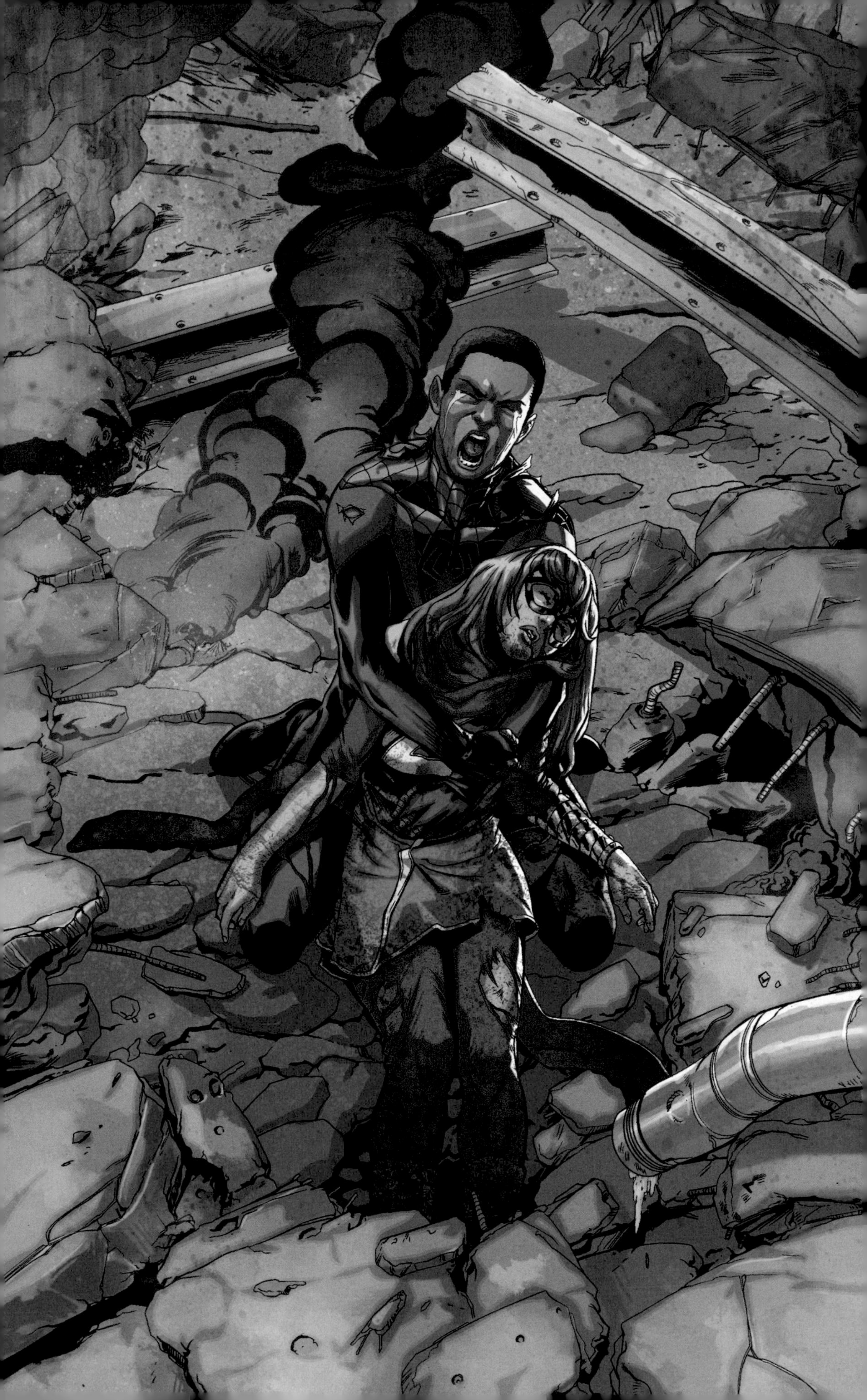

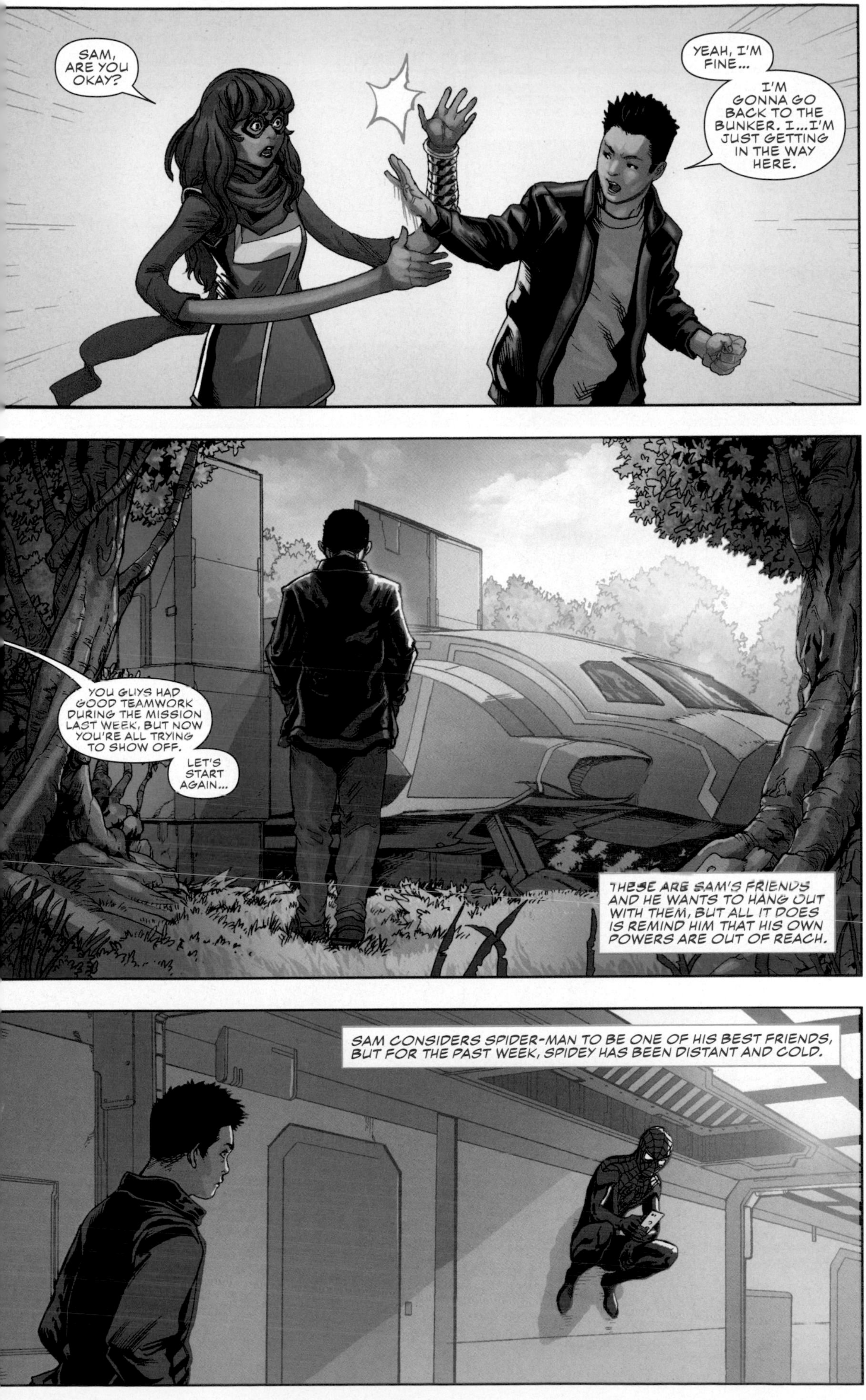
SAM, ARE YOU OKAY?
YEAH, I'M FINE...
I'M GONNA GO BACK TO THE BUNKER. I...I'M JUST GETTING IN THE WAY HERE.
YOU GUYS HAD GOOD TEAMWORK DURING THE MISSION LAST WEEK, BUT NOW YOU'RE ALL TRYING TO SHOW OFF.
LET'S START AGAIN...
THESE ARE SAM'S FRIENDS AND HE WANTS TO HANG OUT WITH THEM, BUT ALL IT DOES IS REMIND HIM THAT HIS OWN POWERS ARE OUT OF REACH.
SAM CONSIDERS SPIDER-MAN TO BE ONE OF HIS BEST FRIENDS, BUT FOR THE PAST WEEK, SPIDEY HAS BEEN DISTANT AND COLD.

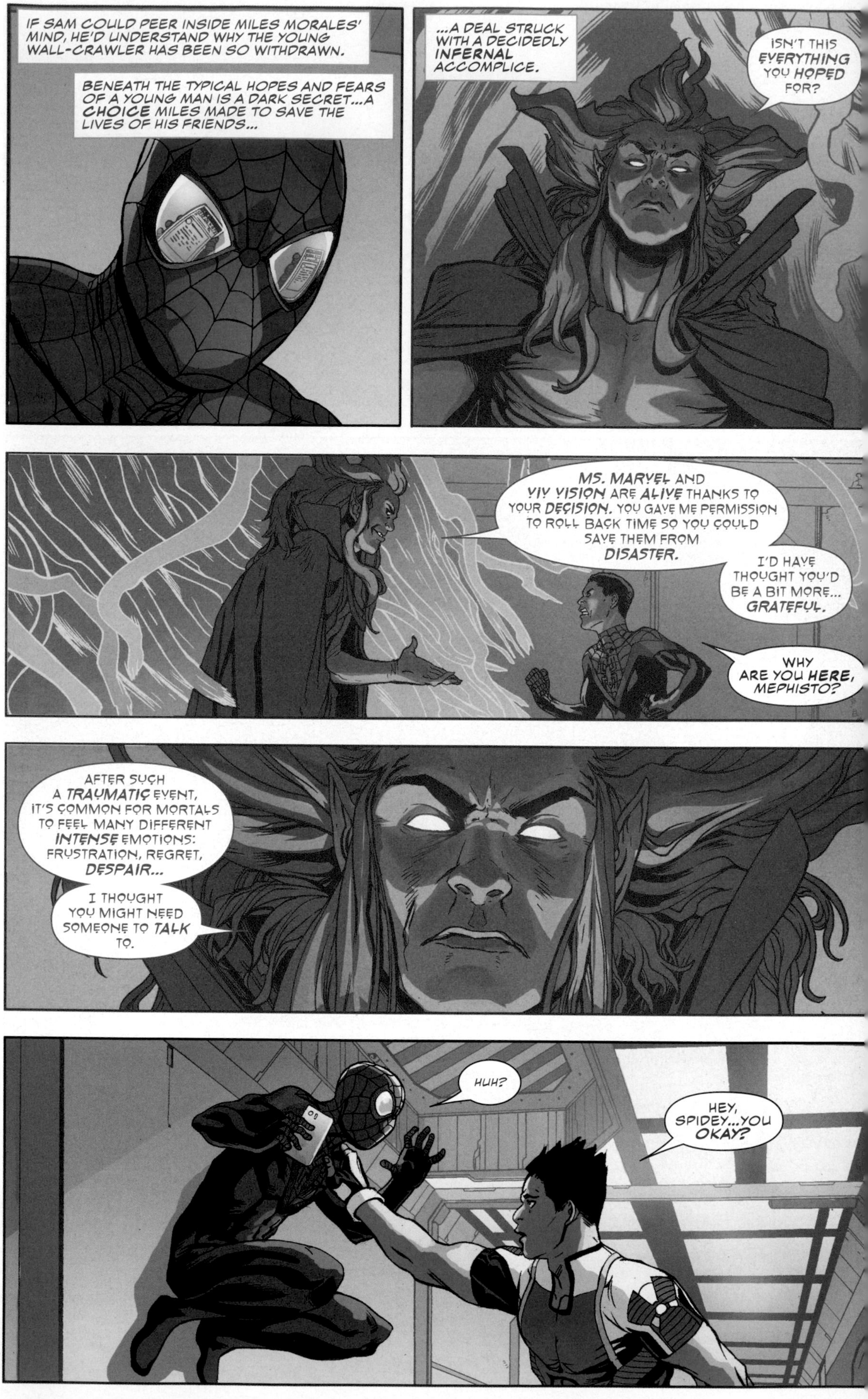

IF SAM COULD PEER INSIDE MILES MORALES' MIND, HE'D UNDERSTAND WHY THE YOUNG WALL-CRAWLER HAS BEEN SO WITHDRAWN.
BENEATH THE TYPICAL HOPES AND FEARS OF A YOUNG MAN IS A DARK SECRET...A CHOICE MILES MADE TO SAVE THE LIVES OF HIS FRIENDS...
...A DEAL STRUCK WITH A DECIDEDLY INFERNAL ACCOMPLICE.
ISN'T THIS EVERYTHING YOU HOPED FOR?
MS. MARVEL AND VIV VISION ARE ALIVE THANKS TO YOUR DECISION. YOU GAVE ME PERMISSION TO ROLL BACK TIME SO YOU COULD SAVE THEM FROM DISASTER.
I'D HAVE THOUGHT YOU'D BE A BIT MORE... GRATEFUL.
WHY ARE YOU HERE, MEPHISTO?
AFTER SUCH A TRAUMATIC EVENT, IT'S COMMON FOR MORTALS TO FEEL MANY DIFFERENT INTENSE EMOTIONS: FRUSTRATION, REGRET, DESPAIR...
I THOUGHT YOU MIGHT NEED SOMEONE TO TALK TO.
HUH?
HEY, SPIDEY...YOU OKAY?

WHEN SOCIETY BECAME DISILLUSIONED WITH ITS HEROES, THE NEXT GENERATION MADE A VOW TO DO BETTER. TO MAKE A DIFFERENCE. TO CHANGE THE WORLD. THEY ARE THE...

CHAMPIONS

BEAT THE DEVIL

JIM ZUB
WRITER

STEVEN CUMMINGS *(#1-4)* &
JUANAN RAMÍREZ *(#5-6)*
ARTISTS

MARCIO MENYZ *WITH*
ERICK ARCINIEGA *(#1)* & **FEDERICO BLEE** *(#3)*
COLOR ARTISTS

VC's CLAYTON COWLES
LETTERER

KIM JACINTO & **RAIN BEREDO**
COVER ART

ASSISTANT EDITOR: **SHANNON ANDREWS**
ASSOCIATE EDITOR: **ALANNA SMITH** *EDITOR:* **TOM BREVOORT**

COLLECTION EDITOR: **JENNIFER GRÜNWALD**
ASSISTANT EDITOR: **CAITLIN O'CONNELL**
ASSOCIATE MANAGING EDITOR: **KATERI WOODY**
EDITOR, SPECIAL PROJECTS: **MARK D. BEAZLEY**
VP PRODUCTION & SPECIAL PROJECTS: **JEFF YOUNGQUIST**
BOOK DESIGNER: **STACIE ZUCKER**

SVP PRINT, SALES & MARKETING: **DAVID GABRIEL**
DIRECTOR, LICENSED PUBLISHING: **SVEN LARSEN**
EDITOR IN CHIEF: **C.B. CEBULSKI**
CHIEF CREATIVE OFFICER: **JOE QUESADA**
PRESIDENT: **DAN BUCKLEY**
EXECUTIVE PRODUCER: **ALAN FINE**

CHAMPIONS BY JIM ZUB VOL.1 BEAT THE DEVIL. Contains material originally published in magazine form as CHAMPIONS #1-6. First printing 2019. ISBN 978-1-302-91671-8. Published by MARVEL WORLDWIDE, INC., a subsidiary of MARVEL ENTERTAINMENT, LLC. OFFICE OF PUBLICATION: 135 West 50th Street, New York, NY 10020. **Printed in Canada.** DAN BUCKLEY, President, Marvel Entertainment; JOHN NEE, Publisher; JOE QUESADA, Chief Creative Officer; TOM BREVOORT, SVP of Publishing; DAVID BOGART, Associate Publisher & SVP of Talent Affairs; DAVID GABRIEL, SVP of Sales & Marketing, Publishing; JEFF YOUNGQUIST, VP of Production & Special Projects; DAN CARR, Executive Director of Publishing Technology; ALEX MORALES, Director of Publishing Operations; DAN EDINGTON, Managing Editor; SUSAN CRESPI, Production Manager; STAN LEE, Chairman Emeritus. For information regarding advertising in Marvel Comics or on Marvel.com, please contact Vit DeBellis, Custom Solutions & Integrated Advertising Manager, at vdebellis@marvel.com. For Marvel subscription inquiries, please call 888-511-5480. **Manufactured between 6/14/2019 and 7/10/2019 by SOLISCO PRINTERS, SCOTT, QC, CANADA.**

10 9 8 7 6 5 4 3 2 1

1

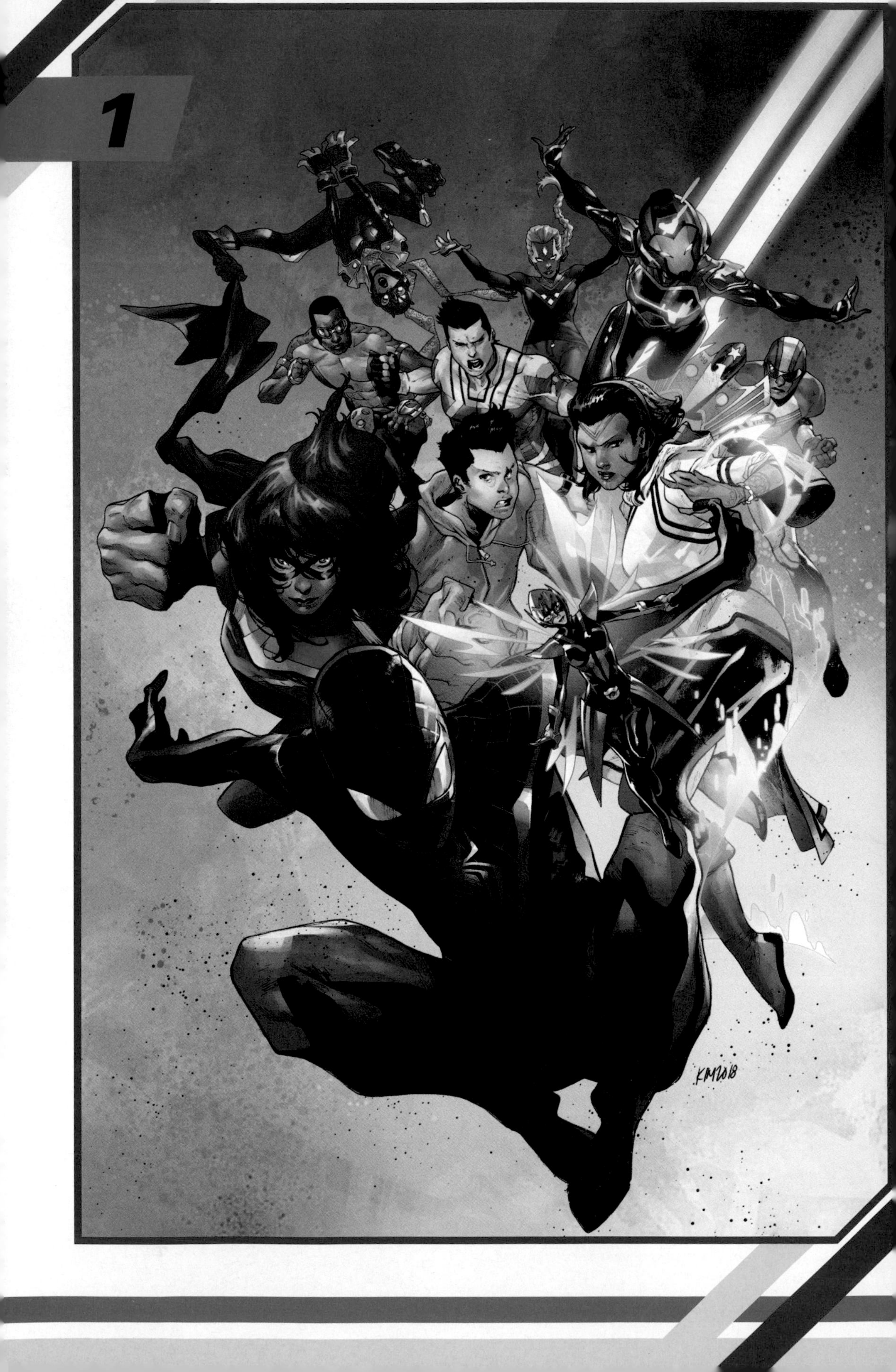
KIM2018

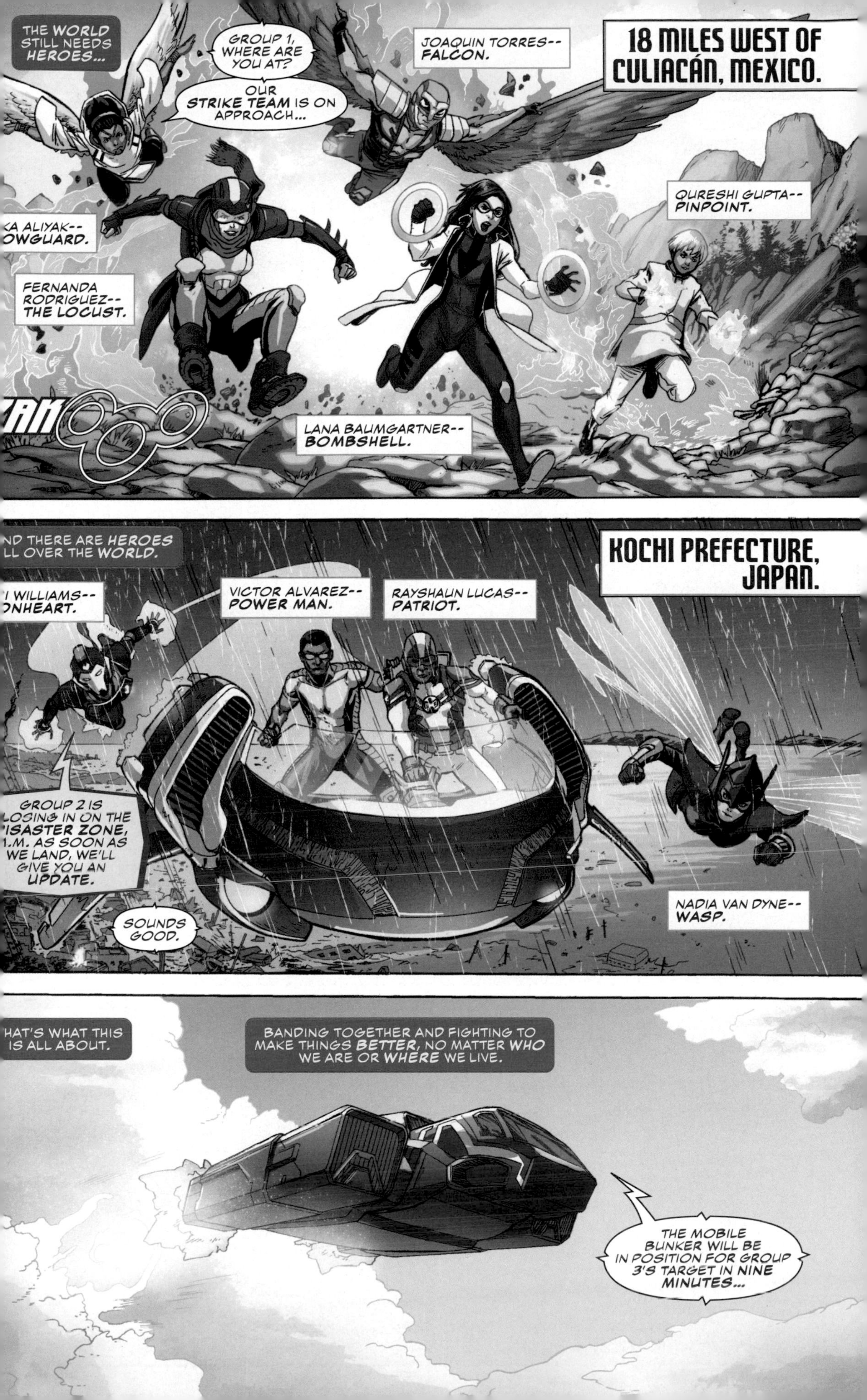
THE WORLD STILL NEEDS HEROES...
GROUP 1, WHERE ARE YOU AT?
OUR STRIKE TEAM IS ON APPROACH...
JOAQUIN TORRES-- FALCON.
18 MILES WEST OF CULIACÁN, MEXICO.
KA ALIYAK-- OWGUARD.
FERNANDA RODRIGUEZ-- THE LOCUST.
QURESHI GUPTA-- PINPOINT.
LANA BAUMGARTNER-- BOMBSHELL.
ND THERE ARE HEROES LL OVER THE WORLD.
KOCHI PREFECTURE, JAPAN.
I WILLIAMS-- ONHEART.
VICTOR ALVAREZ-- POWER MAN.
RAYSHAUN LUCAS-- PATRIOT.
GROUP 2 IS LOSING IN ON THE DISASTER ZONE, M.M. AS SOON AS WE LAND, WE'LL GIVE YOU AN UPDATE.
SOUNDS GOOD.
NADIA VAN DYNE-- WASP.
HAT'S WHAT THIS IS ALL ABOUT.
BANDING TOGETHER AND FIGHTING TO MAKE THINGS BETTER, NO MATTER WHO WE ARE OR WHERE WE LIVE.
THE MOBILE BUNKER WILL BE IN POSITION FOR GROUP 3'S TARGET IN NINE MINUTES...

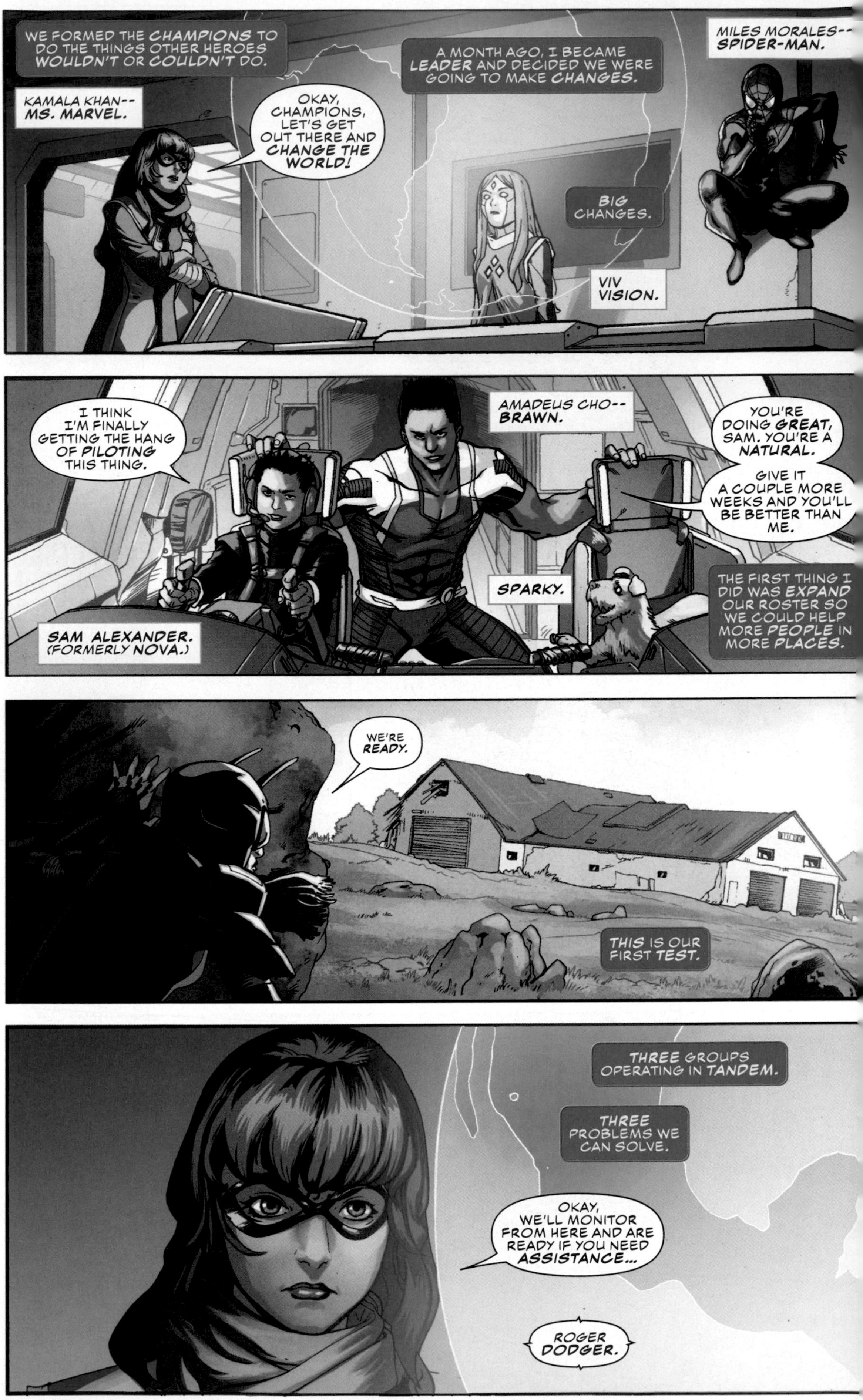

WE FORMED THE CHAMPIONS TO DO THE THINGS OTHER HEROES WOULDN'T OR COULDN'T DO.
KAMALA KHAN-- MS. MARVEL.
OKAY, CHAMPIONS, LET'S GET OUT THERE AND CHANGE THE WORLD!
A MONTH AGO, I BECAME LEADER AND DECIDED WE WERE GOING TO MAKE CHANGES.
BIG CHANGES.
VIV VISION.
MILES MORALES-- SPIDER-MAN.
I THINK I'M FINALLY GETTING THE HANG OF PILOTING THIS THING.
AMADEUS CHO-- BRAWN.
YOU'RE DOING GREAT, SAM. YOU'RE A NATURAL.
GIVE IT A COUPLE MORE WEEKS AND YOU'LL BE BETTER THAN ME.
SPARKY.
SAM ALEXANDER. (FORMERLY NOVA.)
THE FIRST THING I DID WAS EXPAND OUR ROSTER SO WE COULD HELP MORE PEOPLE IN MORE PLACES.
WE'RE READY.
THIS IS OUR FIRST TEST.
THREE GROUPS OPERATING IN TANDEM.
THREE PROBLEMS WE CAN SOLVE.
OKAY, WE'LL MONITOR FROM HERE AND ARE READY IF YOU NEED ASSISTANCE...
ROGER DODGER.

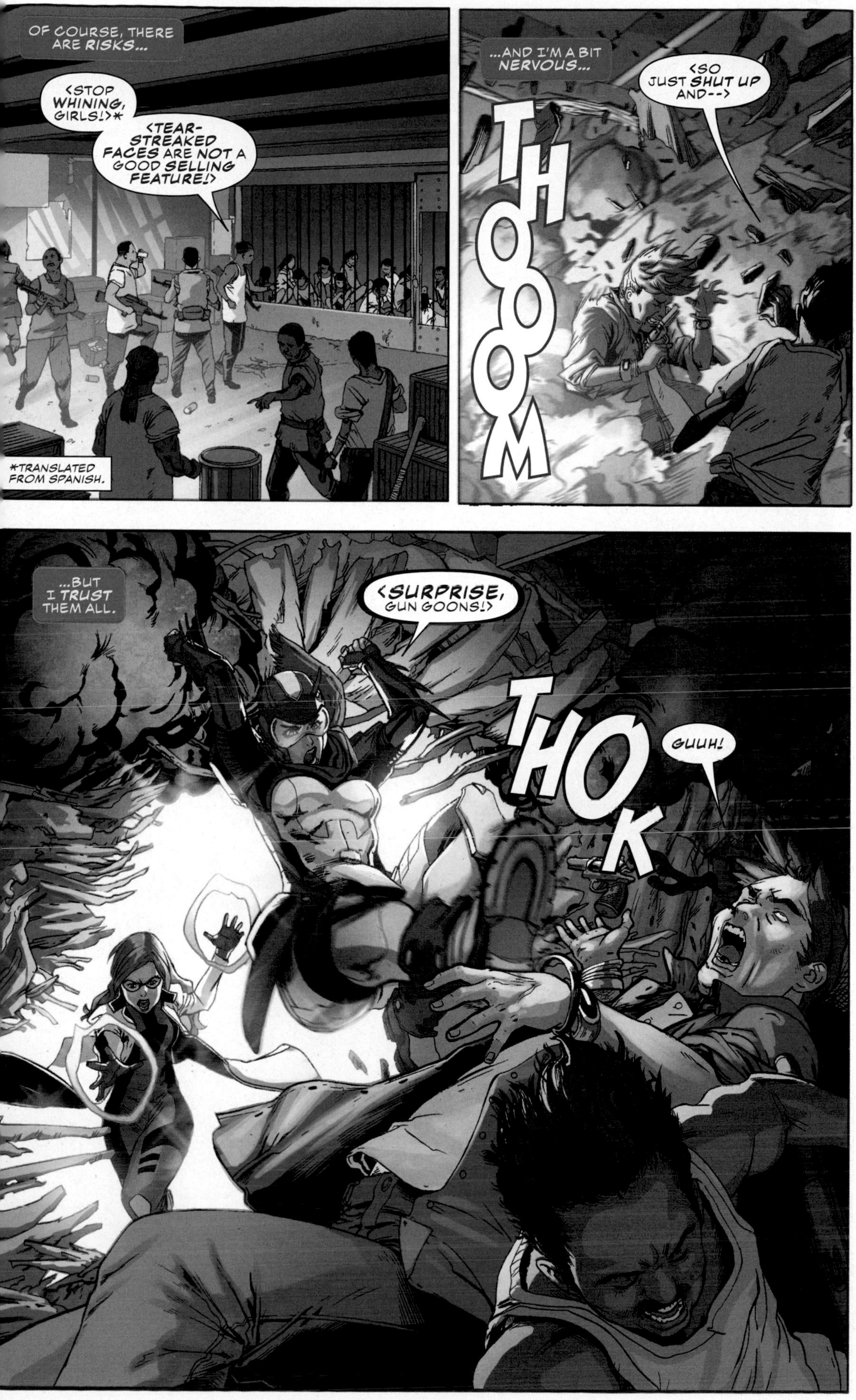

OF COURSE, THERE ARE RISKS...
<STOP WHINING, GIRLS!>*
<TEAR-STREAKED FACES ARE NOT A GOOD SELLING FEATURE!>
*TRANSLATED FROM SPANISH.
...AND I'M A BIT NERVOUS...
<SO JUST SHUT UP AND-->
THOOOOM
...BUT I TRUST THEM ALL.
<SURPRISE, GUN GOONS!>
THOK
GUUH!

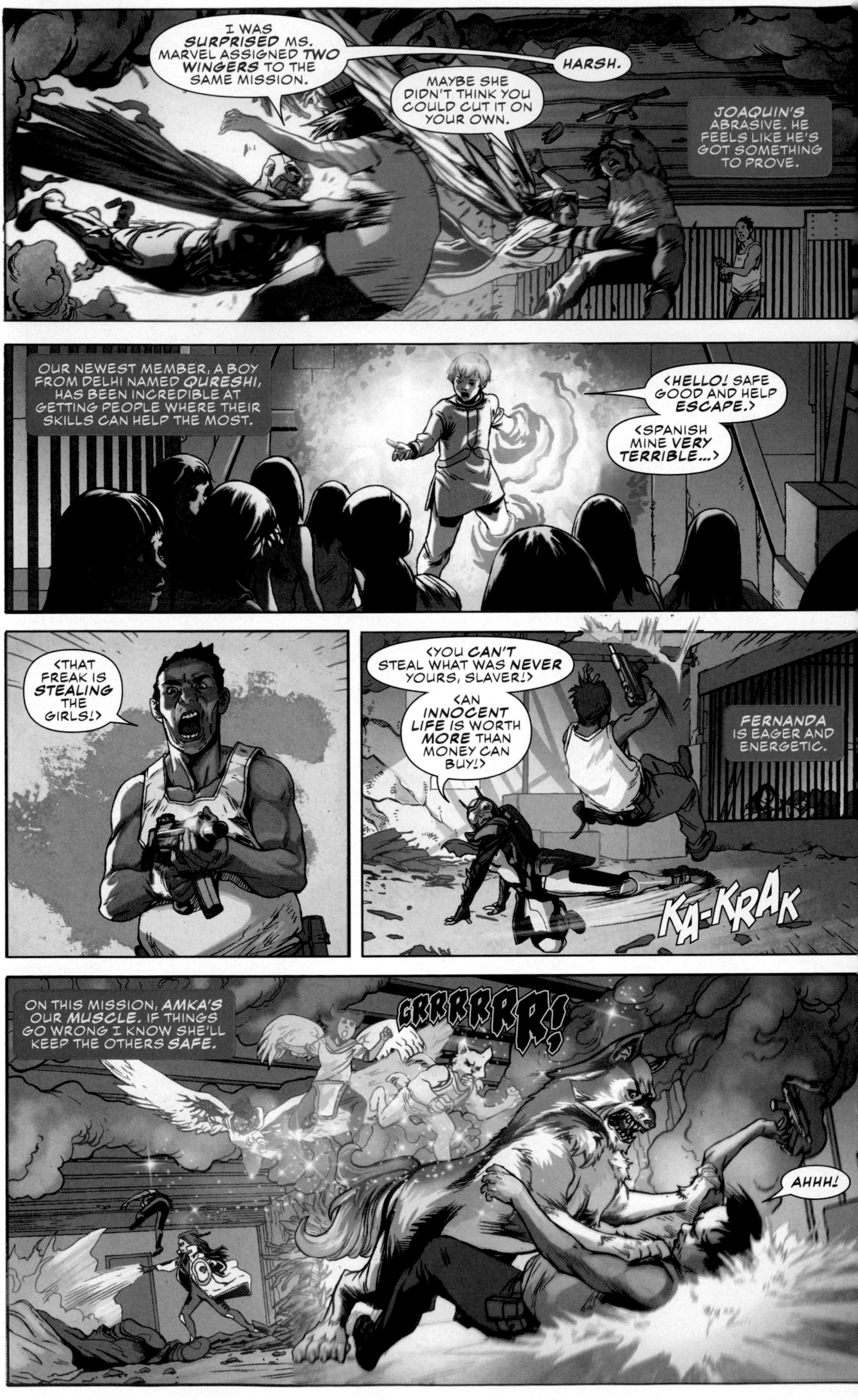
I WAS SURPRISED MS. MARVEL ASSIGNED TWO WINGERS TO THE SAME MISSION.
HARSH.
MAYBE SHE DIDN'T THINK YOU COULD CUT IT ON YOUR OWN.
JOAQUIN'S ABRASIVE. HE FEELS LIKE HE'S GOT SOMETHING TO PROVE.
OUR NEWEST MEMBER, A BOY FROM DELHI NAMED QURESHI, HAS BEEN INCREDIBLE AT GETTING PEOPLE WHERE THEIR SKILLS CAN HELP THE MOST.
<HELLO! SAFE GOOD AND HELP ESCAPE.>
<SPANISH MINE VERY TERRIBLE...>
<THAT FREAK IS STEALING THE GIRLS!>
<YOU CAN'T STEAL WHAT WAS NEVER YOURS, SLAVER!>
<AN INNOCENT LIFE IS WORTH MORE THAN MONEY CAN BUY!>
FERNANDA IS EAGER AND ENERGETIC.
KA-KRAK
ON THIS MISSION, AMKA'S OUR MUSCLE. IF THINGS GO WRONG I KNOW SHE'LL KEEP THE OTHERS SAFE.
GRRRRRR!
AHHH!

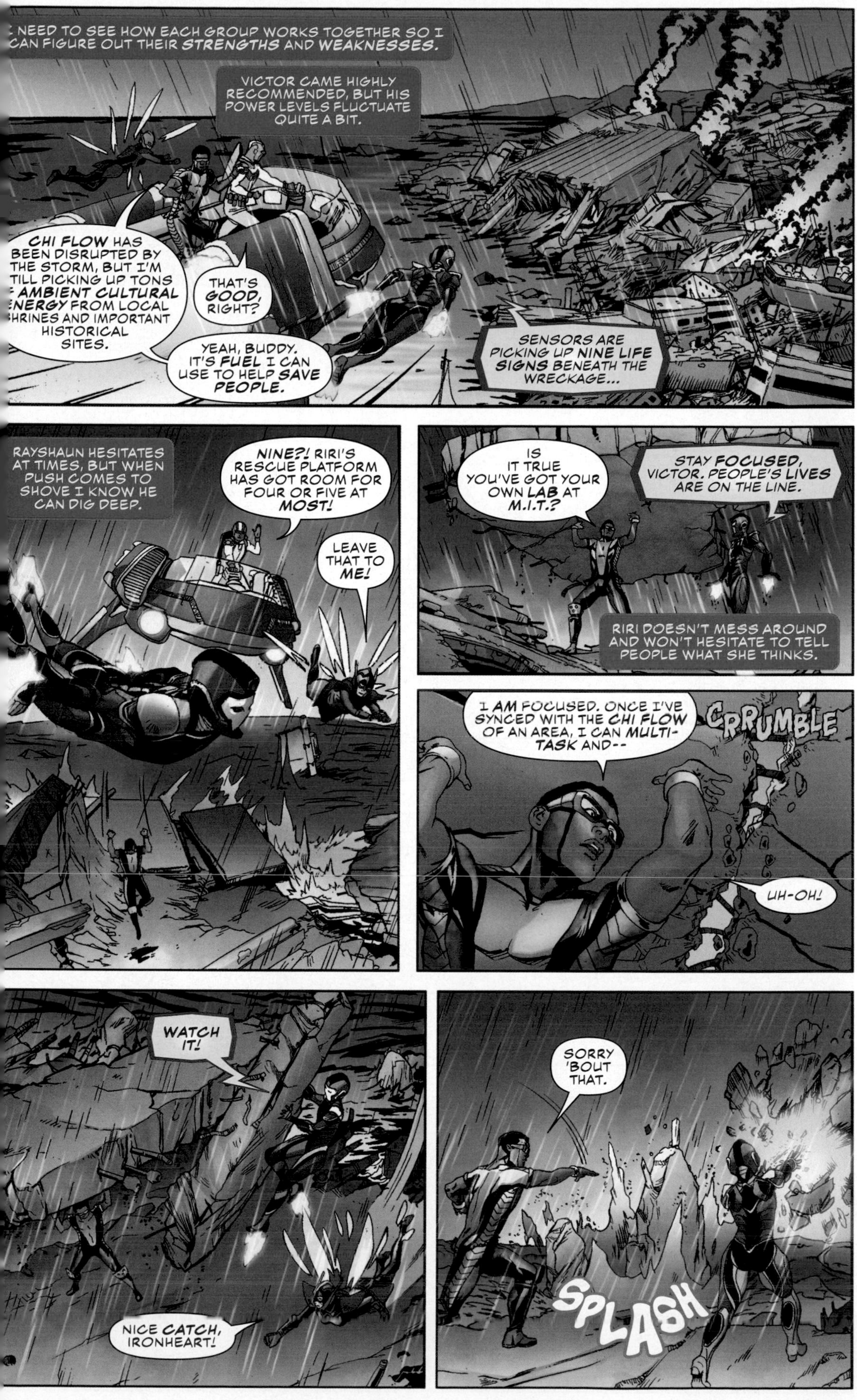

I NEED TO SEE HOW EACH GROUP WORKS TOGETHER SO I CAN FIGURE OUT THEIR STRENGTHS AND WEAKNESSES.
VICTOR CAME HIGHLY RECOMMENDED, BUT HIS POWER LEVELS FLUCTUATE QUITE A BIT.
CHI FLOW HAS BEEN DISRUPTED BY THE STORM, BUT I'M TILL PICKING UP TONS F AMBIENT CULTURAL ENERGY FROM LOCAL SHRINES AND IMPORTANT HISTORICAL SITES.
THAT'S GOOD, RIGHT?
YEAH, BUDDY. IT'S FUEL I CAN USE TO HELP SAVE PEOPLE.
SENSORS ARE PICKING UP NINE LIFE SIGNS BENEATH THE WRECKAGE...
RAYSHAUN HESITATES AT TIMES, BUT WHEN PUSH COMES TO SHOVE I KNOW HE CAN DIG DEEP.
NINE?! RIRI'S RESCUE PLATFORM HAS GOT ROOM FOR FOUR OR FIVE AT MOST!
LEAVE THAT TO ME!
IS IT TRUE YOU'VE GOT YOUR OWN LAB AT M.I.T.?
STAY FOCUSED, VICTOR. PEOPLE'S LIVES ARE ON THE LINE.
RIRI DOESN'T MESS AROUND AND WON'T HESITATE TO TELL PEOPLE WHAT SHE THINKS.
I AM FOCUSED. ONCE I'VE SYNCED WITH THE CHI FLOW OF AN AREA, I CAN MULTI-TASK AND--
CRRUMBLE
UH-OH!
WATCH IT!
NICE CATCH, IRONHEART!
SORRY 'BOUT THAT.
SPLASH

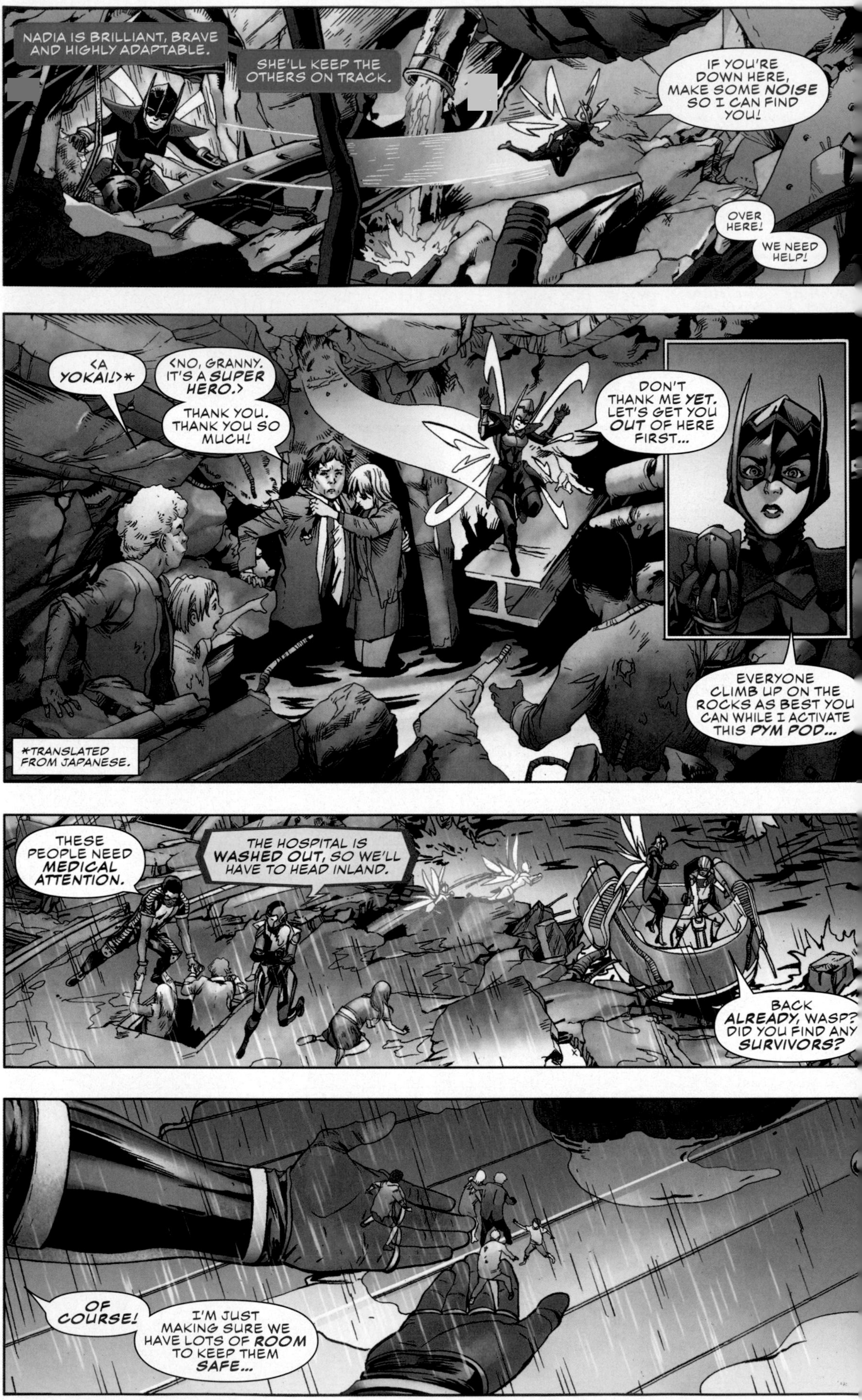
NADIA IS BRILLIANT, BRAVE AND HIGHLY ADAPTABLE.
SHE'LL KEEP THE OTHERS ON TRACK.
IF YOU'RE DOWN HERE, MAKE SOME NOISE SO I CAN FIND YOU!
OVER HERE!
WE NEED HELP!
<A YOKAI!>*
<NO, GRANNY. IT'S A SUPER HERO.>
THANK YOU. THANK YOU SO MUCH!
DON'T THANK ME YET. LET'S GET YOU OUT OF HERE FIRST...
EVERYONE CLIMB UP ON THE ROCKS AS BEST YOU CAN WHILE I ACTIVATE THIS PYM POD...
*TRANSLATED FROM JAPANESE.
THESE PEOPLE NEED MEDICAL ATTENTION.
THE HOSPITAL IS WASHED OUT, SO WE'LL HAVE TO HEAD INLAND.
BACK ALREADY, WASP? DID YOU FIND ANY SURVIVORS?
OF COURSE!
I'M JUST MAKING SURE WE HAVE LOTS OF ROOM TO KEEP THEM SAFE...

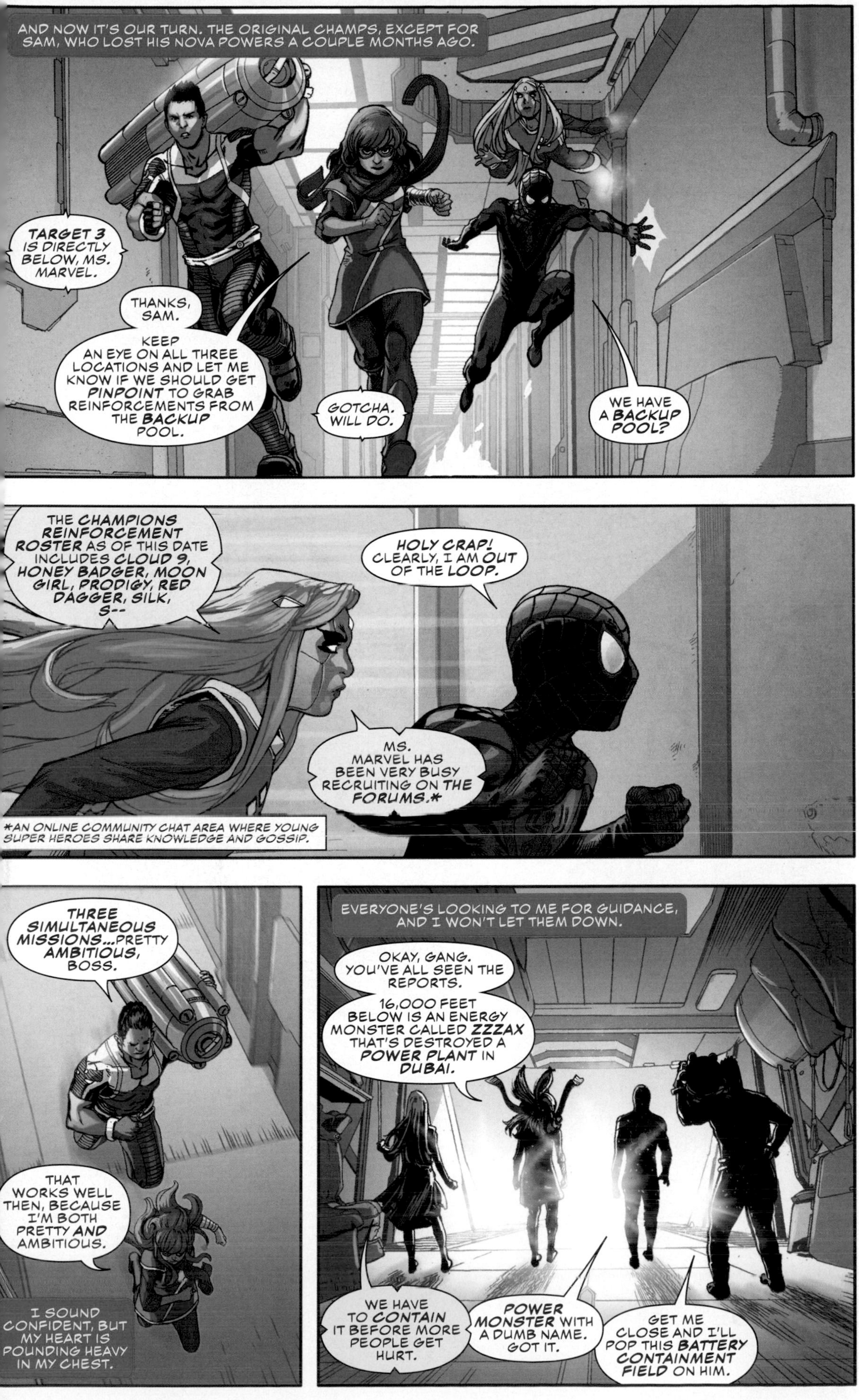

AND NOW IT'S OUR TURN. THE ORIGINAL CHAMPS, EXCEPT FOR SAM, WHO LOST HIS NOVA POWERS A COUPLE MONTHS AGO.
TARGET 3 IS DIRECTLY BELOW, MS. MARVEL.
THANKS, SAM.
KEEP AN EYE ON ALL THREE LOCATIONS AND LET ME KNOW IF WE SHOULD GET PINPOINT TO GRAB REINFORCEMENTS FROM THE BACKUP POOL.
GOTCHA. WILL DO.
WE HAVE A BACKUP POOL?
THE CHAMPIONS REINFORCEMENT ROSTER AS OF THIS DATE INCLUDES CLOUD 9, HONEY BADGER, MOON GIRL, PRODIGY, RED DAGGER, SILK, S--
HOLY CRAP! CLEARLY, I AM OUT OF THE LOOP.
MS. MARVEL HAS BEEN VERY BUSY RECRUITING ON THE FORUMS.*
*AN ONLINE COMMUNITY CHAT AREA WHERE YOUNG SUPER HEROES SHARE KNOWLEDGE AND GOSSIP.
THREE SIMULTANEOUS MISSIONS...PRETTY AMBITIOUS, BOSS.
THAT WORKS WELL THEN, BECAUSE I'M BOTH PRETTY AND AMBITIOUS.
I SOUND CONFIDENT, BUT MY HEART IS POUNDING HEAVY IN MY CHEST.
EVERYONE'S LOOKING TO ME FOR GUIDANCE, AND I WON'T LET THEM DOWN.
OKAY, GANG. YOU'VE ALL SEEN THE REPORTS.
16,000 FEET BELOW IS AN ENERGY MONSTER CALLED ZZZAX THAT'S DESTROYED A POWER PLANT IN DUBAI.
WE HAVE TO CONTAIN IT BEFORE MORE PEOPLE GET HURT.
POWER MONSTER WITH A DUMB NAME. GOT IT.
GET ME CLOSE AND I'LL POP THIS BATTERY CONTAINMENT FIELD ON HIM.

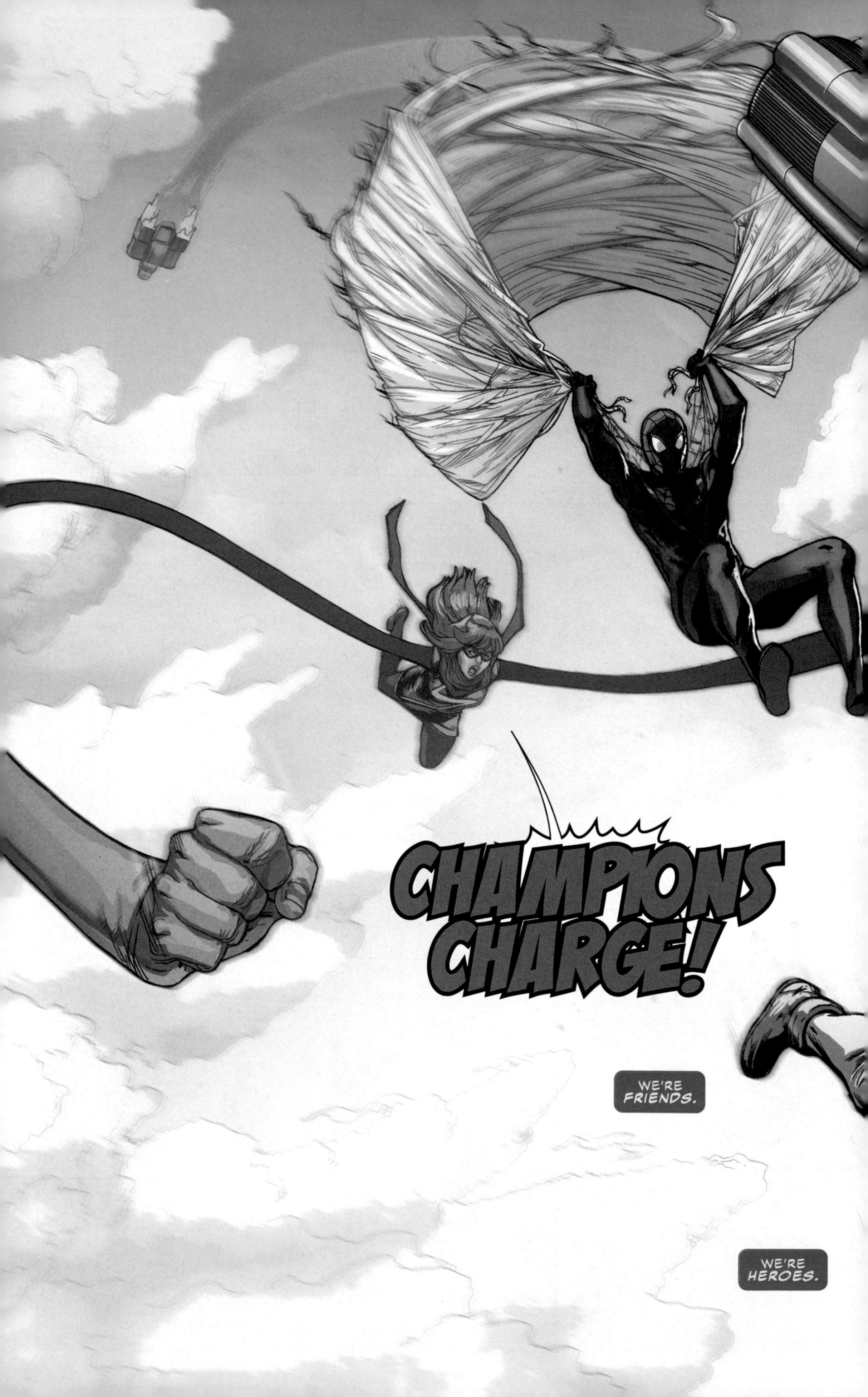
CHAMPIONS CHARGE!
WE'RE FRIENDS.
WE'RE HEROES.

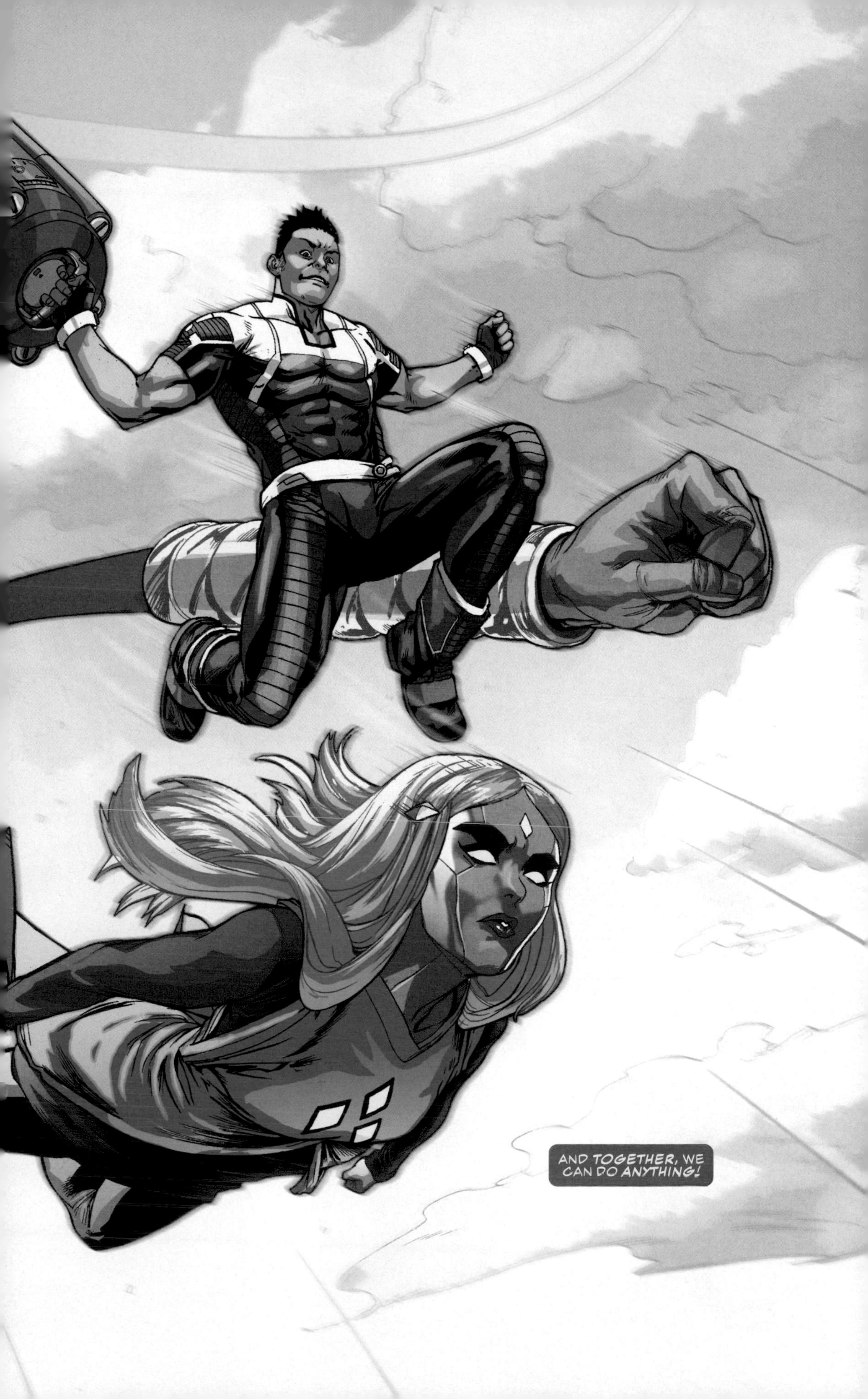
AND TOGETHER, WE CAN DO ANYTHING!

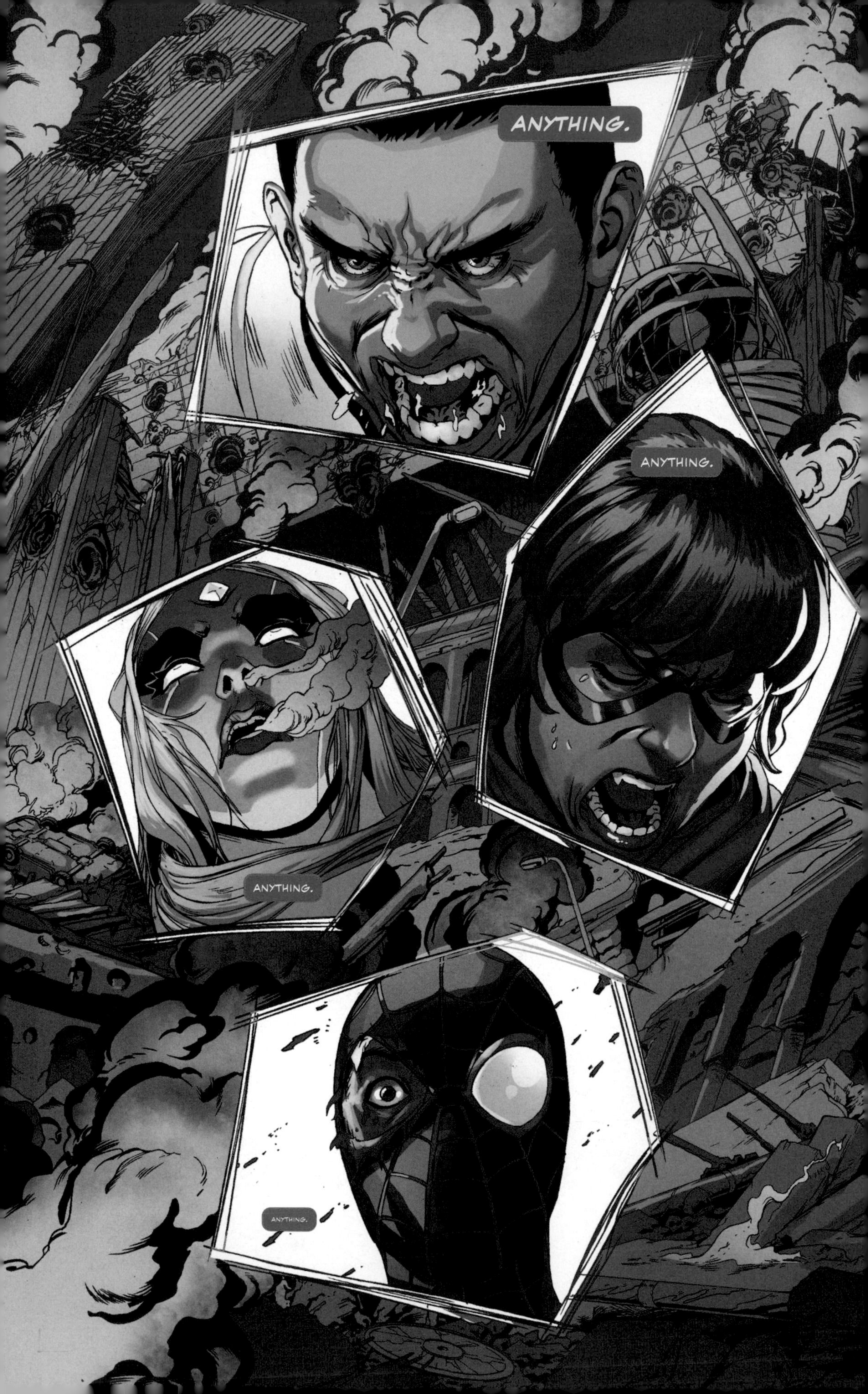
ANYTHING.
ANYTHING.
ANYTHING.
ANYTHING.

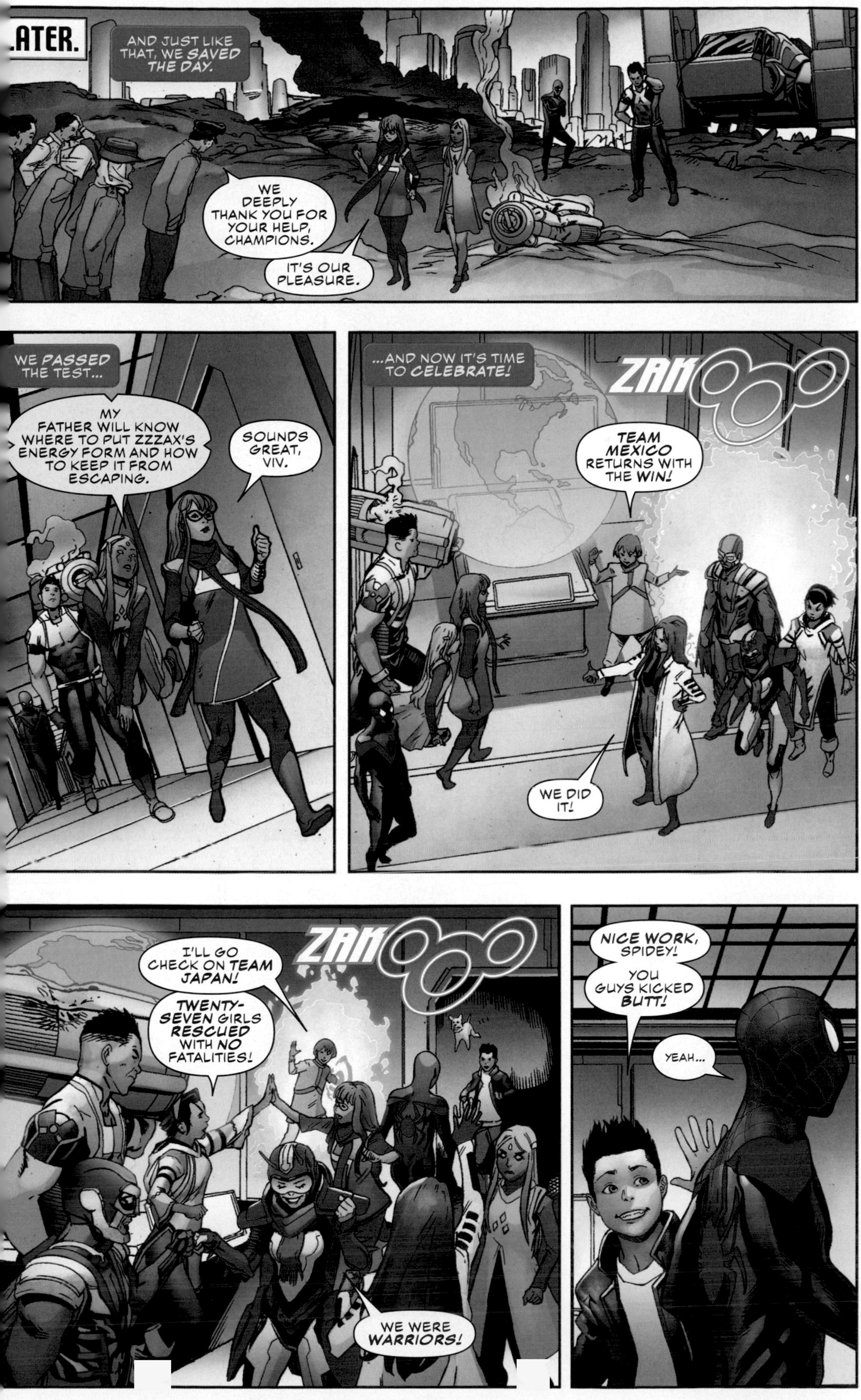
LATER.
AND JUST LIKE THAT, WE SAVED THE DAY.
WE DEEPLY THANK YOU FOR YOUR HELP, CHAMPIONS.
IT'S OUR PLEASURE.
WE PASSED THE TEST...
MY FATHER WILL KNOW WHERE TO PUT ZZZAX'S ENERGY FORM AND HOW TO KEEP IT FROM ESCAPING.
SOUNDS GREAT, VIV.
...AND NOW IT'S TIME TO CELEBRATE!
ZAK
TEAM MEXICO RETURNS WITH THE WIN!
WE DID IT!
ZAK
I'LL GO CHECK ON TEAM JAPAN!
TWENTY-SEVEN GIRLS RESCUED WITH NO FATALITIES!
WE WERE WARRIORS!
NICE WORK, SPIDEY!
YOU GUYS KICKED BUTT!
YEAH...

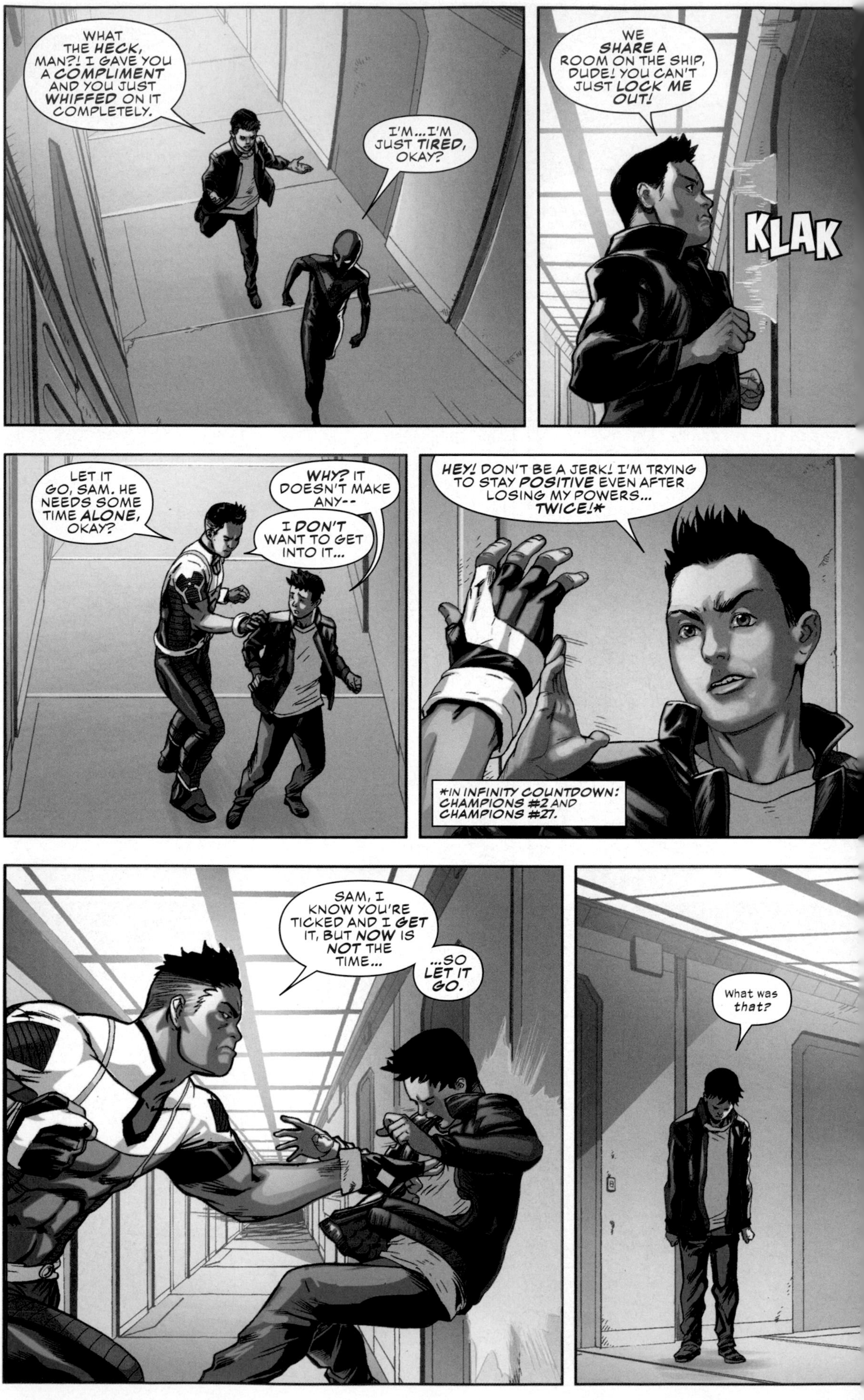
WHAT THE HECK, MAN?! I GAVE YOU A COMPLIMENT AND YOU JUST WHIFFED ON IT COMPLETELY.
I'M...I'M JUST TIRED, OKAY?
WE SHARE A ROOM ON THE SHIP, DUDE! YOU CAN'T JUST LOCK ME OUT!
KLAK
LET IT GO, SAM. HE NEEDS SOME TIME ALONE, OKAY?
WHY? IT DOESN'T MAKE ANY--
I DON'T WANT TO GET INTO IT...
HEY! DON'T BE A JERK! I'M TRYING TO STAY POSITIVE EVEN AFTER LOSING MY POWERS... TWICE!*
*IN INFINITY COUNTDOWN: CHAMPIONS #2 AND CHAMPIONS #27.
SAM, I KNOW YOU'RE TICKED AND I GET IT, BUT NOW IS NOT THE TIME...
...SO LET IT GO.
What was that?

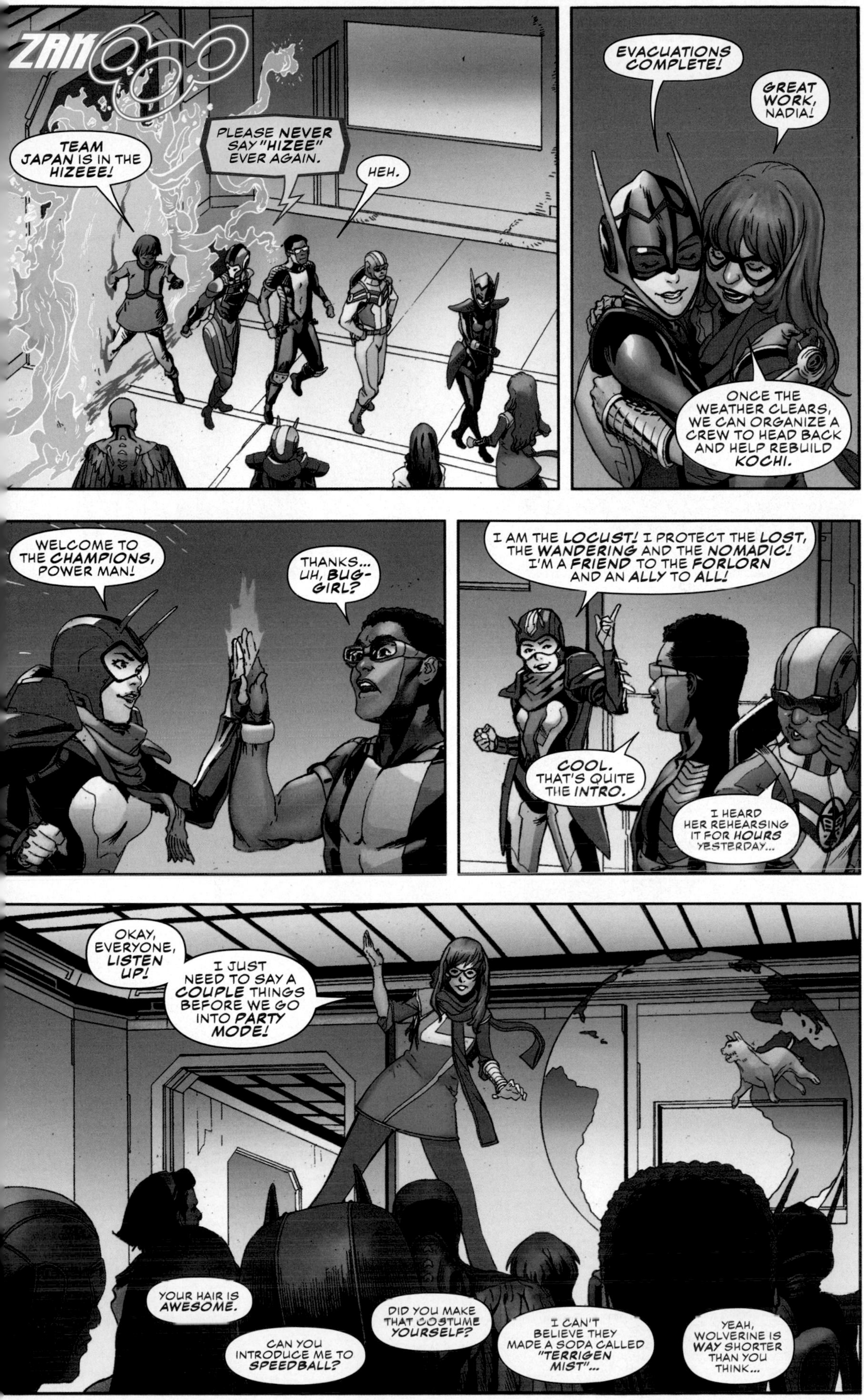
ZAM
TEAM JAPAN IS IN THE HIZEEE!
PLEASE NEVER SAY "HIZEE" EVER AGAIN.
HEH.
EVACUATIONS COMPLETE!
GREAT WORK, NADIA!
ONCE THE WEATHER CLEARS, WE CAN ORGANIZE A CREW TO HEAD BACK AND HELP REBUILD KOCHI.
WELCOME TO THE CHAMPIONS, POWER MAN!
THANKS... UH, BUG-GIRL?
I AM THE LOCUST! I PROTECT THE LOST, THE WANDERING AND THE NOMADIC! I'M A FRIEND TO THE FORLORN AND AN ALLY TO ALL!
COOL. THAT'S QUITE THE INTRO.
I HEARD HER REHEARSING IT FOR HOURS YESTERDAY...
OKAY, EVERYONE, LISTEN UP!
I JUST NEED TO SAY A COUPLE THINGS BEFORE WE GO INTO PARTY MODE!
YOUR HAIR IS AWESOME.
CAN YOU INTRODUCE ME TO SPEEDBALL?
DID YOU MAKE THAT COSTUME YOURSELF?
I CAN'T BELIEVE THEY MADE A SODA CALLED "TERRIGEN MIST"...
YEAH, WOLVERINE IS WAY SHORTER THAN YOU THINK...

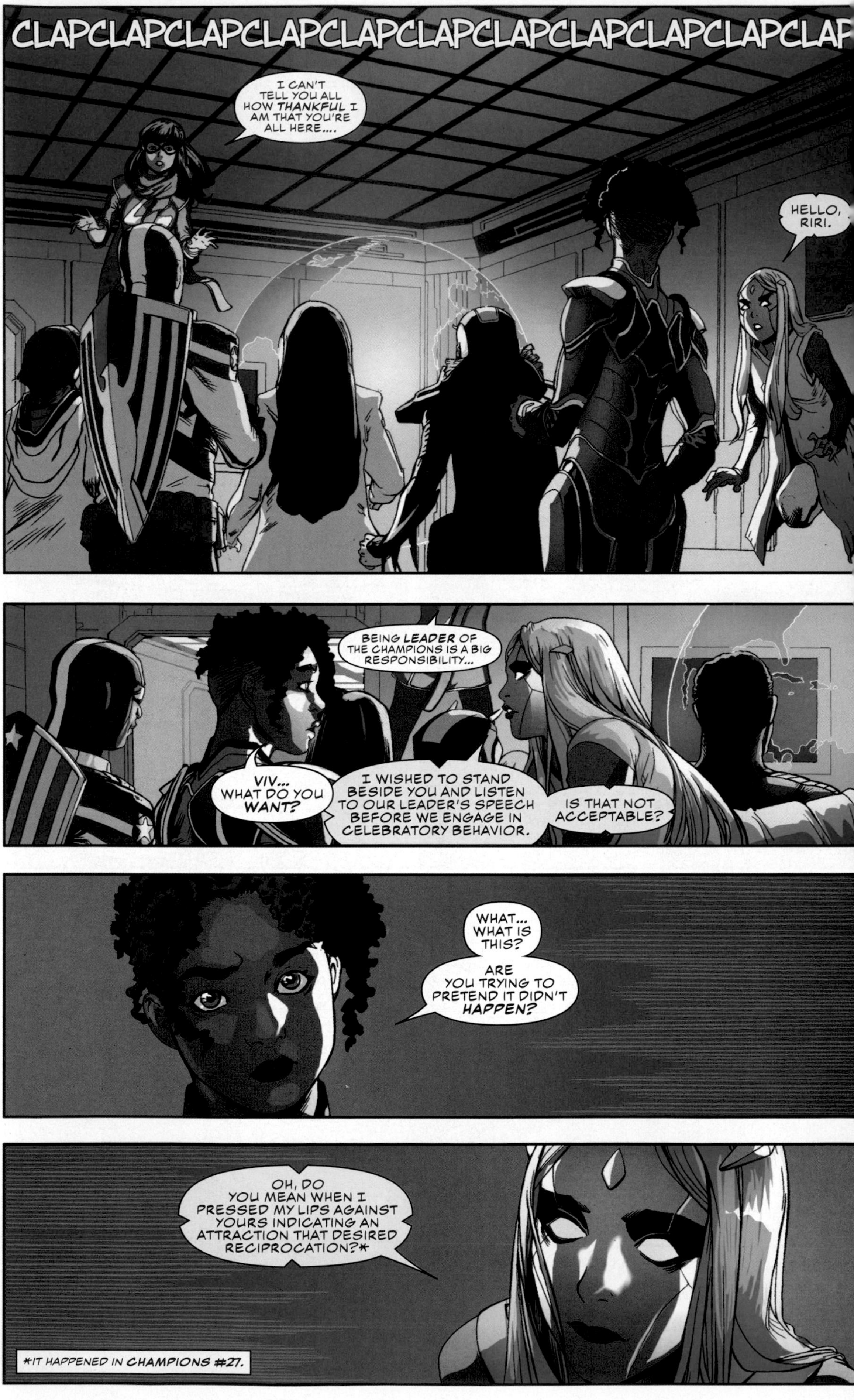
CLAPCLAPCLAPCLAPCLAPCLAPCLAPCLAPCLAPCLAPCLAP
I CAN'T TELL YOU ALL HOW THANKFUL I AM THAT YOU'RE ALL HERE....
HELLO, RIRI.
BEING LEADER OF THE CHAMPIONS IS A BIG RESPONSIBILITY...
VIV... WHAT DO YOU WANT?
I WISHED TO STAND BESIDE YOU AND LISTEN TO OUR LEADER'S SPEECH BEFORE WE ENGAGE IN CELEBRATORY BEHAVIOR.
IS THAT NOT ACCEPTABLE?
WHAT... WHAT IS THIS?
ARE YOU TRYING TO PRETEND IT DIDN'T HAPPEN?
OH, DO YOU MEAN WHEN I PRESSED MY LIPS AGAINST YOURS INDICATING AN ATTRACTION THAT DESIRED RECIPROCATION?*
*IT HAPPENED IN CHAMPIONS #27.

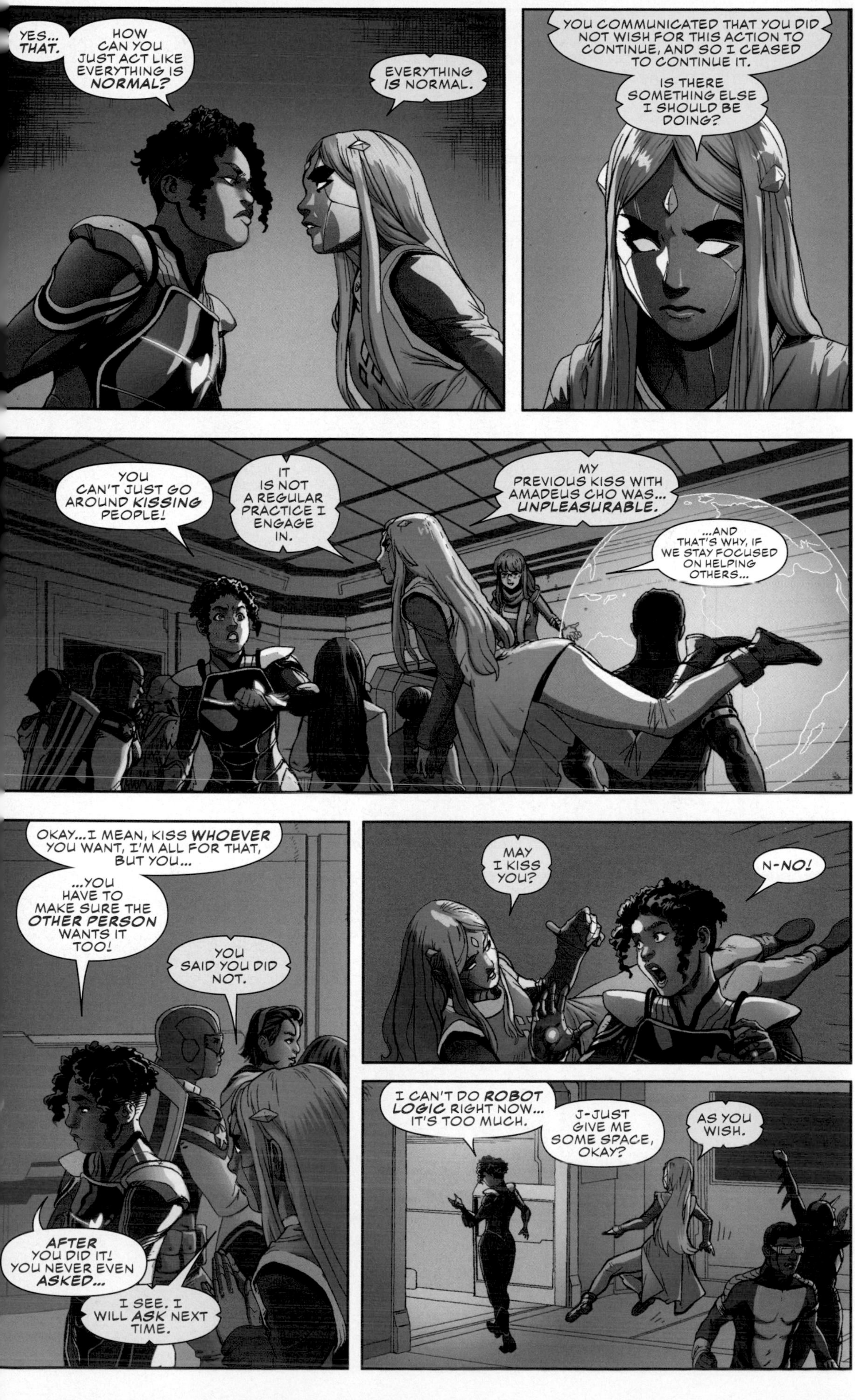
YES... THAT.
HOW CAN YOU JUST ACT LIKE EVERYTHING IS NORMAL?
EVERYTHING IS NORMAL.
YOU COMMUNICATED THAT YOU DID NOT WISH FOR THIS ACTION TO CONTINUE, AND SO I CEASED TO CONTINUE IT.
IS THERE SOMETHING ELSE I SHOULD BE DOING?
YOU CAN'T JUST GO AROUND KISSING PEOPLE!
IT IS NOT A REGULAR PRACTICE I ENGAGE IN.
MY PREVIOUS KISS WITH AMADEUS CHO WAS... UNPLEASURABLE.
...AND THAT'S WHY, IF WE STAY FOCUSED ON HELPING OTHERS...
OKAY...I MEAN, KISS WHOEVER YOU WANT, I'M ALL FOR THAT, BUT YOU...
...YOU HAVE TO MAKE SURE THE OTHER PERSON WANTS IT TOO!
YOU SAID YOU DID NOT.
AFTER YOU DID IT! YOU NEVER EVEN ASKED...
I SEE. I WILL ASK NEXT TIME.
MAY I KISS YOU?
N-NO!
I CAN'T DO ROBOT LOGIC RIGHT NOW... IT'S TOO MUCH.
J-JUST GIVE ME SOME SPACE, OKAY?
AS YOU WISH.

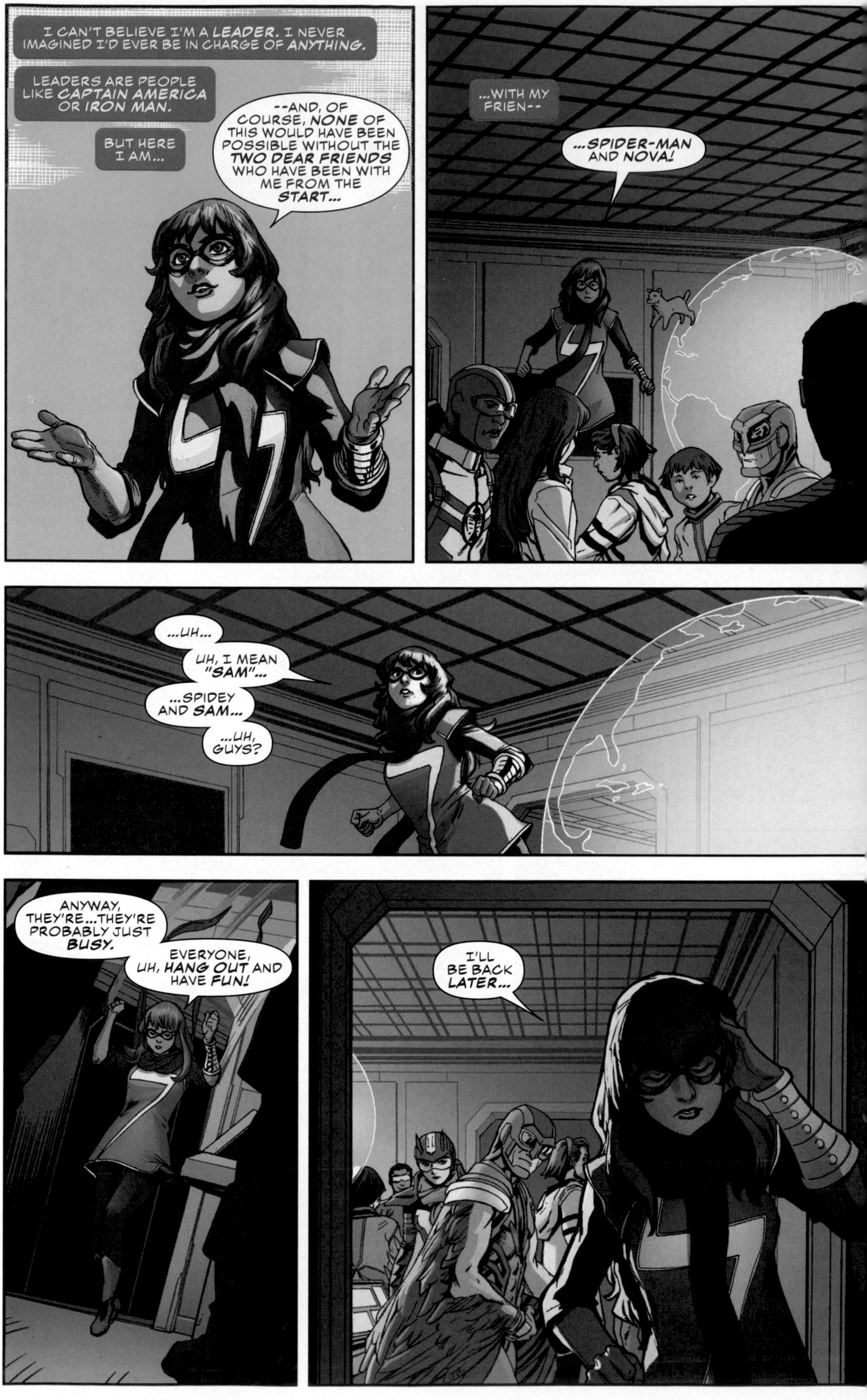
I CAN'T BELIEVE I'M A LEADER. I NEVER IMAGINED I'D EVER BE IN CHARGE OF ANYTHING.
LEADERS ARE PEOPLE LIKE CAPTAIN AMERICA OR IRON MAN.
BUT HERE I AM...
--AND, OF COURSE, NONE OF THIS WOULD HAVE BEEN POSSIBLE WITHOUT THE TWO DEAR FRIENDS WHO HAVE BEEN WITH ME FROM THE START...
...WITH MY FRIEN--
...SPIDER-MAN AND NOVA!
...UH...
UH, I MEAN "SAM"...
...SPIDEY AND SAM...
...UH, GUYS?
ANYWAY, THEY'RE...THEY'RE PROBABLY JUST BUSY.
EVERYONE, UH, HANG OUT AND HAVE FUN!
I'LL BE BACK LATER...

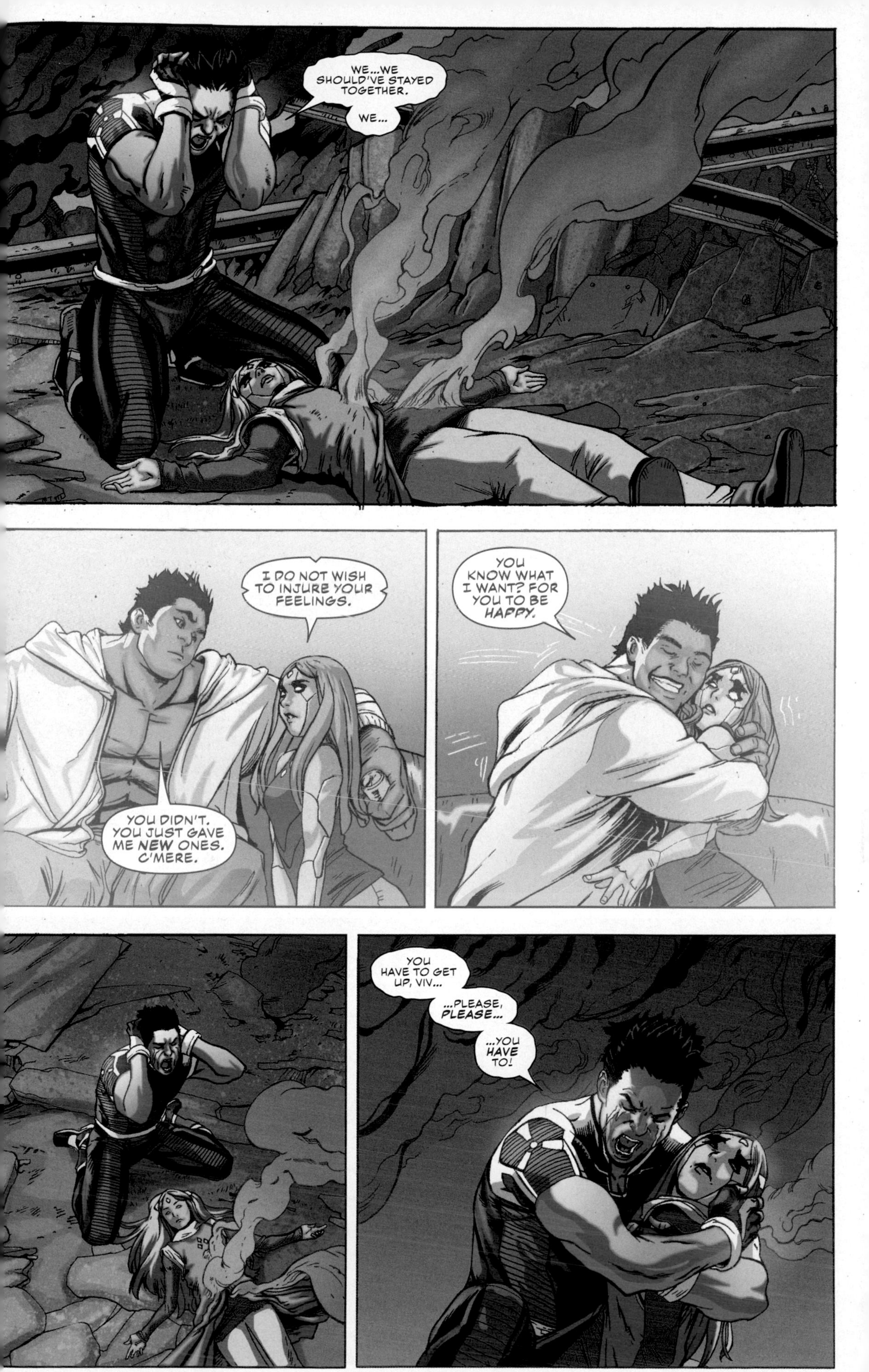
WE...WE SHOULD'VE STAYED TOGETHER.
WE...
I DO NOT WISH TO INJURE YOUR FEELINGS.
YOU DIDN'T. YOU JUST GAVE ME NEW ONES. C'MERE.
YOU KNOW WHAT I WANT? FOR YOU TO BE HAPPY.
YOU HAVE TO GET UP, VIV...
...PLEASE, PLEASE...
...YOU HAVE TO!

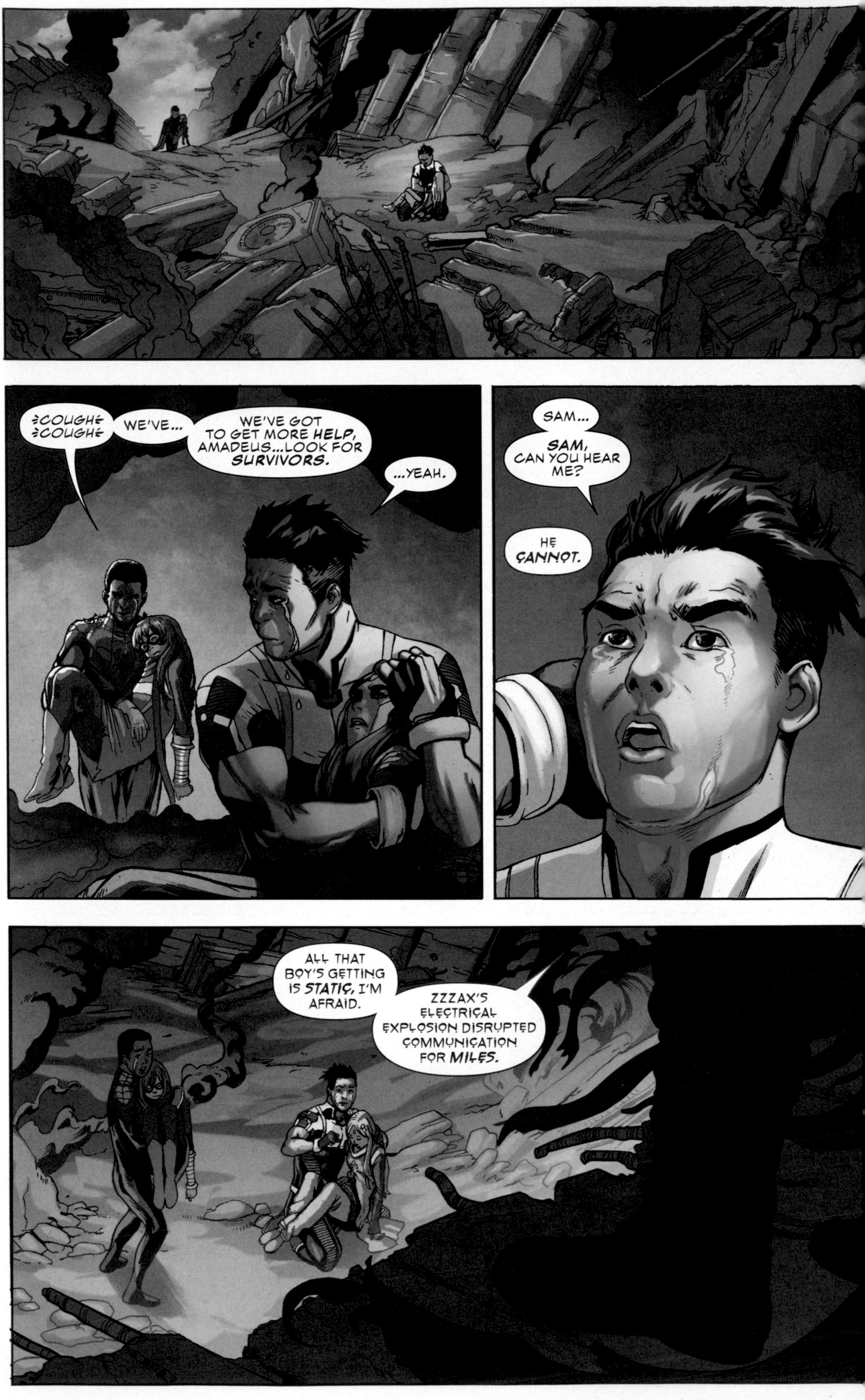

COUGH COUGH
WE'VE...
WE'VE GOT TO GET MORE HELP, AMADEUS...LOOK FOR SURVIVORS.
...YEAH.
SAM...
SAM, CAN YOU HEAR ME?
HE CANNOT.
ALL THAT BOY'S GETTING IS STATIC, I'M AFRAID.
ZZZAX'S ELECTRICAL EXPLOSION DISRUPTED COMMUNICATION FOR MILES.

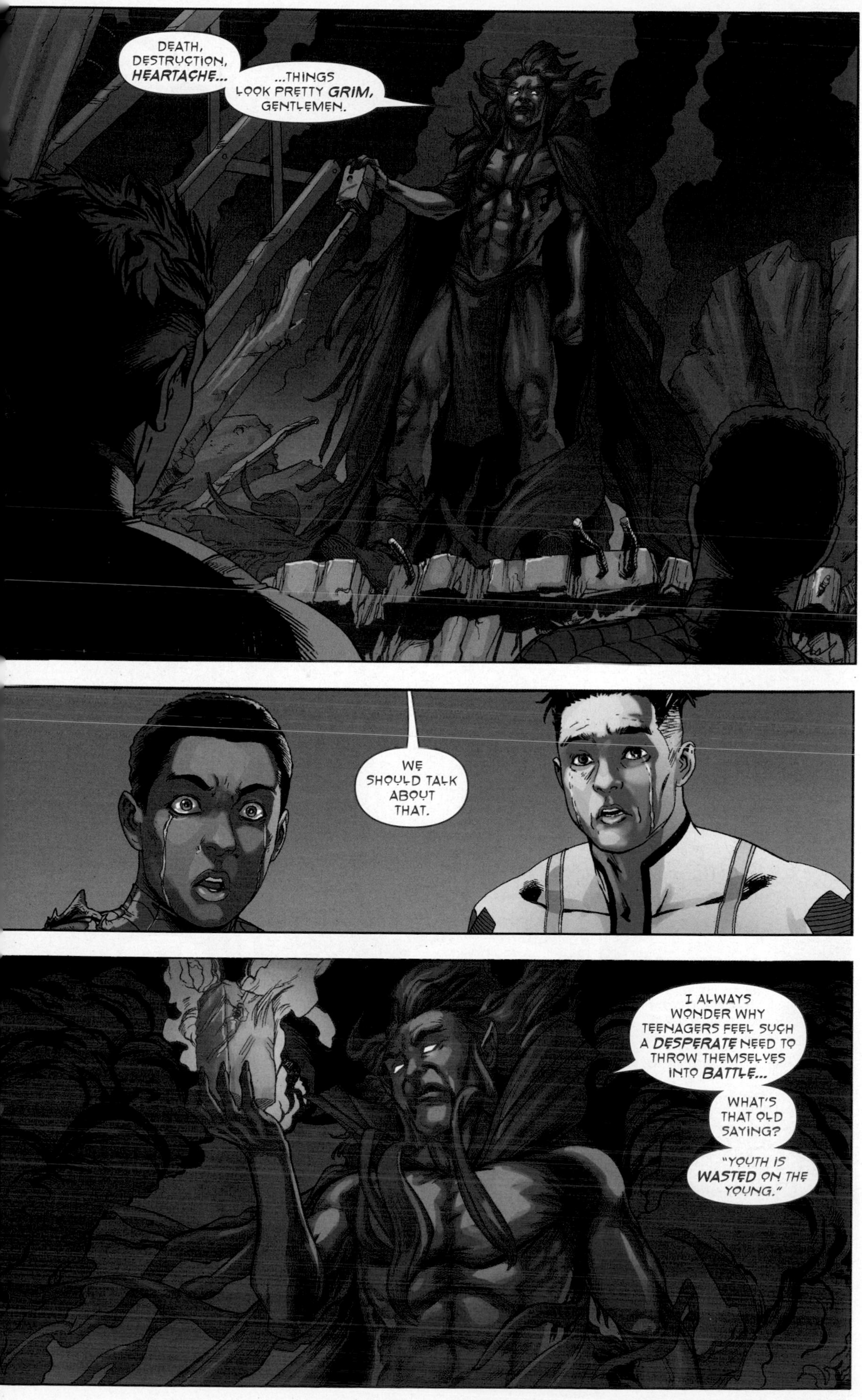
DEATH, DESTRUCTION, HEARTACHE...
...THINGS LOOK PRETTY GRIM, GENTLEMEN.
WE SHOULD TALK ABOUT THAT.
I ALWAYS WONDER WHY TEENAGERS FEEL SUCH A DESPERATE NEED TO THROW THEMSELVES INTO BATTLE...
WHAT'S THAT OLD SAYING?
"YOUTH IS WASTED ON THE YOUNG."

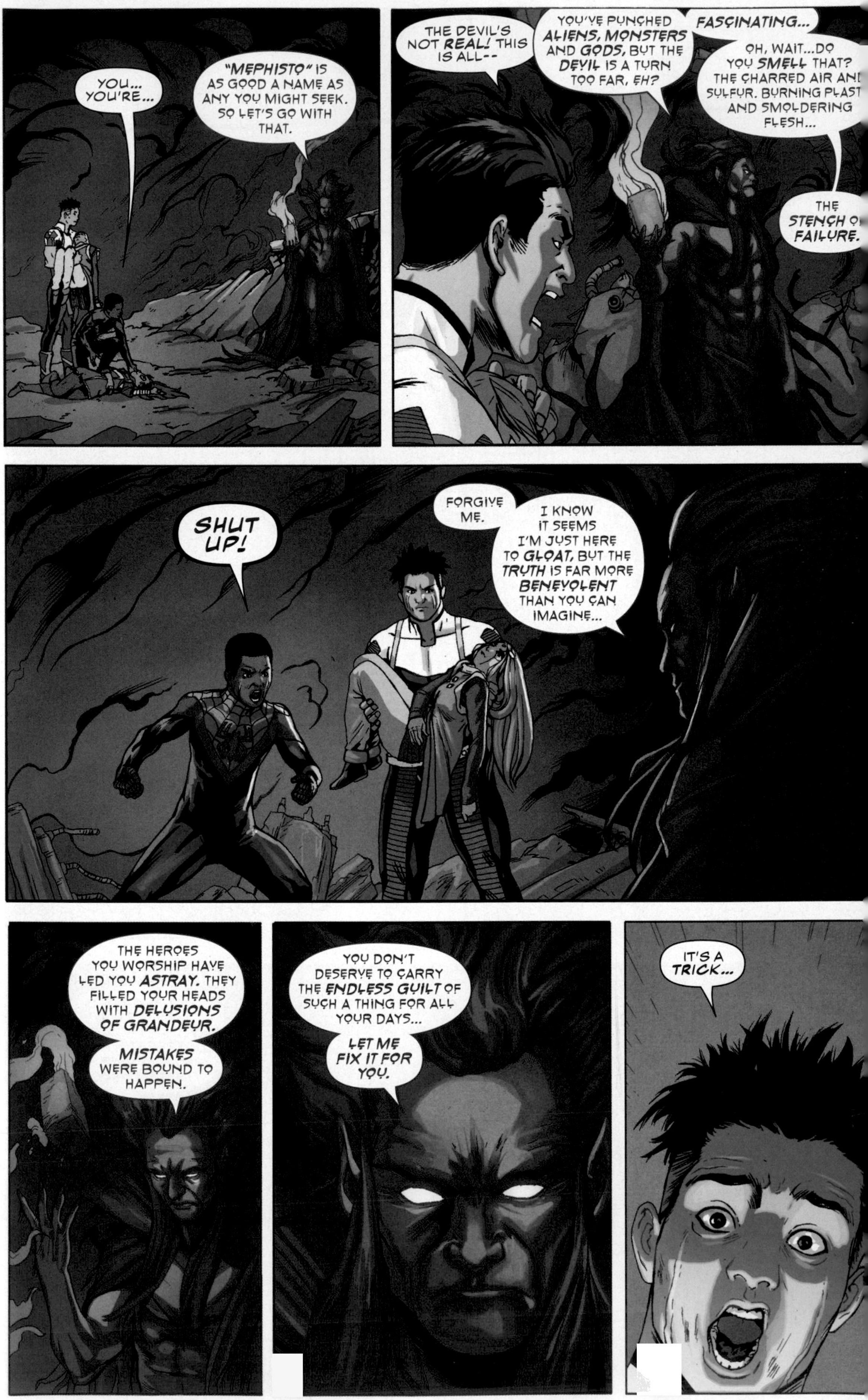
YOU... YOU'RE...
"MEPHISTO" IS AS GOOD A NAME AS ANY YOU MIGHT SEEK. SO LET'S GO WITH THAT.
THE DEVIL'S NOT REAL! THIS IS ALL--
YOU'VE PUNCHED ALIENS, MONSTERS AND GODS, BUT THE DEVIL IS A TURN TOO FAR, EH?
FASCINATING...
OH, WAIT...DO YOU SMELL THAT? THE CHARRED AIR AND SULFUR. BURNING PLAST AND SMOLDERING FLESH...
THE STENCH OF FAILURE.
SHUT UP!
FORGIVE ME.
I KNOW IT SEEMS I'M JUST HERE TO GLOAT, BUT THE TRUTH IS FAR MORE BENEVOLENT THAN YOU CAN IMAGINE...
THE HEROES YOU WORSHIP HAVE LED YOU ASTRAY. THEY FILLED YOUR HEADS WITH DELUSIONS OF GRANDEUR.
MISTAKES WERE BOUND TO HAPPEN.
YOU DON'T DESERVE TO CARRY THE ENDLESS GUILT OF SUCH A THING FOR ALL YOUR DAYS...
LET ME FIX IT FOR YOU.
IT'S A TRICK...

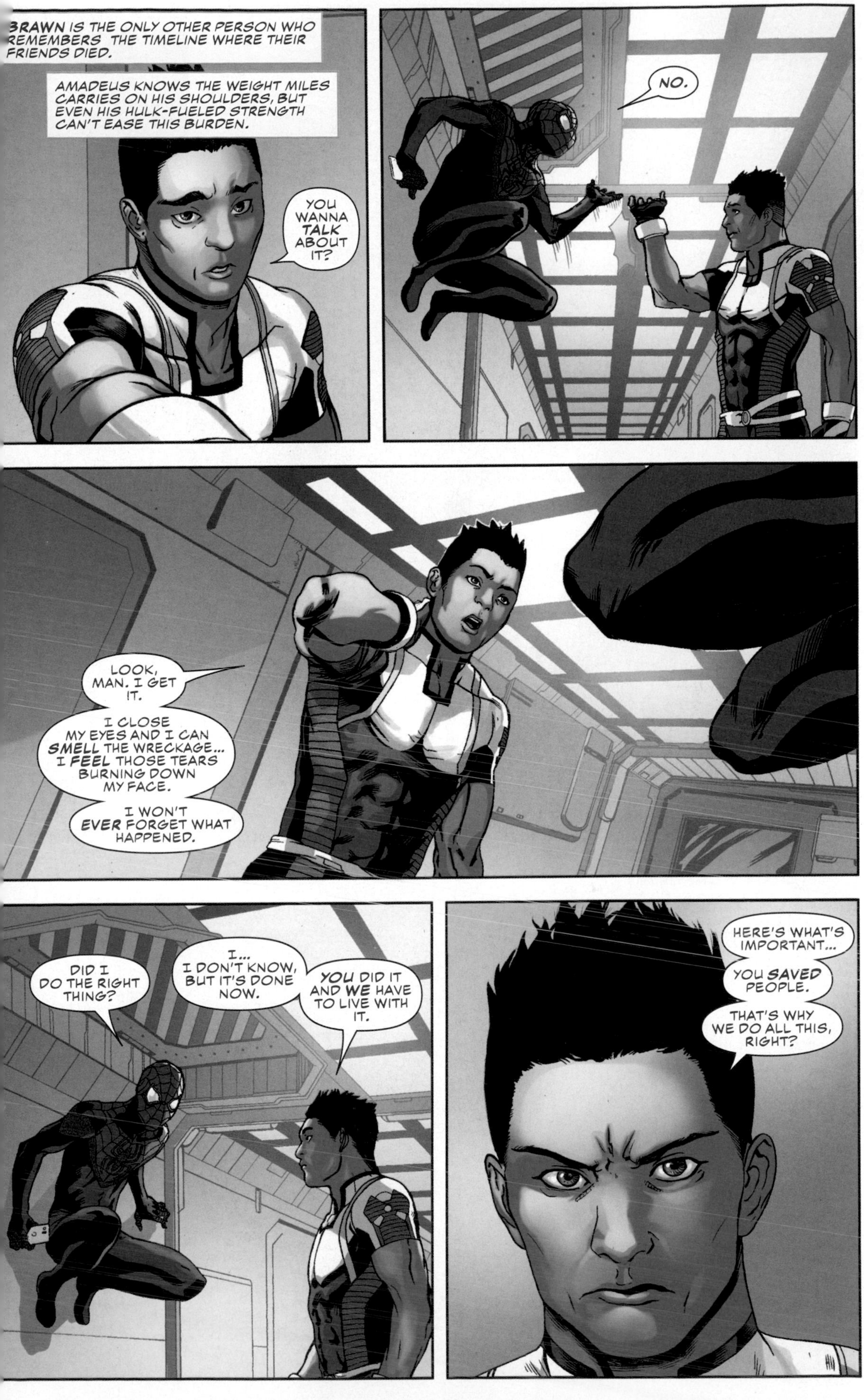
BRAWN IS THE ONLY OTHER PERSON WHO REMEMBERS THE TIMELINE WHERE THEIR FRIENDS DIED.
AMADEUS KNOWS THE WEIGHT MILES CARRIES ON HIS SHOULDERS, BUT EVEN HIS HULK-FUELED STRENGTH CAN'T EASE THIS BURDEN.
YOU WANNA TALK ABOUT IT?
NO.
LOOK, MAN. I GET IT.
I CLOSE MY EYES AND I CAN SMELL THE WRECKAGE... I FEEL THOSE TEARS BURNING DOWN MY FACE.
I WON'T EVER FORGET WHAT HAPPENED.
DID I DO THE RIGHT THING?
I... I DON'T KNOW, BUT IT'S DONE NOW.
YOU DID IT AND WE HAVE TO LIVE WITH IT.
HERE'S WHAT'S IMPORTANT...
YOU SAVED PEOPLE.
THAT'S WHY WE DO ALL THIS, RIGHT?

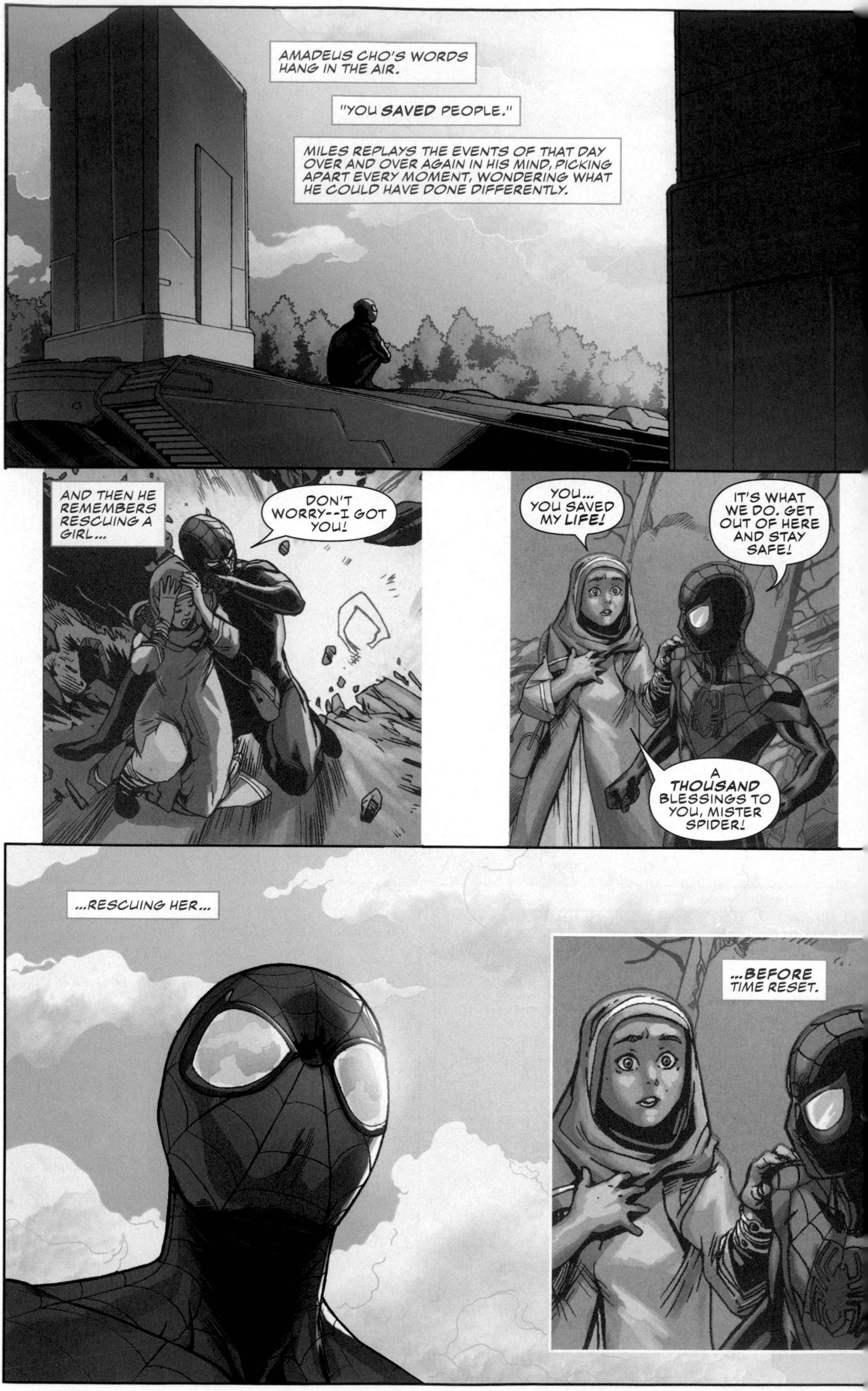
AMADEUS CHO'S WORDS HANG IN THE AIR.
"YOU SAVED PEOPLE."
MILES REPLAYS THE EVENTS OF THAT DAY OVER AND OVER AGAIN IN HIS MIND, PICKING APART EVERY MOMENT, WONDERING WHAT HE COULD HAVE DONE DIFFERENTLY.
AND THEN HE REMEMBERS RESCUING A GIRL...
DON'T WORRY--I GOT YOU!
YOU... YOU SAVED MY LIFE!
IT'S WHAT WE DO. GET OUT OF HERE AND STAY SAFE!
A THOUSAND BLESSINGS TO YOU, MISTER SPIDER!
...RESCUING HER...
...BEFORE TIME RESET.

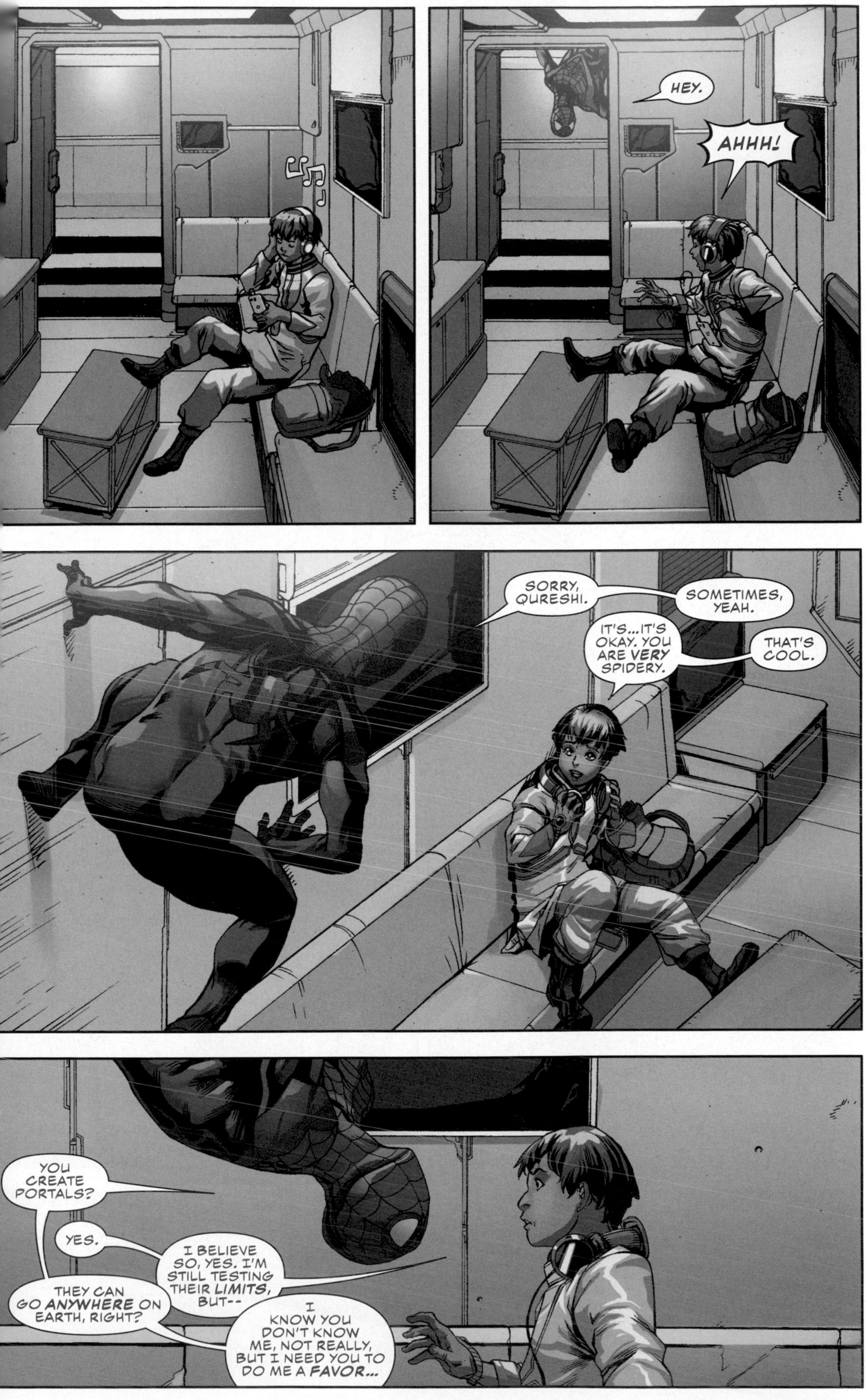
HEY.
AHHH!
SORRY, QURESHI.
IT'S...IT'S OKAY. YOU ARE VERY SPIDERY.
SOMETIMES, YEAH.
THAT'S COOL.
YOU CREATE PORTALS?
YES.
I BELIEVE SO, YES. I'M STILL TESTING THEIR LIMITS, BUT--
THEY CAN GO ANYWHERE ON EARTH, RIGHT?
I KNOW YOU DON'T KNOW ME, NOT REALLY, BUT I NEED YOU TO DO ME A FAVOR...

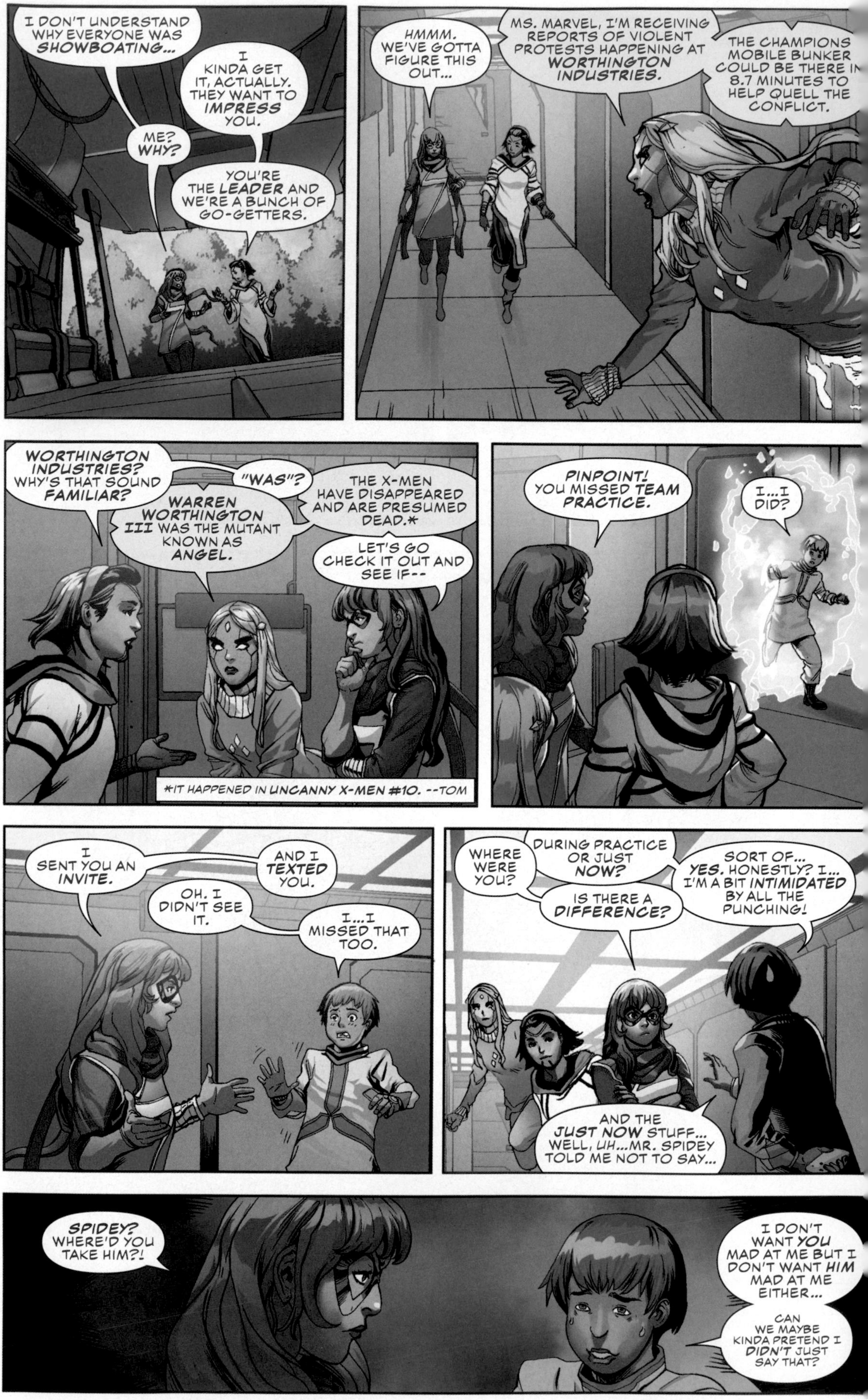
I DON'T UNDERSTAND WHY EVERYONE WAS SHOWBOATING...
I KINDA GET IT, ACTUALLY. THEY WANT TO IMPRESS YOU.
ME? WHY?
YOU'RE THE LEADER AND WE'RE A BUNCH OF GO-GETTERS.
HMMM. WE'VE GOTTA FIGURE THIS OUT...
MS. MARVEL, I'M RECEIVING REPORTS OF VIOLENT PROTESTS HAPPENING AT WORTHINGTON INDUSTRIES.
THE CHAMPIONS MOBILE BUNKER COULD BE THERE IN 8.7 MINUTES TO HELP QUELL THE CONFLICT.
WORTHINGTON INDUSTRIES? WHY'S THAT SOUND FAMILIAR?
WARREN WORTHINGTON III WAS THE MUTANT KNOWN AS ANGEL.
"WAS"?
THE X-MEN HAVE DISAPPEARED AND ARE PRESUMED DEAD.*
LET'S GO CHECK IT OUT AND SEE IF--
*IT HAPPENED IN UNCANNY X-MEN #10. --TOM
PINPOINT! YOU MISSED TEAM PRACTICE.
I...I DID?
I SENT YOU AN INVITE.
AND I TEXTED YOU.
OH. I DIDN'T SEE IT.
I...I MISSED THAT TOO.
WHERE WERE YOU?
DURING PRACTICE OR JUST NOW?
IS THERE A DIFFERENCE?
SORT OF... YES. HONESTLY? I... I'M A BIT INTIMIDATED BY ALL THE PUNCHING!
AND THE JUST NOW STUFF... WELL, UH...MR. SPIDEY TOLD ME NOT TO SAY...
SPIDEY? WHERE'D YOU TAKE HIM?!
I DON'T WANT YOU MAD AT ME BUT I DON'T WANT HIM MAD AT ME EITHER...
CAN WE MAYBE KINDA PRETEND I DIDN'T JUST SAY THAT?

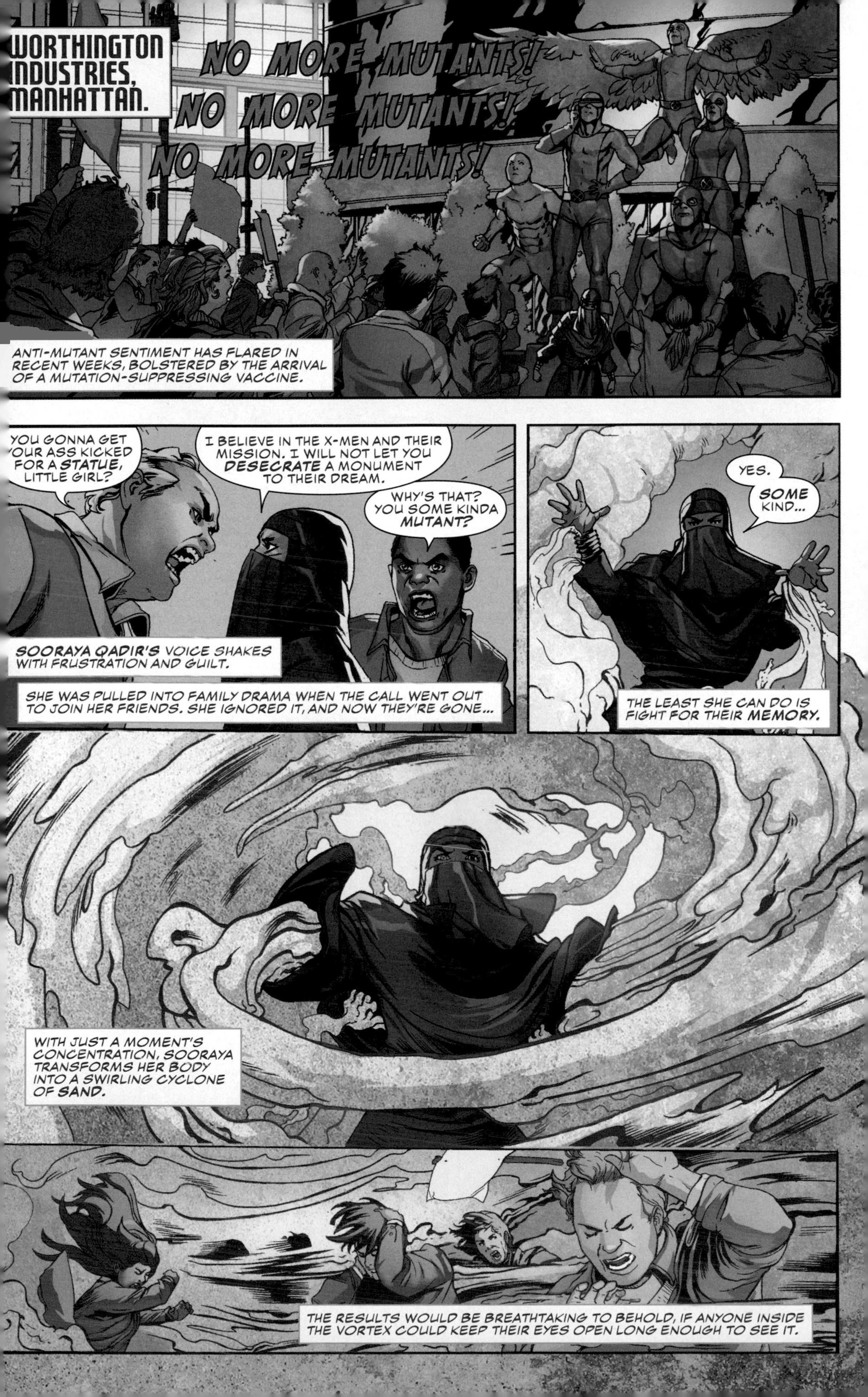
WORTHINGTON INDUSTRIES, MANHATTAN.
NO MORE MUTANTS! NO MORE MUTANTS! NO MORE MUTANTS!
ANTI-MUTANT SENTIMENT HAS FLARED IN RECENT WEEKS, BOLSTERED BY THE ARRIVAL OF A MUTATION-SUPPRESSING VACCINE.
YOU GONNA GET YOUR ASS KICKED FOR A STATUE, LITTLE GIRL?
I BELIEVE IN THE X-MEN AND THEIR MISSION. I WILL NOT LET YOU DESECRATE A MONUMENT TO THEIR DREAM.
WHY'S THAT? YOU SOME KINDA MUTANT?
SOORAYA QADIR'S VOICE SHAKES WITH FRUSTRATION AND GUILT.
SHE WAS PULLED INTO FAMILY DRAMA WHEN THE CALL WENT OUT TO JOIN HER FRIENDS. SHE IGNORED IT, AND NOW THEY'RE GONE...
YES.
SOME KIND...
THE LEAST SHE CAN DO IS FIGHT FOR THEIR MEMORY.
WITH JUST A MOMENT'S CONCENTRATION, SOORAYA TRANSFORMS HER BODY INTO A SWIRLING CYCLONE OF SAND.
THE RESULTS WOULD BE BREATHTAKING TO BEHOLD, IF ANYONE INSIDE THE VORTEX COULD KEEP THEIR EYES OPEN LONG ENOUGH TO SEE IT.

THOOM

OKAY, EVERYBODY!

LET'S CALM THIS DOWN!

NO ONE NEEDS TO GET HURT.

IT'S THE *YOUNG AVENGERS!*

YOU ARE MISTAKEN. WE ARE THE *CHAMPIONS.*

ARREST THAT MUTANT!

SHE TRIED TO *KILL* US!

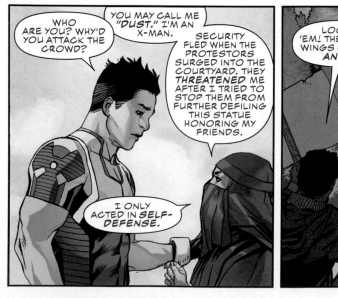

WHO ARE YOU? WHY'D YOU ATTACK THE CROWD?

YOU MAY CALL ME *"DUST."* I'M AN X-MAN.

SECURITY FLED WHEN THE PROTESTORS SURGED INTO THE COURTYARD. THEY *THREATENED* ME AFTER I TRIED TO STOP THEM FROM FURTHER DEFILING THIS STATUE HONORING MY FRIENDS.

I ONLY ACTED IN *SELF-DEFENSE.*

LOOK AT 'EM! THEY'VE GOT WINGS JUST LIKE *ANGEL!*

THEY'RE *MUTANTS!*

BACK OFF. WE'RE NOT *STARTING* ANYTHING, BUT WE'LL HAPPILY *STOP* IT IF YOU TRY TO HURT ANYONE.

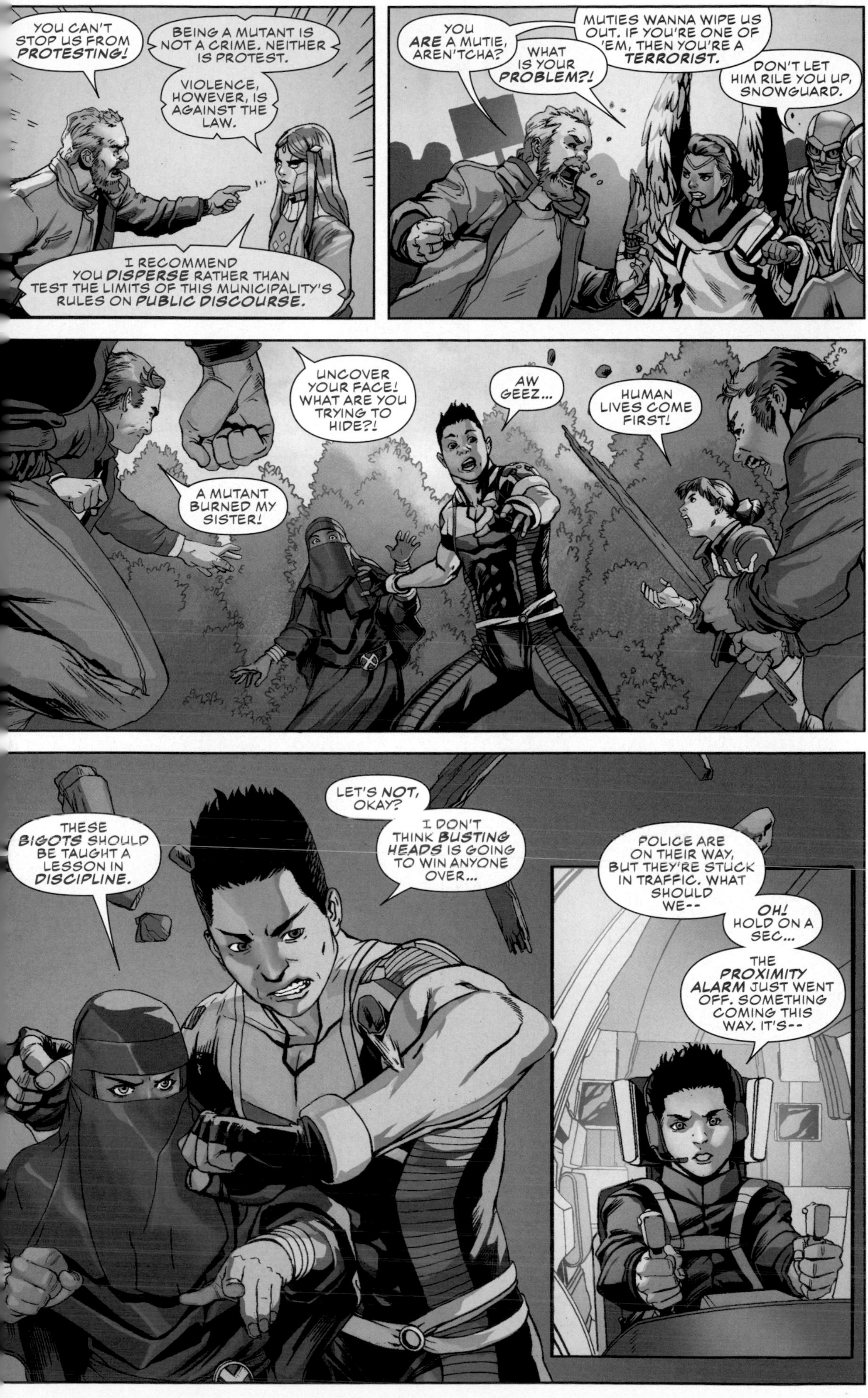
YOU CAN'T STOP US FROM PROTESTING!
BEING A MUTANT IS NOT A CRIME. NEITHER IS PROTEST.
VIOLENCE, HOWEVER, IS AGAINST THE LAW.
I RECOMMEND YOU DISPERSE RATHER THAN TEST THE LIMITS OF THIS MUNICIPALITY'S RULES ON PUBLIC DISCOURSE.
YOU ARE A MUTIE, AREN'TCHA?
MUTIES WANNA WIPE US OUT. IF YOU'RE ONE OF 'EM, THEN YOU'RE A TERRORIST.
WHAT IS YOUR PROBLEM?!
DON'T LET HIM RILE YOU UP, SNOWGUARD.
UNCOVER YOUR FACE! WHAT ARE YOU TRYING TO HIDE?!
A MUTANT BURNED MY SISTER!
AW GEEZ...
HUMAN LIVES COME FIRST!
THESE BIGOTS SHOULD BE TAUGHT A LESSON IN DISCIPLINE.
LET'S NOT, OKAY?
I DON'T THINK BUSTING HEADS IS GOING TO WIN ANYONE OVER...
POLICE ARE ON THEIR WAY, BUT THEY'RE STUCK IN TRAFFIC. WHAT SHOULD WE--
OH! HOLD ON A SEC...
THE PROXIMITY ALARM JUST WENT OFF. SOMETHING COMING THIS WAY. IT'S--

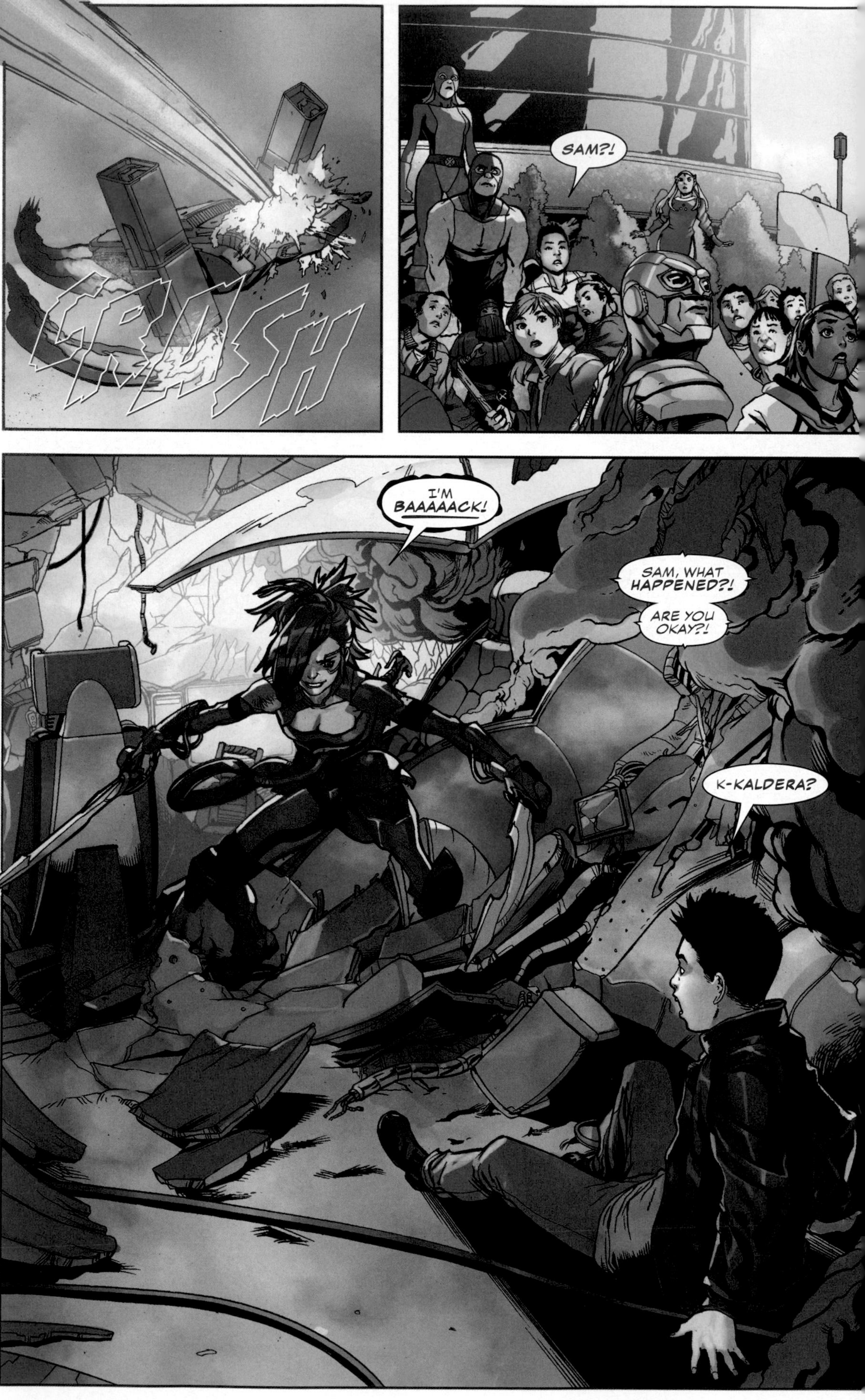
CRASH
SAM?!
I'M BAAAAACK!
SAM, WHAT HAPPENED?!
ARE YOU OKAY?!
K-KALDERA?

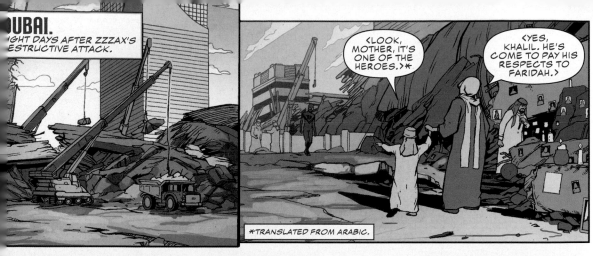

DUBAI.
IGHT DAYS AFTER ZZZAX'S DESTRUCTIVE ATTACK.

<LOOK, MOTHER, IT'S ONE OF THE HEROES.>*

<YES, KHALIL. HE'S COME TO PAY HIS RESPECTS TO FARIDAH.>

*TRANSLATED FROM ARABIC.

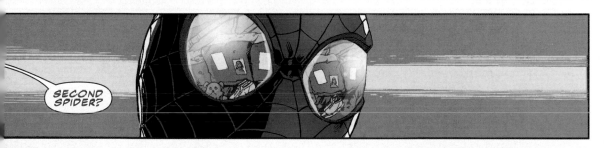

SECOND SPIDER?

DO YOU MEAN ME?

THAT'S HOW YOUR NAME IS TRANSLATED IN ARABIC. THE NEWSPAPERS CALL YOU "THE SECOND SPIDER."

OH. OKAY...

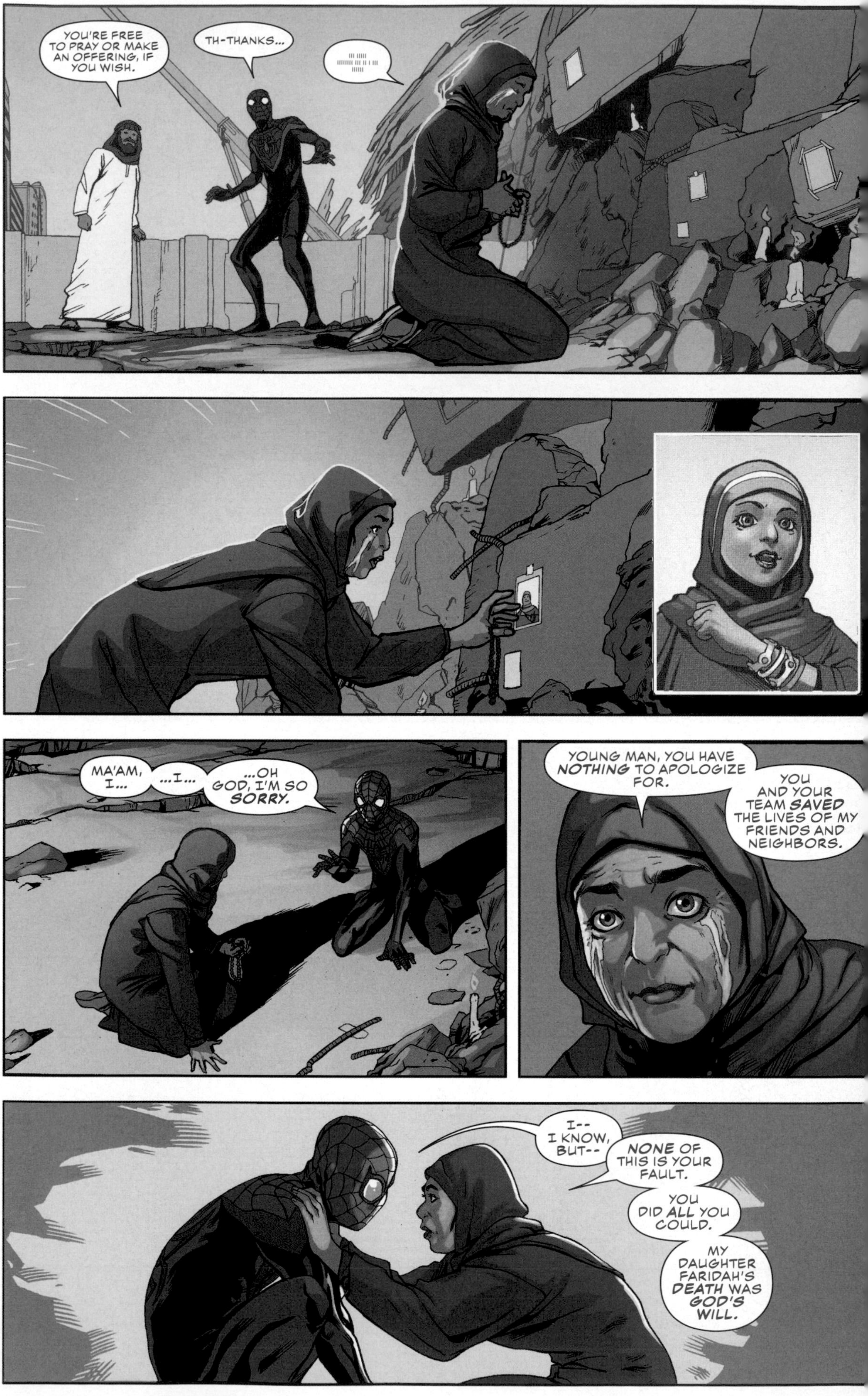
YOU'RE FREE TO PRAY OR MAKE AN OFFERING, IF YOU WISH.
TH-THANKS...
MA'AM, I...
...I...
...OH GOD, I'M SO SORRY.
YOUNG MAN, YOU HAVE NOTHING TO APOLOGIZE FOR.
YOU AND YOUR TEAM SAVED THE LIVES OF MY FRIENDS AND NEIGHBORS.
I-- I KNOW, BUT--
NONE OF THIS IS YOUR FAULT.
YOU DID ALL YOU COULD.
MY DAUGHTER FARIDAH'S DEATH WAS GOD'S WILL.

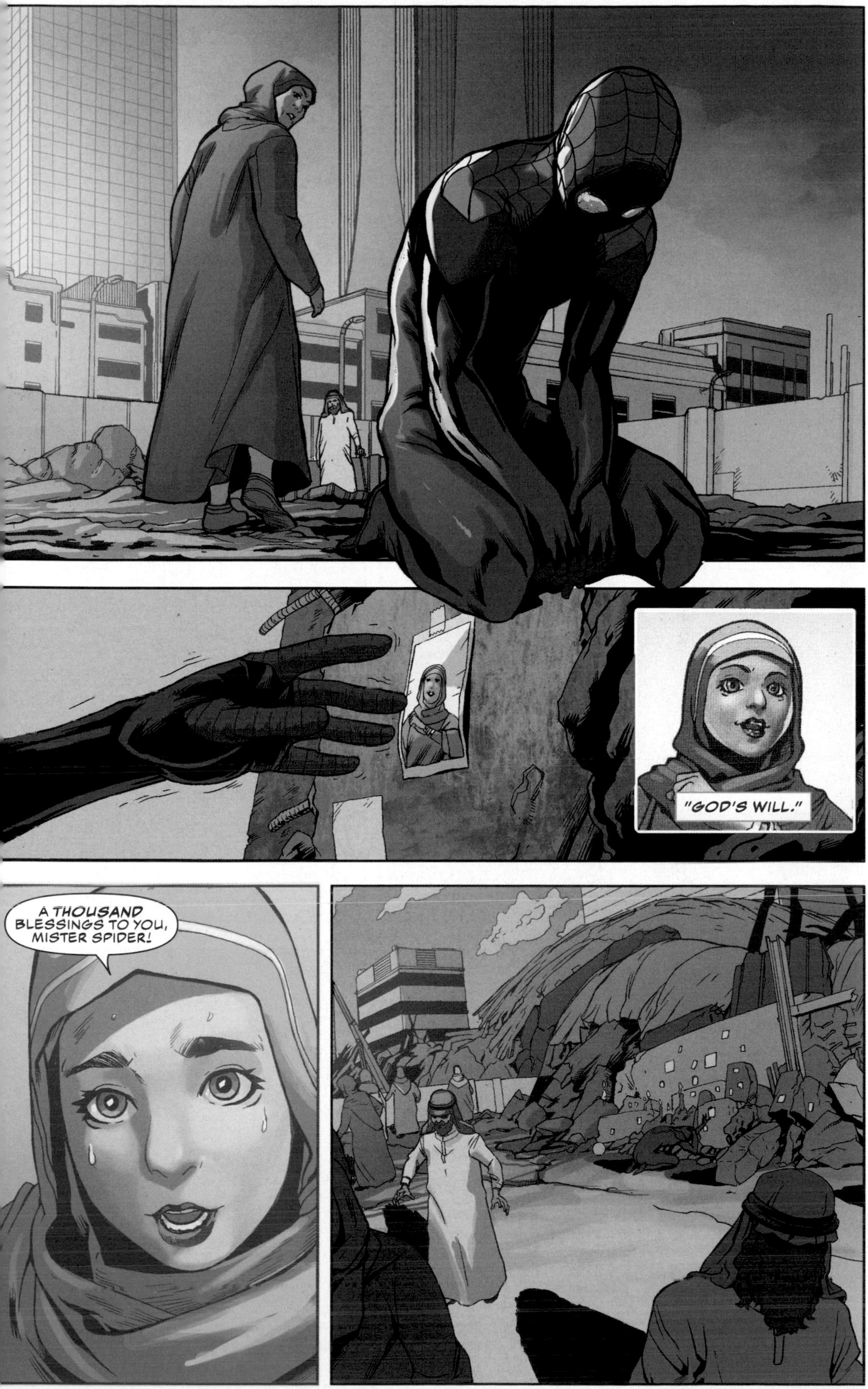
"GOD'S WILL."
A THOUSAND BLESSINGS TO YOU, MISTER SPIDER!

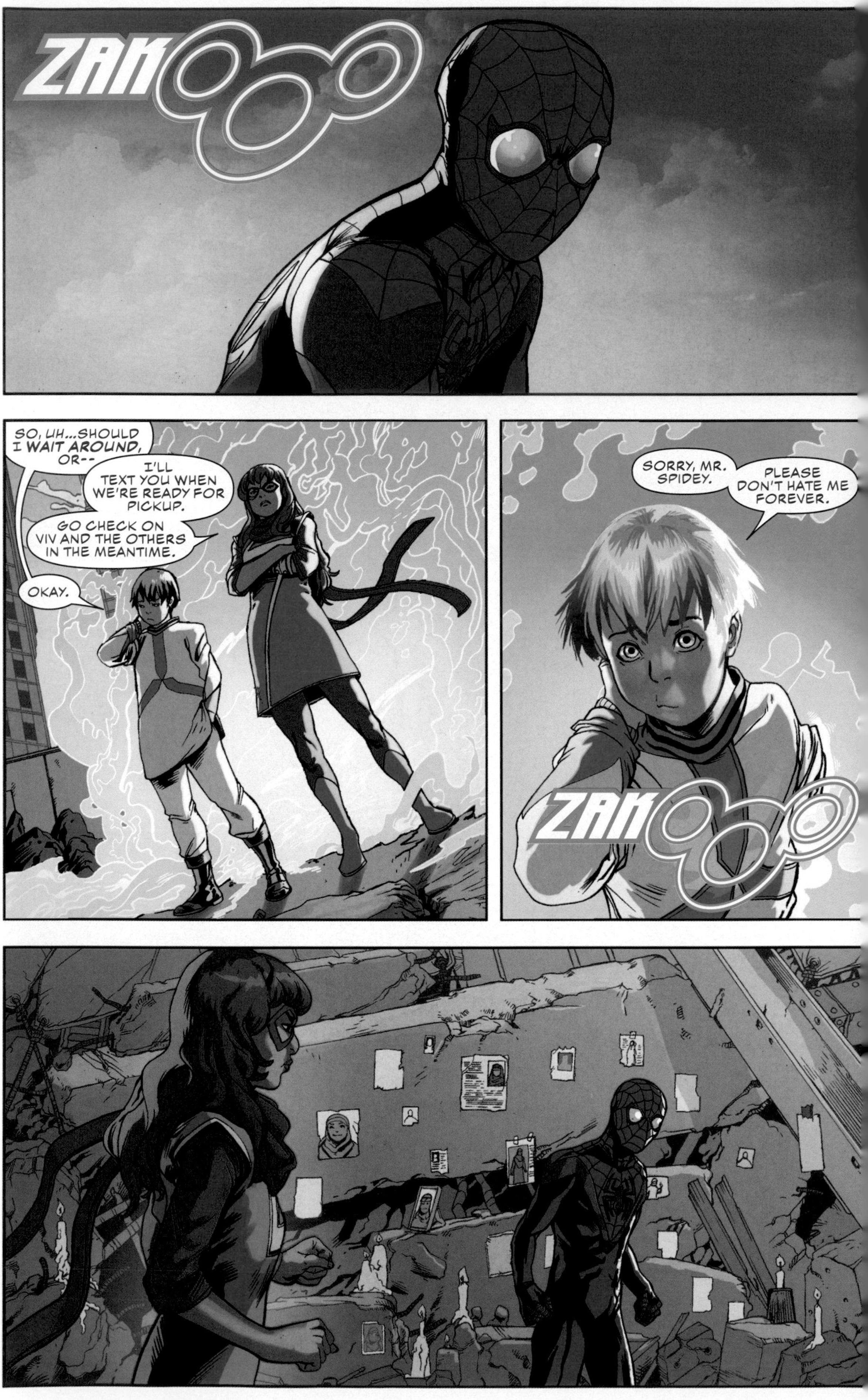
ZAKOOOP
SO, UH...SHOULD I WAIT AROUND, OR--
I'LL TEXT YOU WHEN WE'RE READY FOR PICKUP.
GO CHECK ON VIV AND THE OTHERS IN THE MEANTIME.
OKAY.
SORRY, MR. SPIDEY.
PLEASE DON'T HATE ME FOREVER.
ZAKOOOP

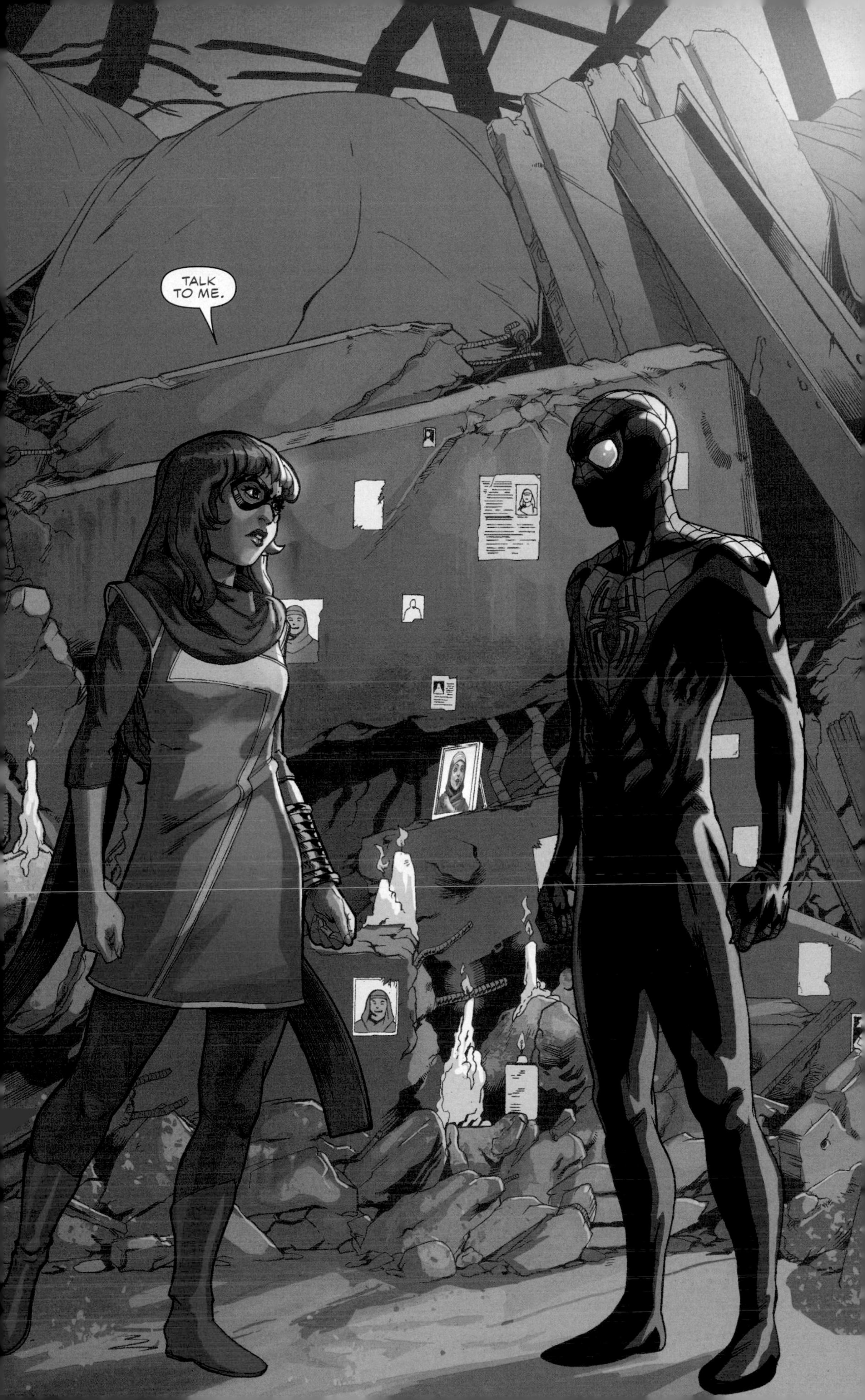
TALK TO ME.

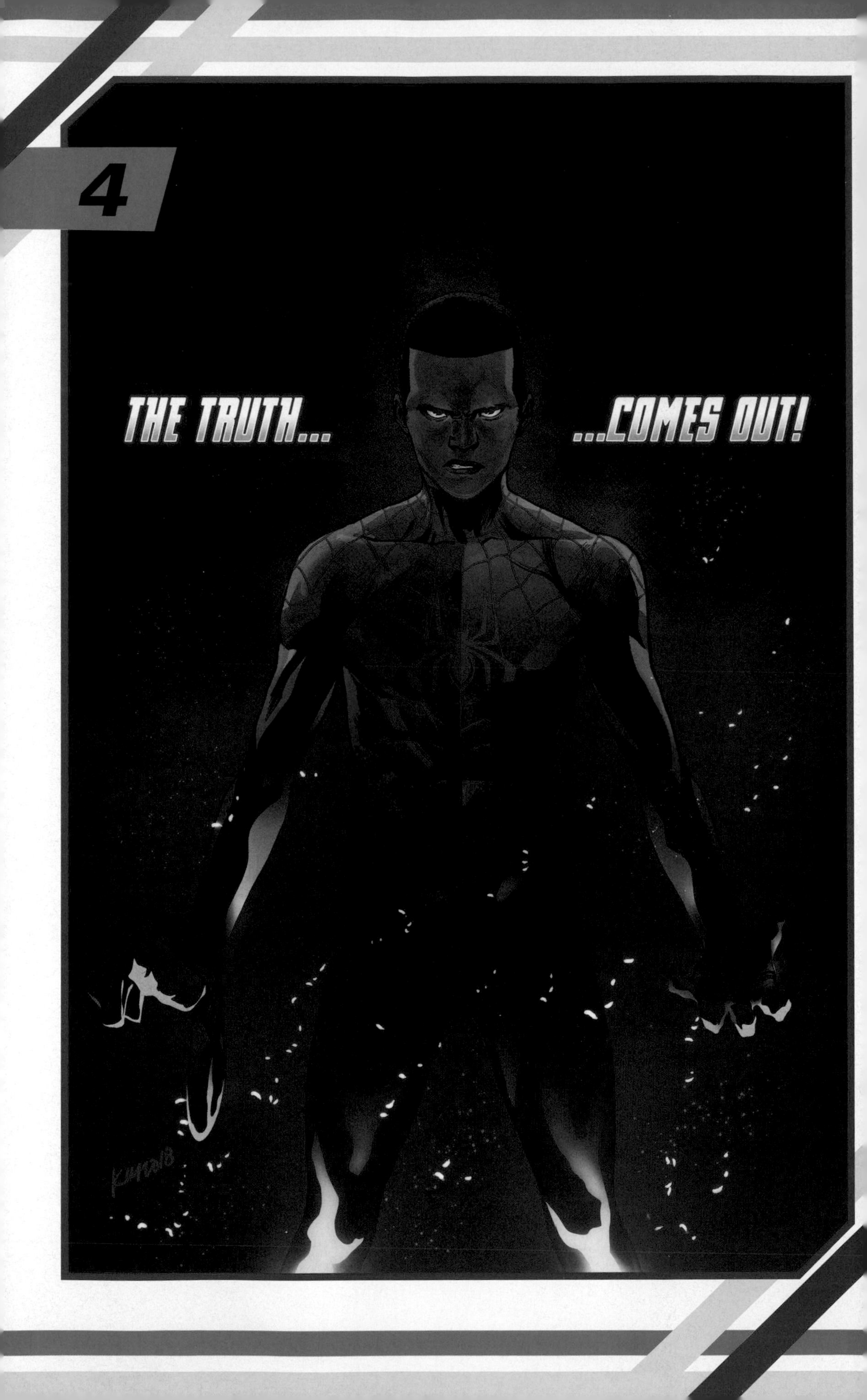
4
THE TRUTH...
...COMES OUT!

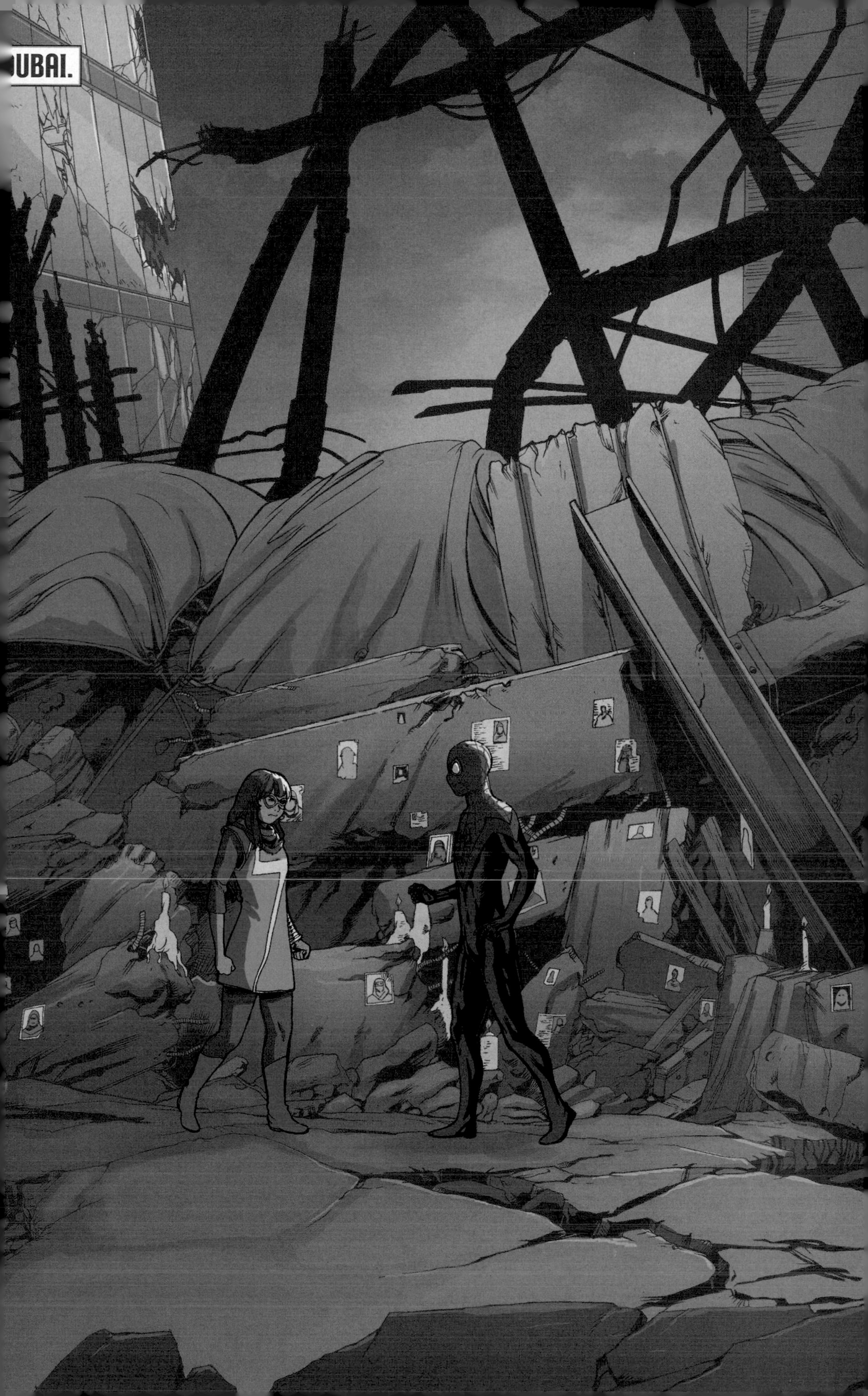

UBAI.

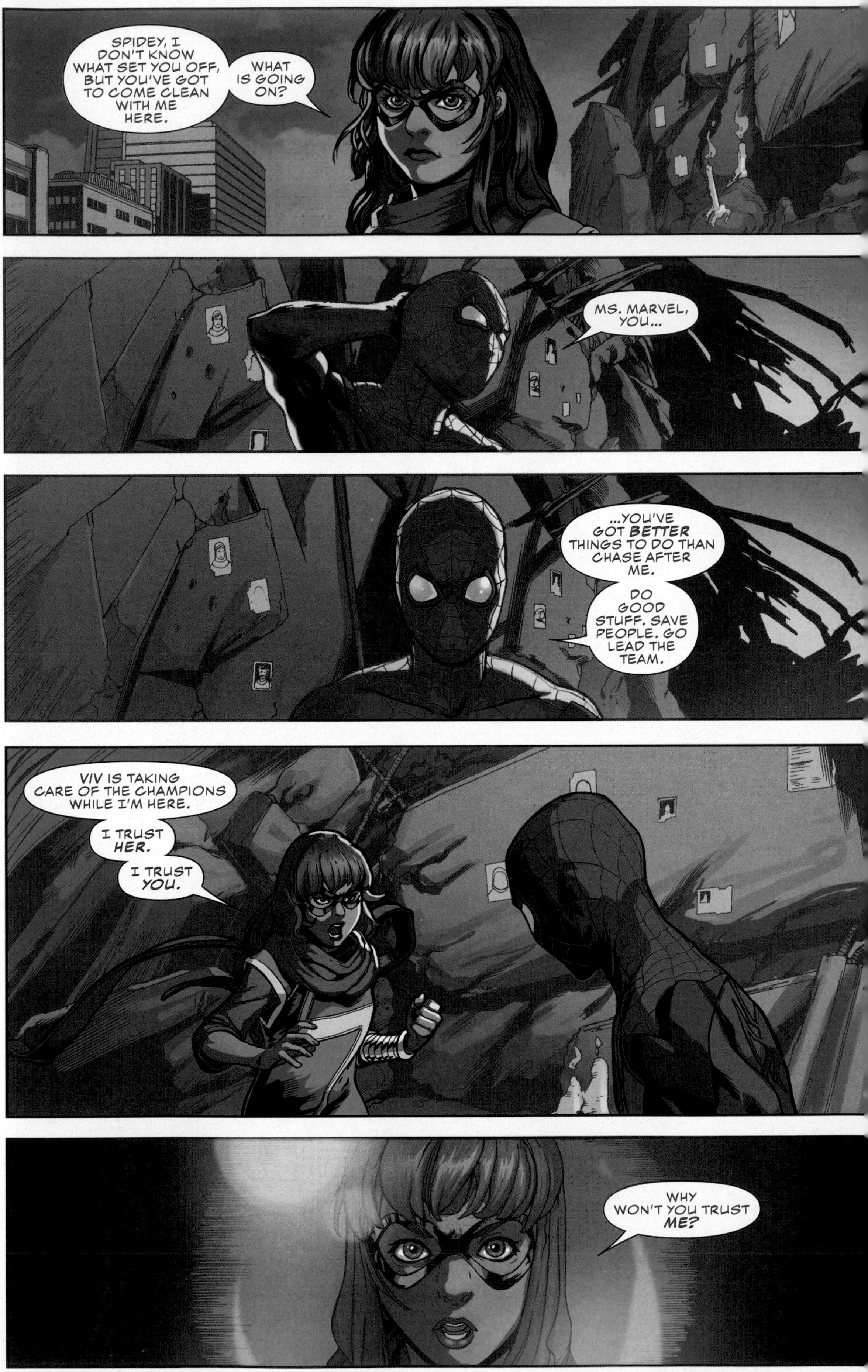
SPIDEY, I DON'T KNOW WHAT SET YOU OFF, BUT YOU'VE GOT TO COME CLEAN WITH ME HERE.
WHAT IS GOING ON?
MS. MARVEL, YOU...
...YOU'VE GOT **BETTER** THINGS TO DO THAN CHASE AFTER ME.
DO GOOD STUFF. SAVE PEOPLE. GO LEAD THE TEAM.
VIV IS TAKING CARE OF THE CHAMPIONS WHILE I'M HERE.
I TRUST ***HER.***
I TRUST ***YOU.***
WHY WON'T YOU TRUST ***ME?***

HE CHAMPIONS MOBILE BUNKER,
OATING ABOVE MANHATTAN.
TIME TO DIE!
KALDERA: FORMER ASSASSIN EMPLOYED BY THE BLACK ORDER. CURRENT SEEKER OF VENGEANCE AGAINST SAM ALEXANDER.
SLASH
AHHHH!
SAM ALEXANDER: FORMER SPACE HERO KNOWN AS "NOVA." CURRENT PILOT OF THE CHAMPIONS MOBILE BUNKER, FOR AS LONG AS IT'S ABLE TO STAY AIRBORNE.
Beat The Devil, Part 4
No Choice

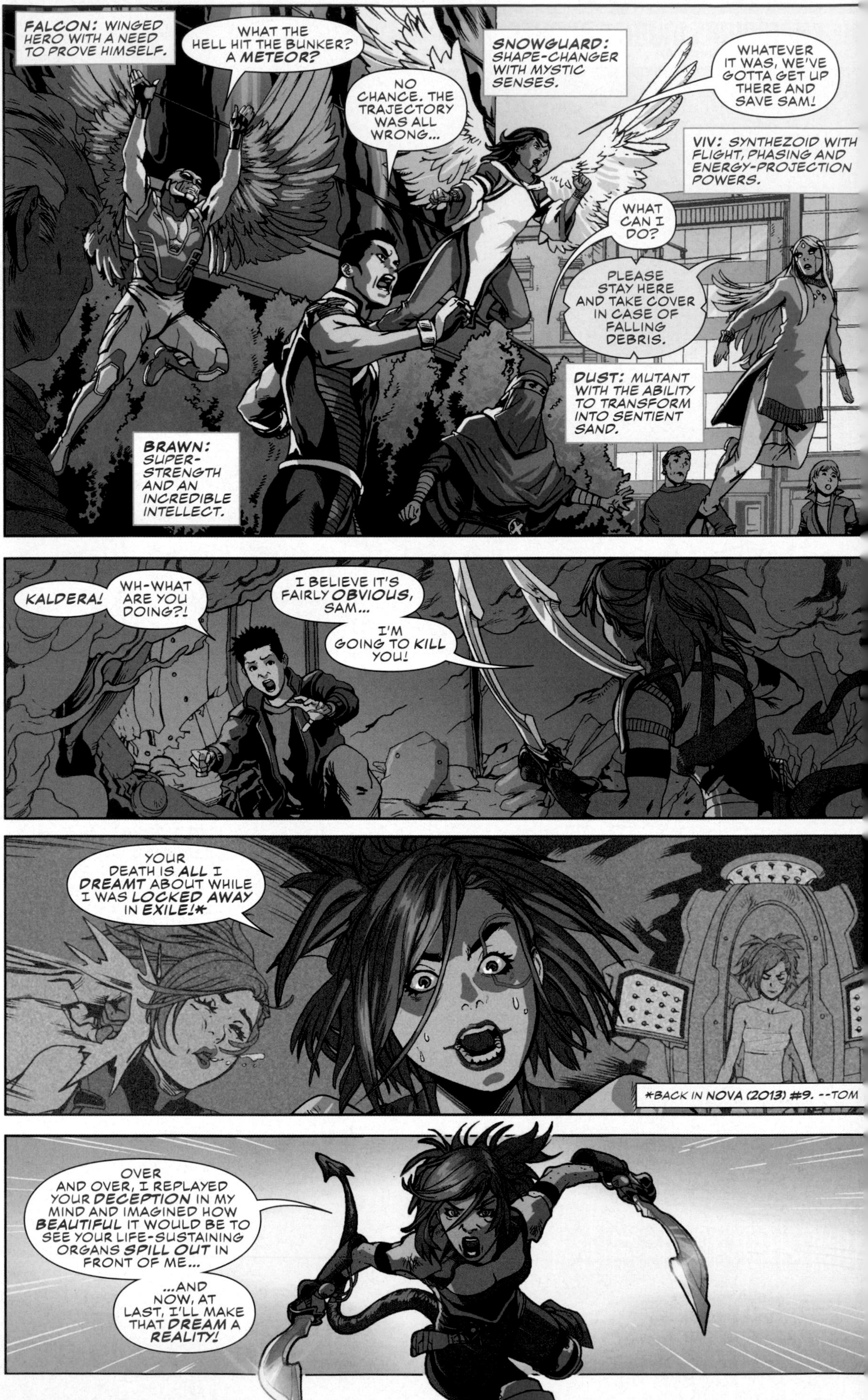

FALCON: WINGED HERO WITH A NEED TO PROVE HIMSELF.
WHAT THE HELL HIT THE BUNKER? A METEOR?
NO CHANCE. THE TRAJECTORY WAS ALL WRONG...
SNOWGUARD: SHAPE-CHANGER WITH MYSTIC SENSES.
WHATEVER IT WAS, WE'VE GOTTA GET UP THERE AND SAVE SAM!
VIV: SYNTHEZOID WITH FLIGHT, PHASING AND ENERGY-PROJECTION POWERS.
WHAT CAN I DO?
PLEASE STAY HERE AND TAKE COVER IN CASE OF FALLING DEBRIS.
DUST: MUTANT WITH THE ABILITY TO TRANSFORM INTO SENTIENT SAND.
BRAWN: SUPER-STRENGTH AND AN INCREDIBLE INTELLECT.
KALDERA!
WH-WHAT ARE YOU DOING?!
I BELIEVE IT'S FAIRLY OBVIOUS, SAM...
I'M GOING TO KILL YOU!
YOUR DEATH IS ALL I DREAMT ABOUT WHILE I WAS LOCKED AWAY IN EXILE!*
*BACK IN NOVA (2013) #9. --TOM
OVER AND OVER, I REPLAYED YOUR DECEPTION IN MY MIND AND IMAGINED HOW BEAUTIFUL IT WOULD BE TO SEE YOUR LIFE-SUSTAINING ORGANS SPILL OUT IN FRONT OF ME...
...AND NOW, AT LAST, I'LL MAKE THAT DREAM A REALITY!

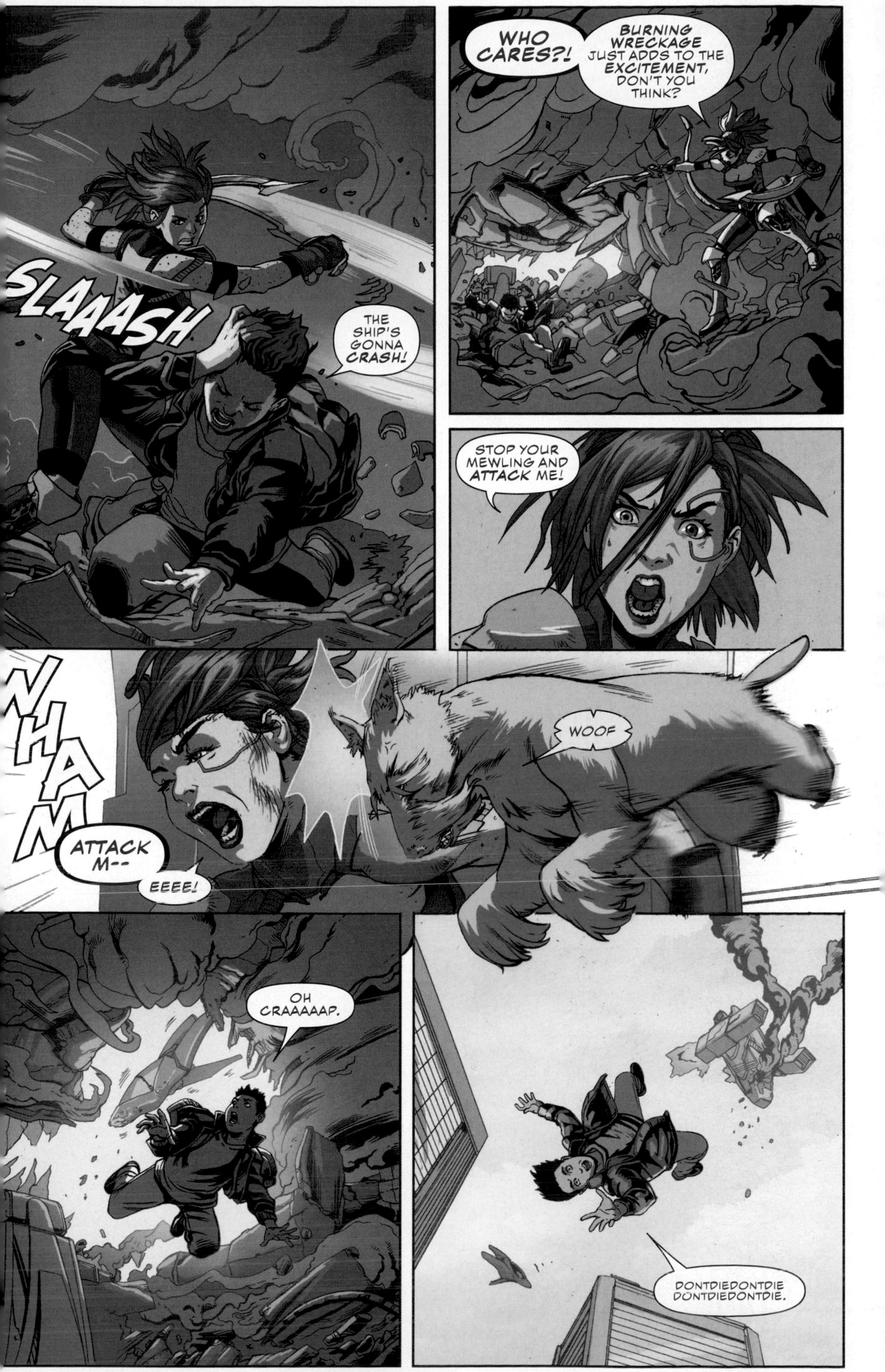
SLAAASH
THE SHIP'S GONNA CRASH!
WHO CARES?!
BURNING WRECKAGE JUST ADDS TO THE EXCITEMENT, DON'T YOU THINK?
STOP YOUR MEWLING AND ATTACK ME!
WHAM
ATTACK M--
EEEE!
WOOF
OH CRAAAAAP.
DONTDIEDONTDIE DONTDIEDONTDIE.

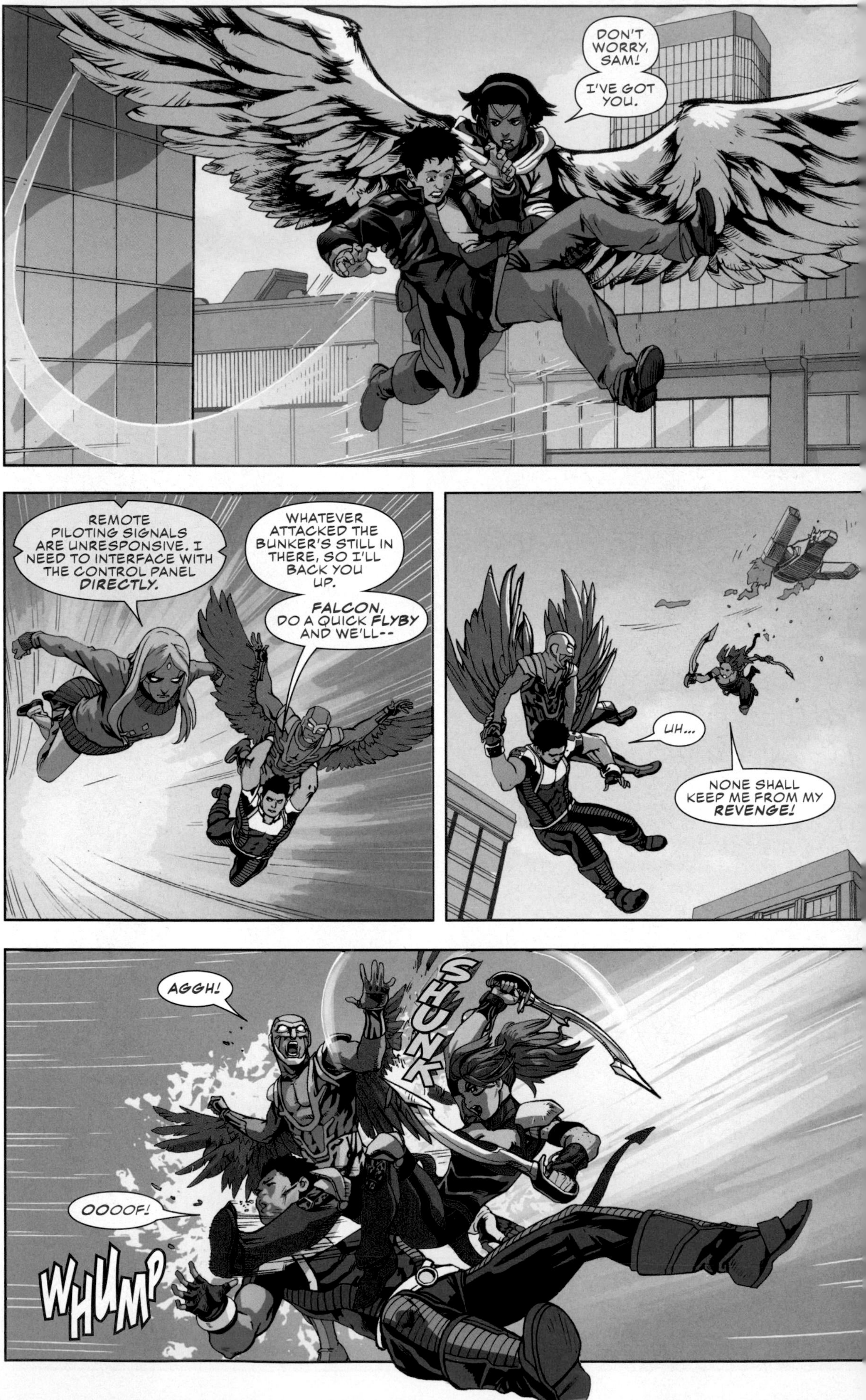
DON'T WORRY, SAM!
I'VE GOT YOU.
REMOTE PILOTING SIGNALS ARE UNRESPONSIVE. I NEED TO INTERFACE WITH THE CONTROL PANEL DIRECTLY.
WHATEVER ATTACKED THE BUNKER'S STILL IN THERE, SO I'LL BACK YOU UP.
FALCON, DO A QUICK FLYBY AND WE'LL--
UH...
NONE SHALL KEEP ME FROM MY REVENGE!
AGGH!
SHUNK
OOOOF!
WHUMP

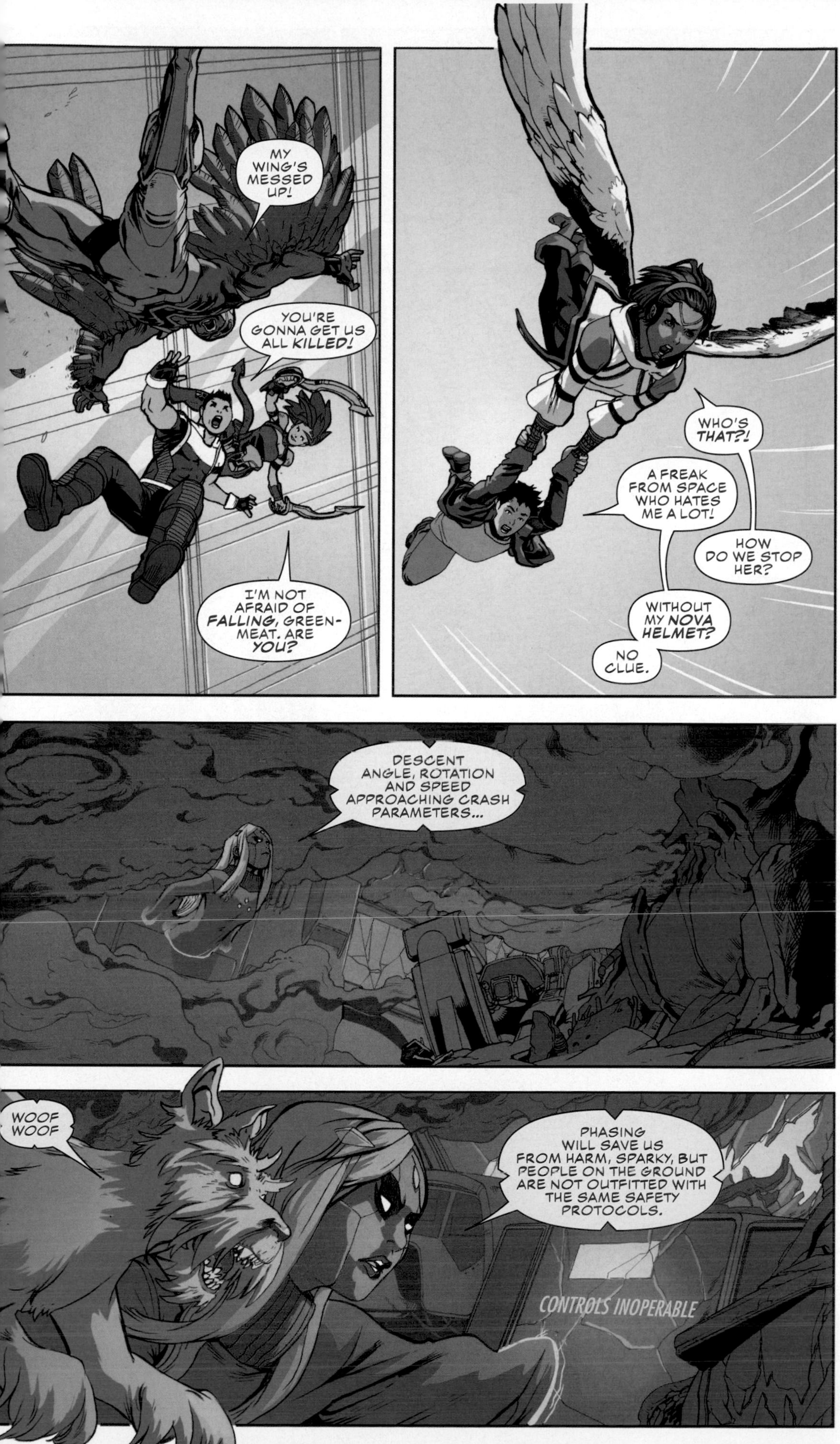
MY WING'S MESSED UP!
YOU'RE GONNA GET US ALL KILLED!
I'M NOT AFRAID OF FALLING, GREEN-MEAT. ARE YOU?
WHO'S THAT?!
A FREAK FROM SPACE WHO HATES ME A LOT!
HOW DO WE STOP HER?
WITHOUT MY NOVA HELMET?
NO CLUE.
DESCENT ANGLE, ROTATION AND SPEED APPROACHING CRASH PARAMETERS...
WOOF WOOF
PHASING WILL SAVE US FROM HARM, SPARKY, BUT PEOPLE ON THE GROUND ARE NOT OUTFITTED WITH THE SAME SAFETY PROTOCOLS.
CONTROLS INOPERABLE

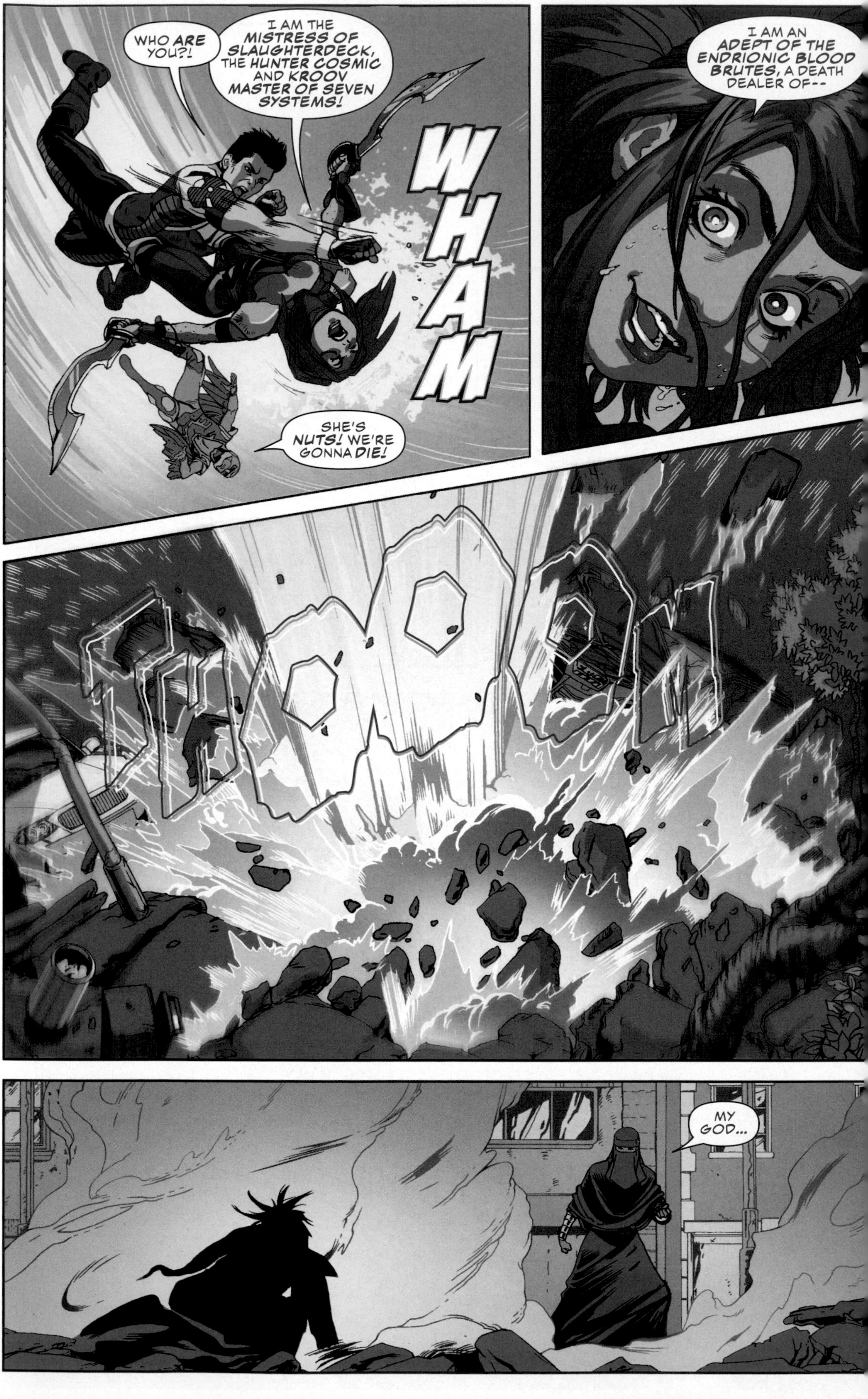
WHO ARE YOU?!
I AM THE MISTRESS OF SLAUGHTERDECK, THE HUNTER COSMIC AND KROOV MASTER OF SEVEN SYSTEMS!
WHAM
SHE'S NUTS! WE'RE GONNA DIE!
I AM AN ADEPT OF THE ENDRIONIC BLOOD BRUTES, A DEATH DEALER OF--
MY GOD...

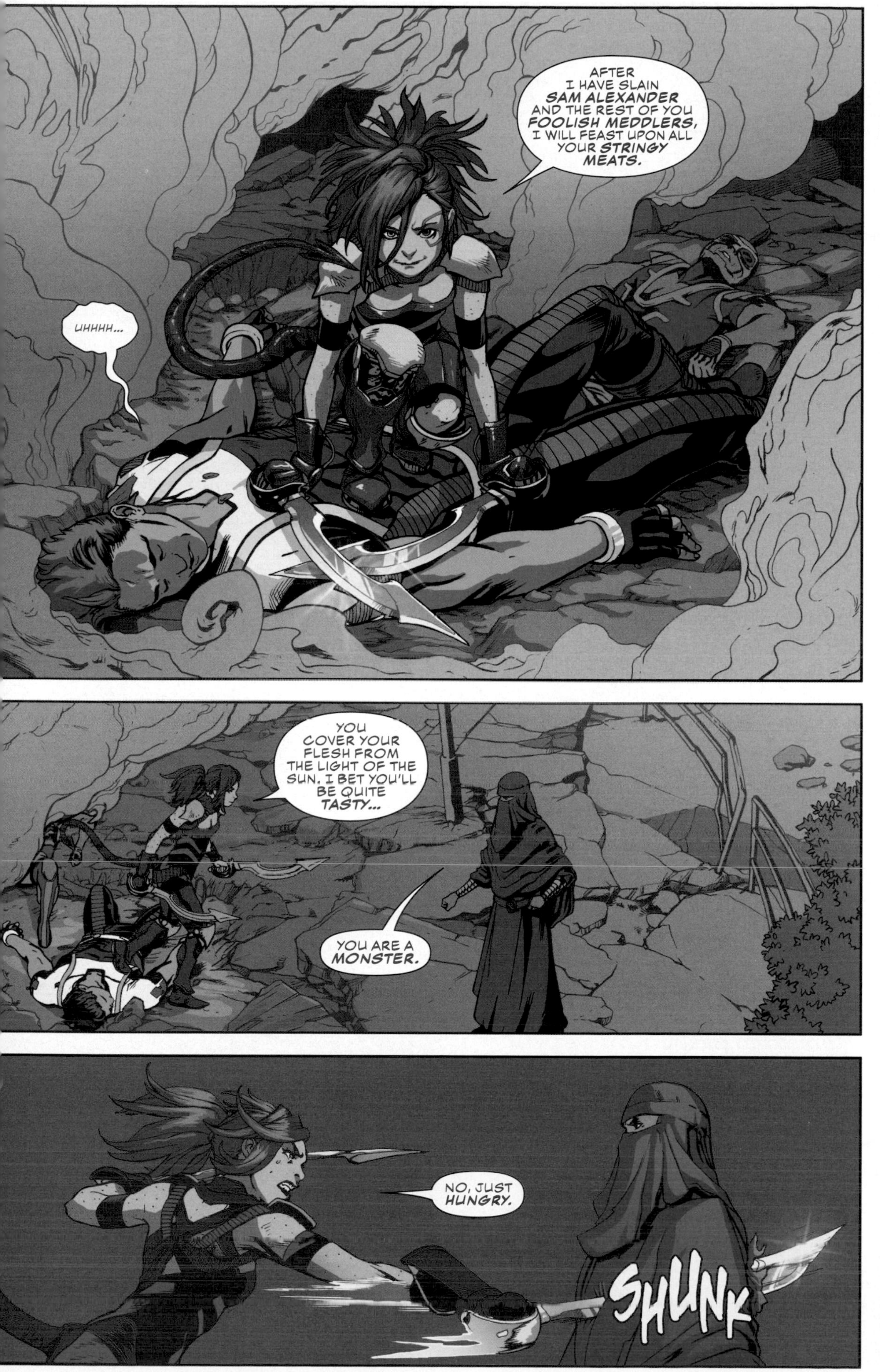
AFTER I HAVE SLAIN SAM ALEXANDER AND THE REST OF YOU FOOLISH MEDDLERS, I WILL FEAST UPON ALL YOUR STRINGY MEATS.
UHHHH...
YOU COVER YOUR FLESH FROM THE LIGHT OF THE SUN. I BET YOU'LL BE QUITE TASTY...
YOU ARE A MONSTER.
NO, JUST HUNGRY.
SHUNK

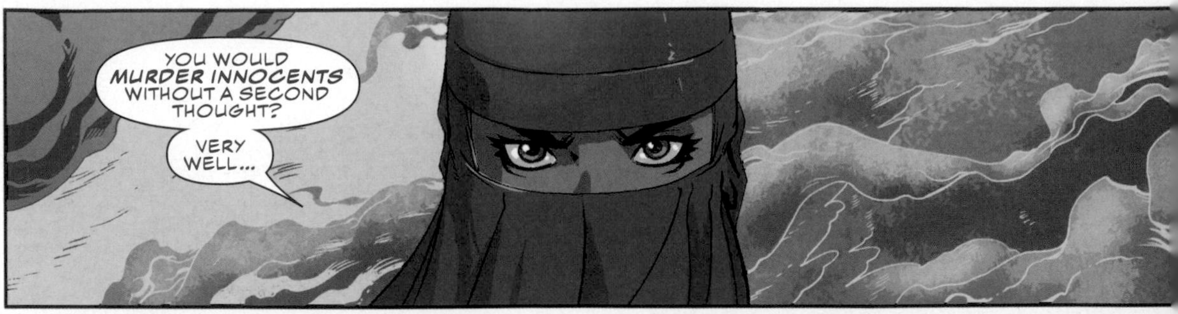
YOU WOULD MURDER INNOCENTS WITHOUT A SECOND THOUGHT?
VERY WELL...

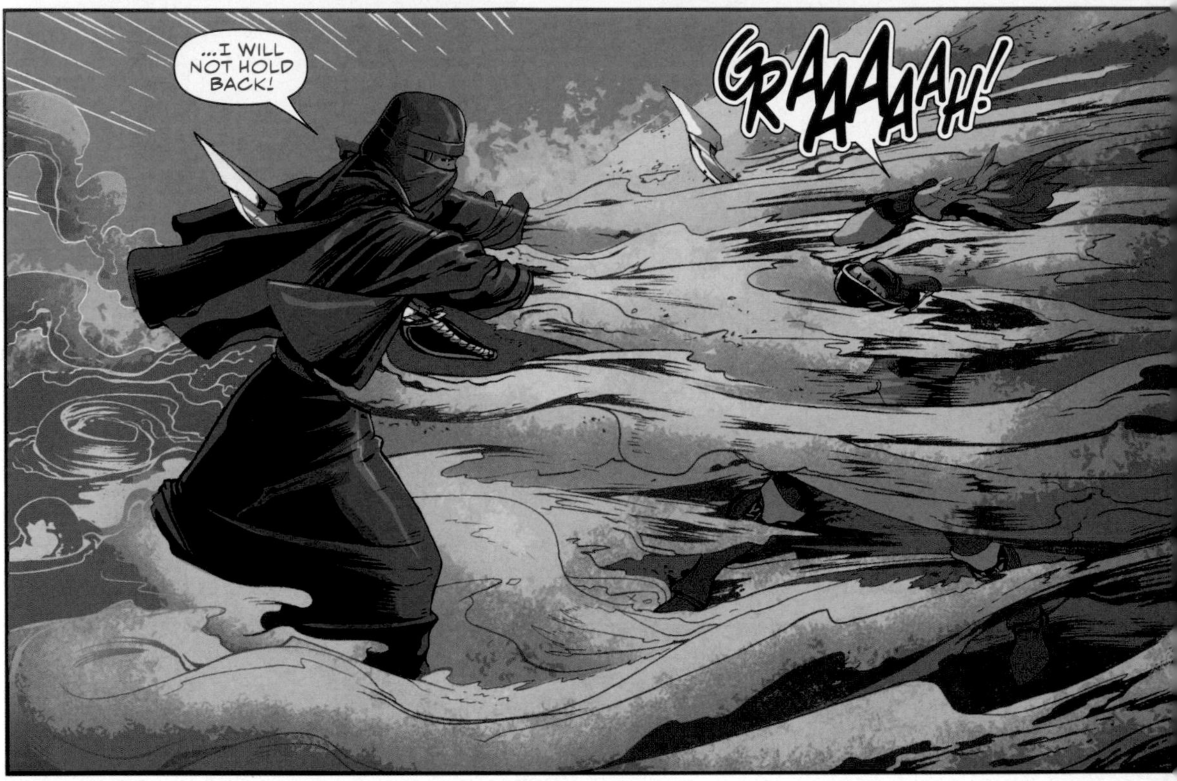
...I WILL NOT HOLD BACK!
GRAAAAAAH!

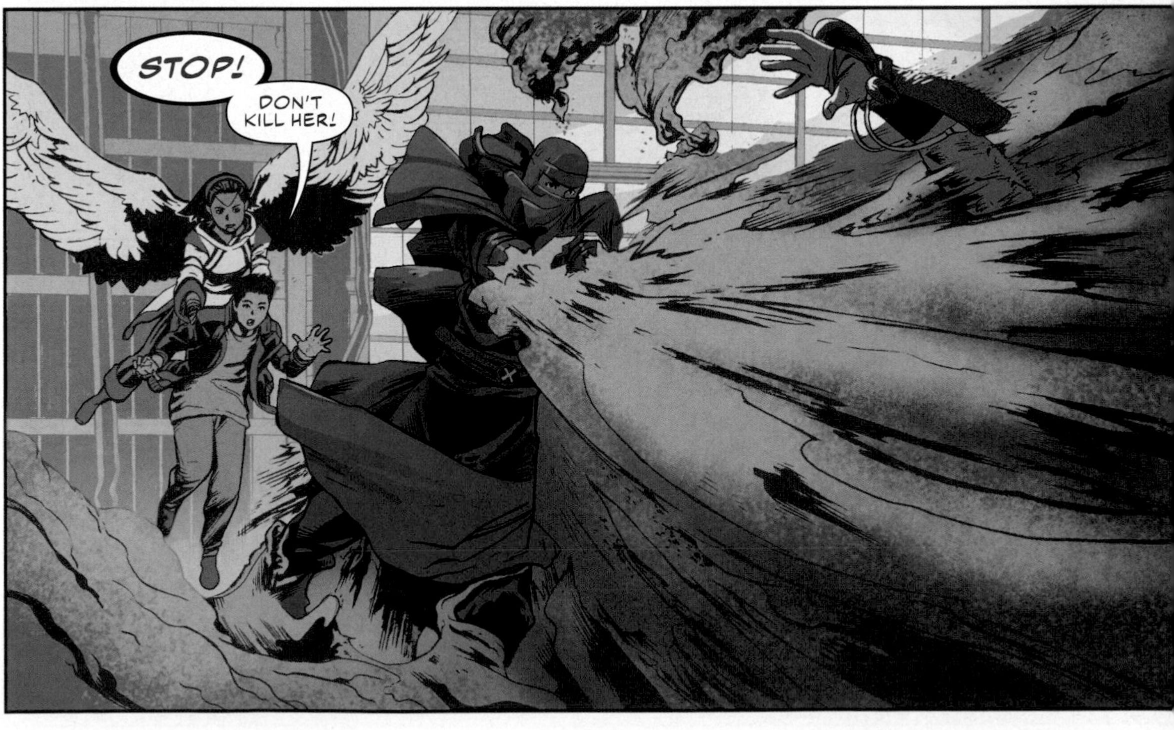
STOP!
DON'T KILL HER!

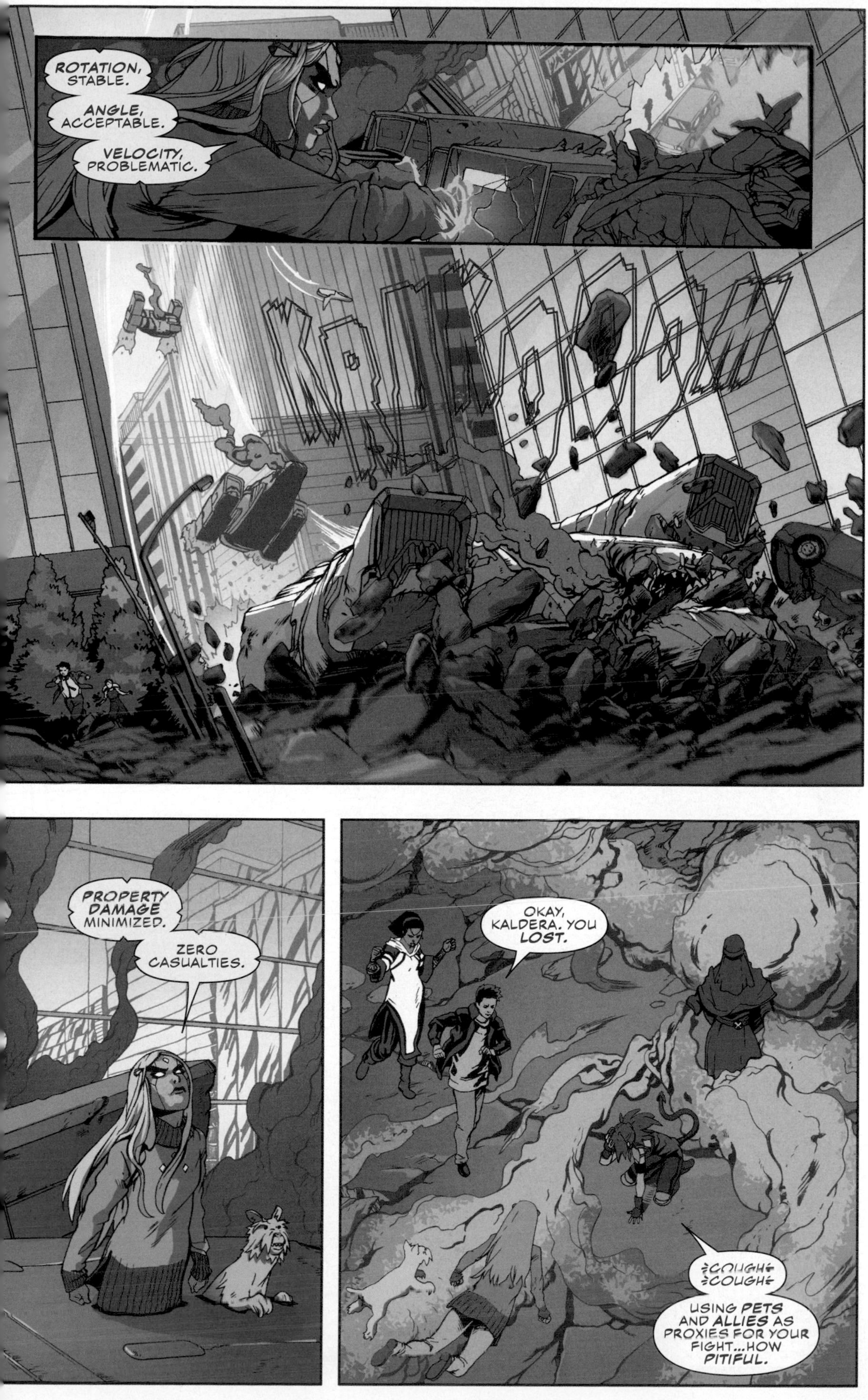
ROTATION, STABLE.
ANGLE, ACCEPTABLE.
VELOCITY, PROBLEMATIC.
PROPERTY DAMAGE MINIMIZED.
ZERO CASUALTIES.
OKAY, KALDERA. YOU LOST.
COUGH COUGH
USING PETS AND ALLIES AS PROXIES FOR YOUR FIGHT...HOW PITIFUL.

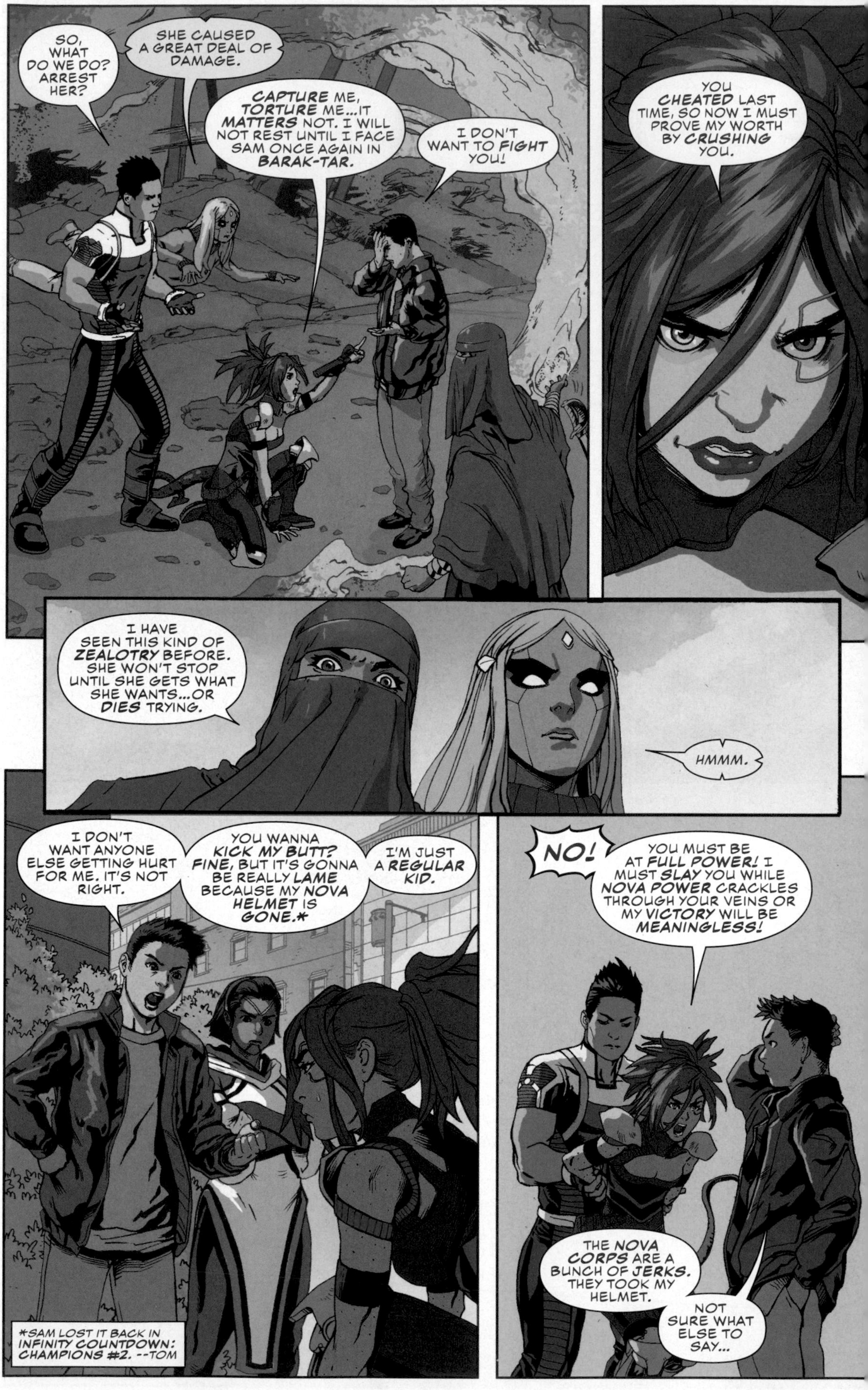
SO, WHAT DO WE DO? ARREST HER?
SHE CAUSED A GREAT DEAL OF DAMAGE.
CAPTURE ME, TORTURE ME...IT MATTERS NOT. I WILL NOT REST UNTIL I FACE SAM ONCE AGAIN IN BARAK-TAR.
I DON'T WANT TO FIGHT YOU!
YOU CHEATED LAST TIME, SO NOW I MUST PROVE MY WORTH BY CRUSHING YOU.
I HAVE SEEN THIS KIND OF ZEALOTRY BEFORE. SHE WON'T STOP UNTIL SHE GETS WHAT SHE WANTS...OR DIES TRYING.
HMMM.
I DON'T WANT ANYONE ELSE GETTING HURT FOR ME. IT'S NOT RIGHT.
YOU WANNA KICK MY BUTT? FINE, BUT IT'S GONNA BE REALLY LAME BECAUSE MY NOVA HELMET IS GONE.*
I'M JUST A REGULAR KID.
*SAM LOST IT BACK IN INFINITY COUNTDOWN: CHAMPIONS #2. --TOM
NO!
YOU MUST BE AT FULL POWER! I MUST SLAY YOU WHILE NOVA POWER CRACKLES THROUGH YOUR VEINS OR MY VICTORY WILL BE MEANINGLESS!
THE NOVA CORPS ARE A BUNCH OF JERKS. THEY TOOK MY HELMET.
NOT SURE WHAT ELSE TO SAY...

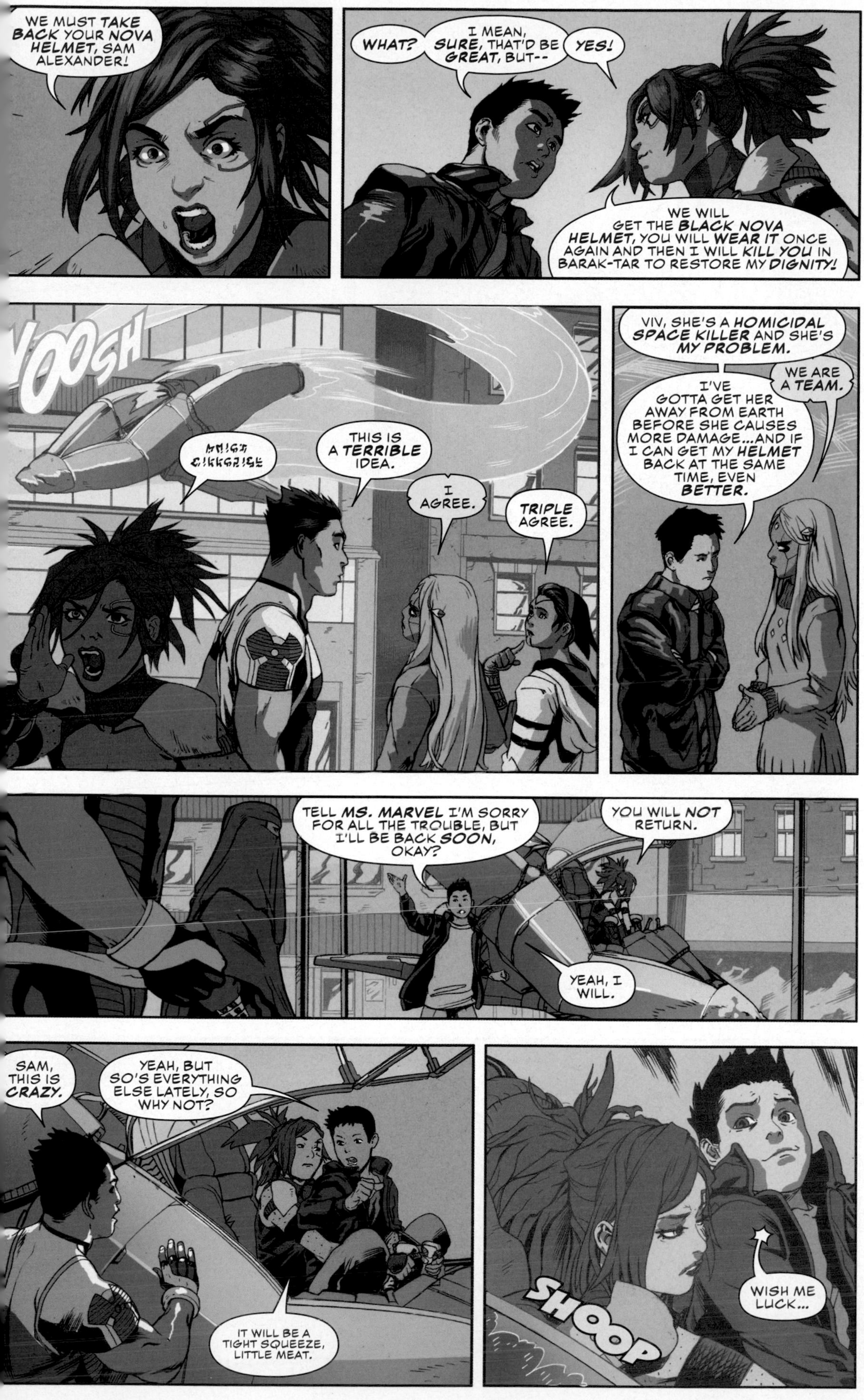
WE MUST TAKE BACK YOUR NOVA HELMET, SAM ALEXANDER!
WHAT?
I MEAN, SURE, THAT'D BE GREAT, BUT--
YES!
WE WILL GET THE BLACK NOVA HELMET, YOU WILL WEAR IT ONCE AGAIN AND THEN I WILL KILL YOU IN BARAK-TAR TO RESTORE MY DIGNITY!
WOOSH
THIS IS A TERRIBLE IDEA.
I AGREE.
TRIPLE AGREE.
VIV, SHE'S A HOMICIDAL SPACE KILLER AND SHE'S MY PROBLEM.
WE ARE A TEAM.
I'VE GOTTA GET HER AWAY FROM EARTH BEFORE SHE CAUSES MORE DAMAGE...AND IF I CAN GET MY HELMET BACK AT THE SAME TIME, EVEN BETTER.
TELL MS. MARVEL I'M SORRY FOR ALL THE TROUBLE, BUT I'LL BE BACK SOON, OKAY?
YOU WILL NOT RETURN.
YEAH, I WILL.
SAM, THIS IS CRAZY.
YEAH, BUT SO'S EVERYTHING ELSE LATELY, SO WHY NOT?
IT WILL BE A TIGHT SQUEEZE, LITTLE MEAT.
SHOOP
WISH ME LUCK...

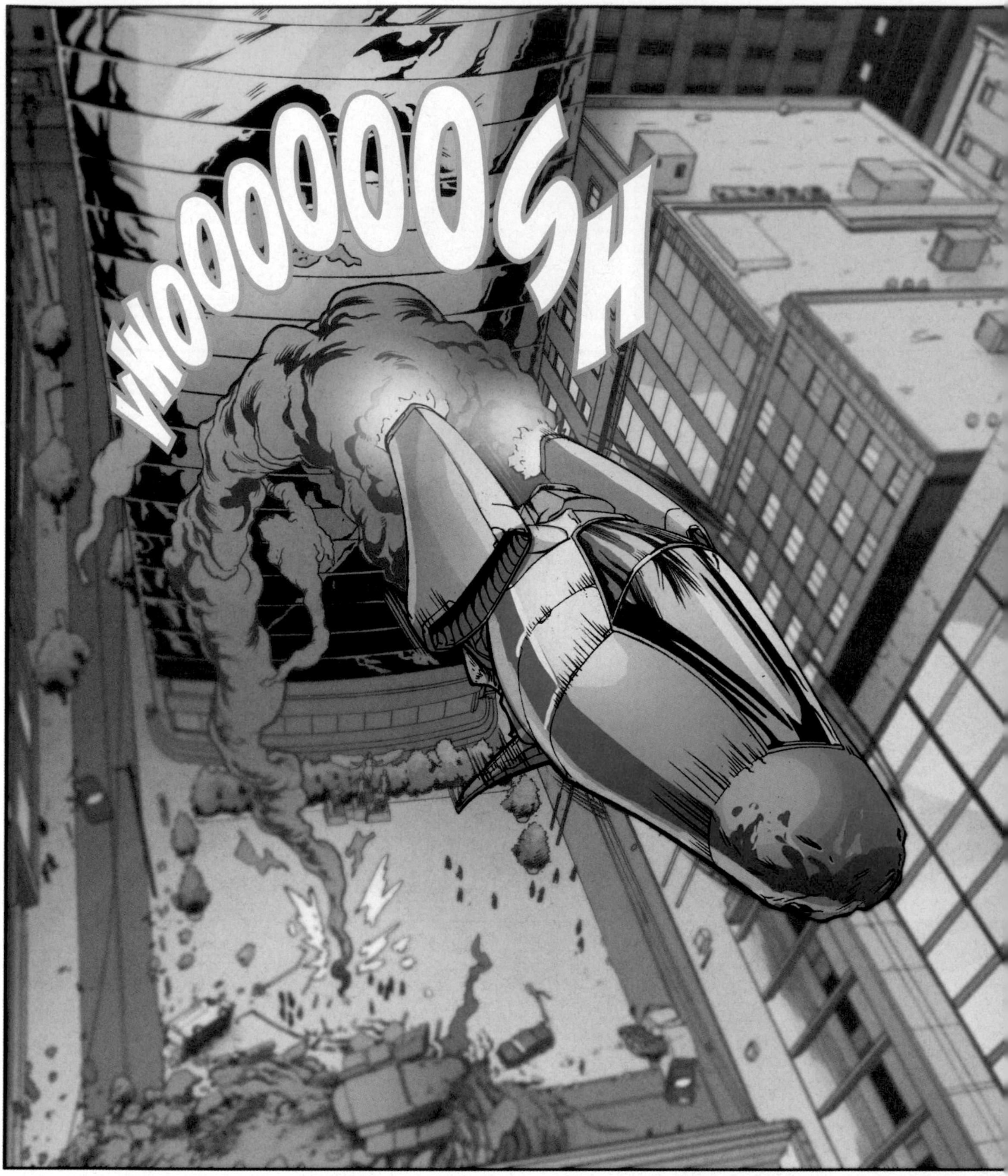
VWOOOOOOSH

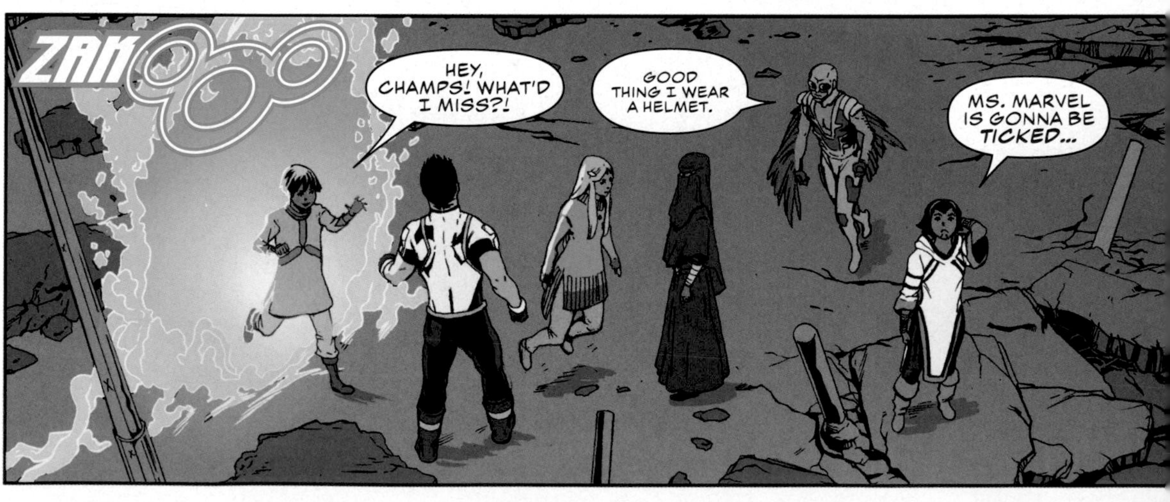
ZAK
HEY, CHAMPS! WHAT'D I MISS?!
GOOD THING I WEAR A HELMET.
MS. MARVEL IS GONNA BE TICKED...

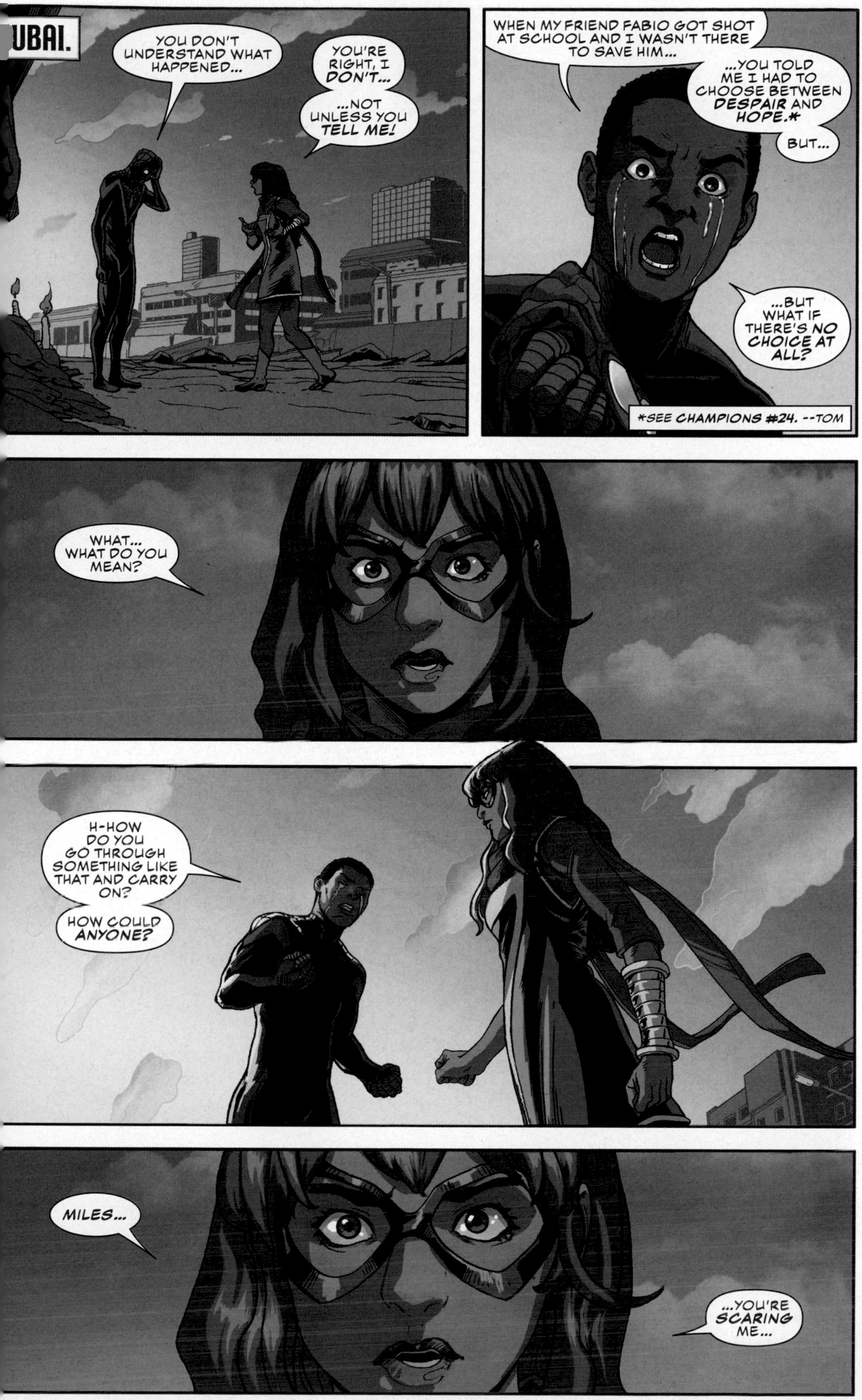
UBAI.
YOU DON'T UNDERSTAND WHAT HAPPENED...
YOU'RE RIGHT, I DON'T...
...NOT UNLESS YOU TELL ME!
WHEN MY FRIEND FABIO GOT SHOT AT SCHOOL AND I WASN'T THERE TO SAVE HIM...
...YOU TOLD ME I HAD TO CHOOSE BETWEEN DESPAIR AND HOPE.*
BUT...
...BUT WHAT IF THERE'S NO CHOICE AT ALL?
*SEE CHAMPIONS #24. --TOM
WHAT... WHAT DO YOU MEAN?
H-HOW DO YOU GO THROUGH SOMETHING LIKE THAT AND CARRY ON?
HOW COULD ANYONE?
MILES...
...YOU'RE SCARING ME...

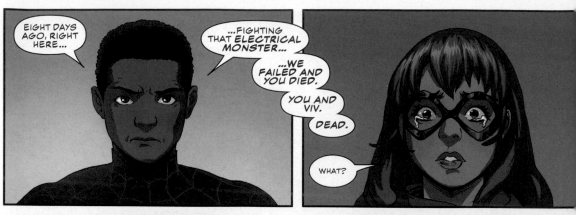

EIGHT DAYS AGO, RIGHT HERE...

...FIGHTING THAT ELECTRICAL MONSTER...

...WE FAILED AND YOU DIED.

YOU AND VIV.

DEAD.

WHAT?

BUT THEN I GOT THE CHANCE TO MAKE IT ALL RIGHT...

...TO CHOOSE "HOPE."

HE CALLS HIMSELF MEPHISTO.

YOU... YOU CAN'T BE SERIOUS.

WH-WHAT DID YOU--

SELL MY SOUL? NO... I WISH I HAD.

AT LEAST THEN I COULD'VE PAID THE PRICE AND BEEN DONE WITH IT.

IT WAS WORSE.

AMADEUS AND I GOT A COSMIC DO-OVER. WE SAVED YOU BOTH--SAVED A BUNCH OF OTHER PEOPLE, TOO.

EXCEPT A GIRL NAMED FARIDAH...

...THE SECOND TIME, I WASN'T THERE TO KEEP HER SAFE.

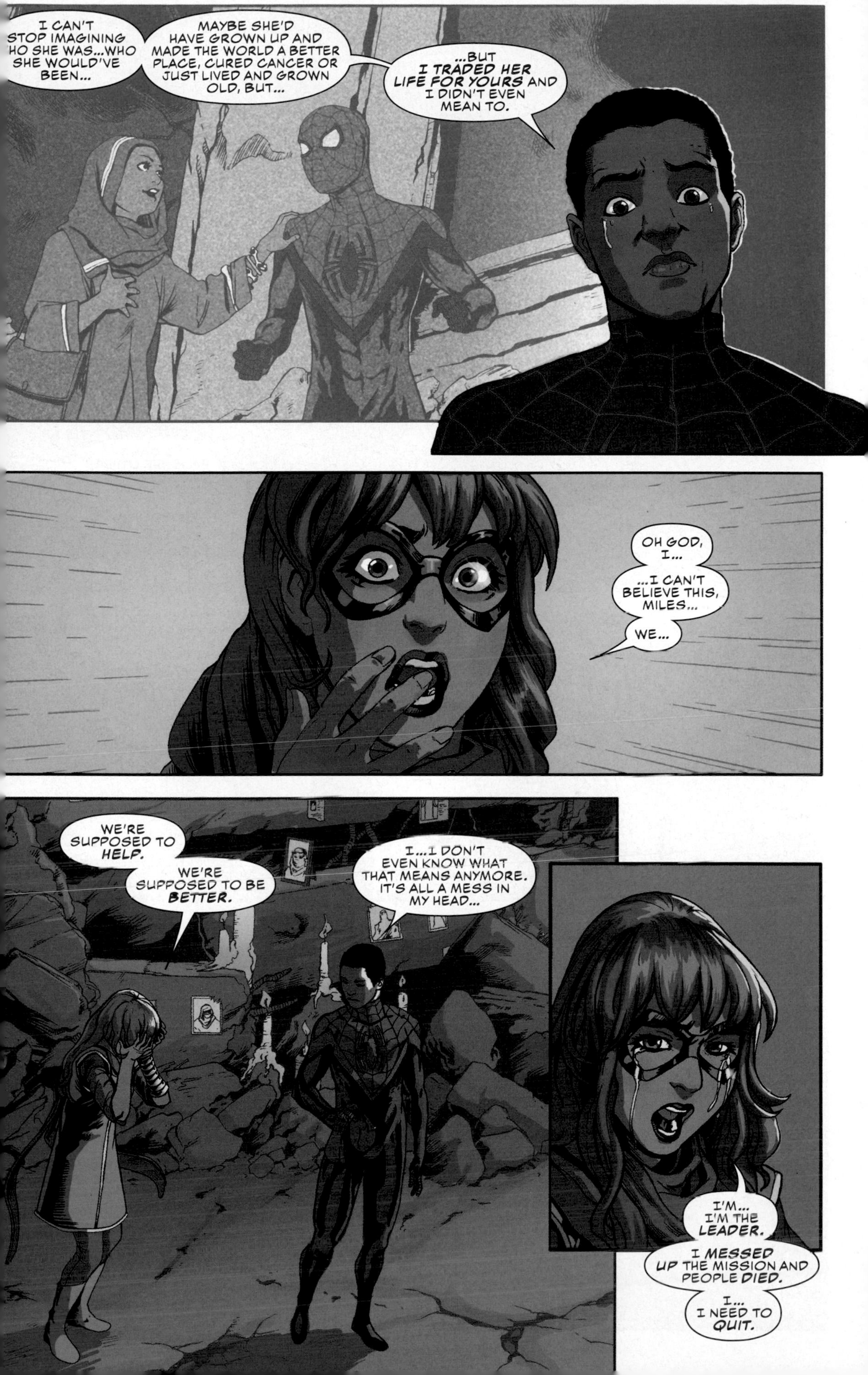
I CAN'T STOP IMAGINING HO SHE WAS...WHO SHE WOULD'VE BEEN...
MAYBE SHE'D HAVE GROWN UP AND MADE THE WORLD A BETTER PLACE, CURED CANCER OR JUST LIVED AND GROWN OLD, BUT...
...BUT I TRADED HER LIFE FOR YOURS AND I DIDN'T EVEN MEAN TO.
OH GOD, I...
...I CAN'T BELIEVE THIS, MILES...
WE...
WE'RE SUPPOSED TO HELP.
WE'RE SUPPOSED TO BE BETTER.
I...I DON'T EVEN KNOW WHAT THAT MEANS ANYMORE. IT'S ALL A MESS IN MY HEAD...
I'M... I'M THE LEADER.
I MESSED UP THE MISSION AND PEOPLE DIED.
I... I NEED TO QUIT.

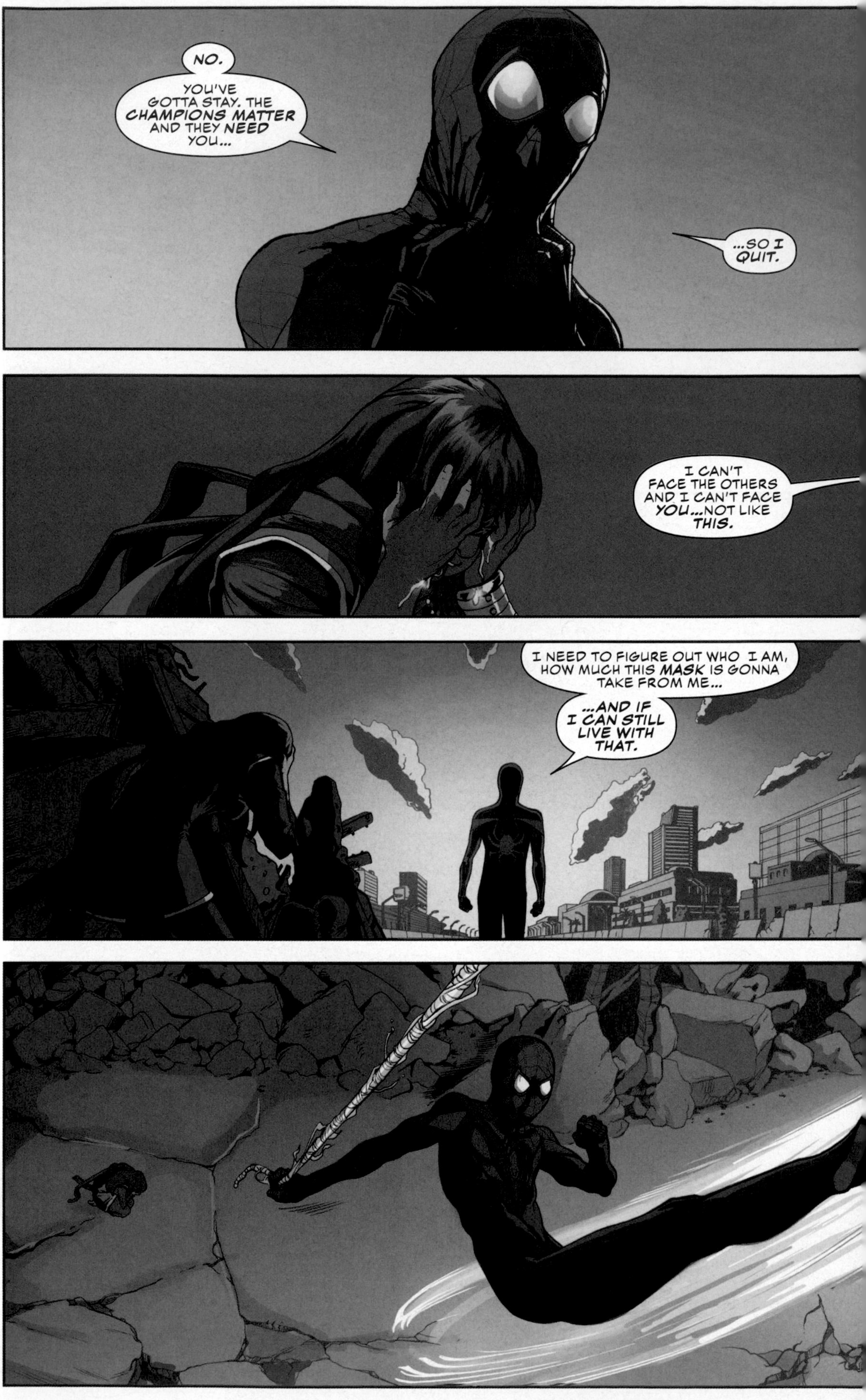
NO.
YOU'VE GOTTA STAY. THE CHAMPIONS MATTER AND THEY NEED YOU...
...SO I QUIT.
I CAN'T FACE THE OTHERS AND I CAN'T FACE YOU...NOT LIKE THIS.
I NEED TO FIGURE OUT WHO I AM, HOW MUCH THIS MASK IS GONNA TAKE FROM ME...
...AND IF I CAN STILL LIVE WITH THAT.

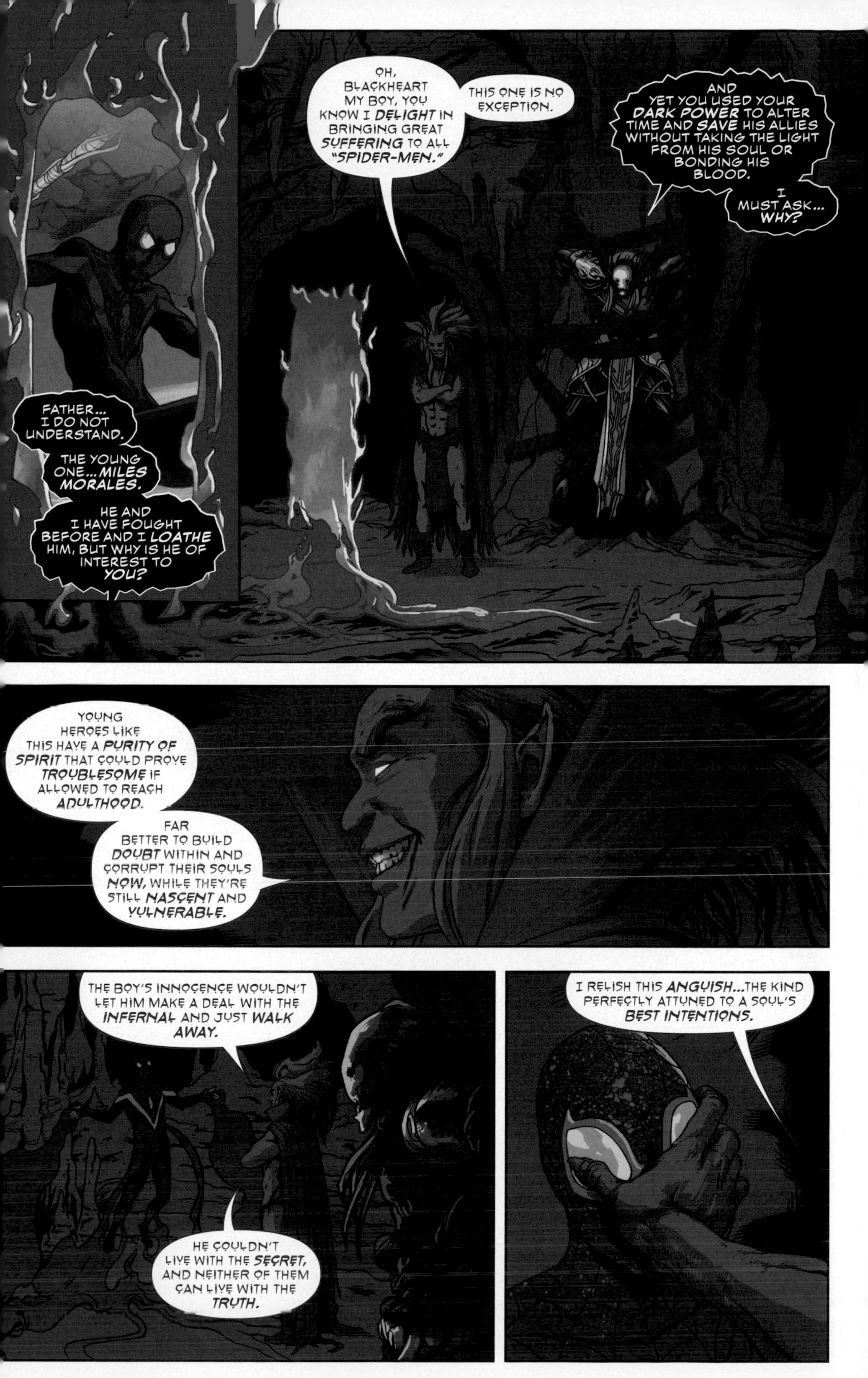
FATHER... I DO NOT UNDERSTAND.
THE YOUNG ONE... MILES MORALES.
HE AND I HAVE FOUGHT BEFORE AND I LOATHE HIM, BUT WHY IS HE OF INTEREST TO YOU?
OH, BLACKHEART MY BOY, YOU KNOW I DELIGHT IN BRINGING GREAT SUFFERING TO ALL "SPIDER-MEN."
THIS ONE IS NO EXCEPTION.
AND YET YOU USED YOUR DARK POWER TO ALTER TIME AND SAVE HIS ALLIES WITHOUT TAKING THE LIGHT FROM HIS SOUL OR BONDING HIS BLOOD.
I MUST ASK... WHY?
YOUNG HEROES LIKE THIS HAVE A PURITY OF SPIRIT THAT COULD PROVE TROUBLESOME IF ALLOWED TO REACH ADULTHOOD.
FAR BETTER TO BUILD DOUBT WITHIN AND CORRUPT THEIR SOULS NOW, WHILE THEY'RE STILL NASCENT AND VULNERABLE.
THE BOY'S INNOCENCE WOULDN'T LET HIM MAKE A DEAL WITH THE INFERNAL AND JUST WALK AWAY.
HE COULDN'T LIVE WITH THE SECRET, AND NEITHER OF THEM CAN LIVE WITH THE TRUTH.
I RELISH THIS ANGUISH... THE KIND PERFECTLY ATTUNED TO A SOUL'S BEST INTENTIONS.

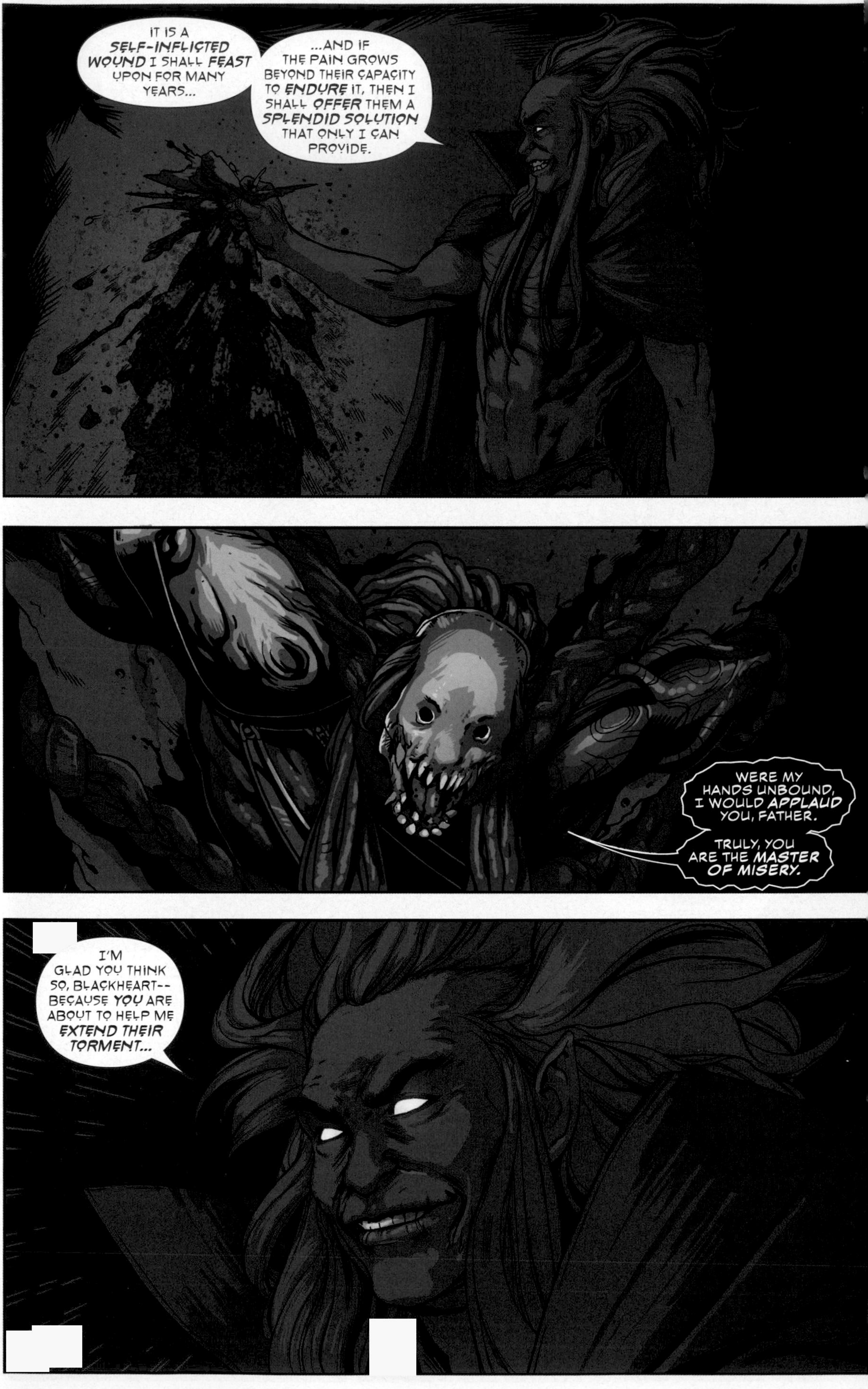
IT IS A SELF-INFLICTED WOUND I SHALL FEAST UPON FOR MANY YEARS...
...AND IF THE PAIN GROWS BEYOND THEIR CAPACITY TO ENDURE IT, THEN I SHALL OFFER THEM A SPLENDID SOLUTION THAT ONLY I CAN PROVIDE.
WERE MY HANDS UNBOUND, I WOULD APPLAUD YOU, FATHER.
TRULY, YOU ARE THE MASTER OF MISERY.
I'M GLAD YOU THINK SO, BLACKHEART-- BECAUSE YOU ARE ABOUT TO HELP ME EXTEND THEIR TORMENT...

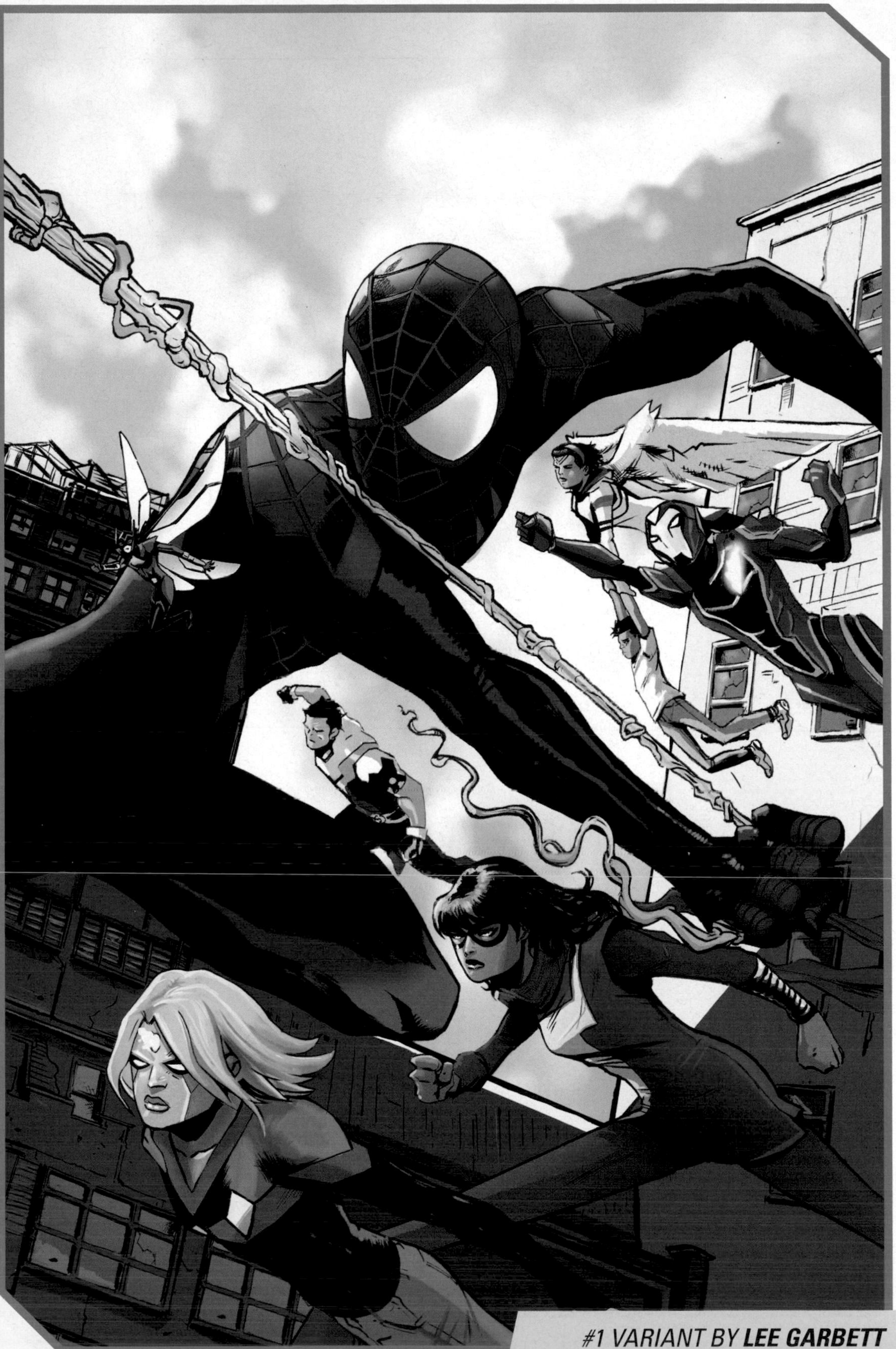

#1 VARIANT BY **LEE GARBETT**

5

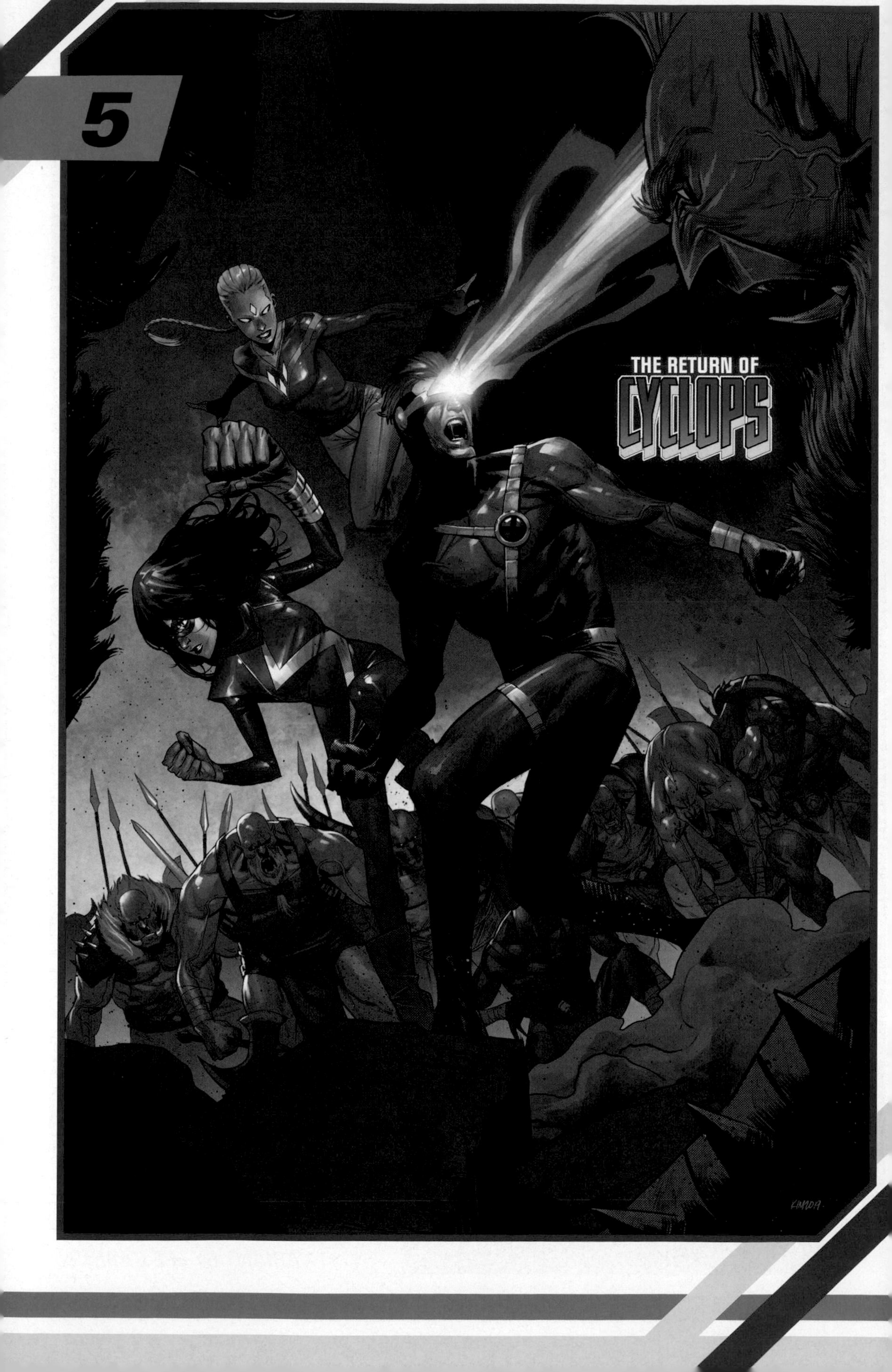
THE RETURN OF
CYCLOPS

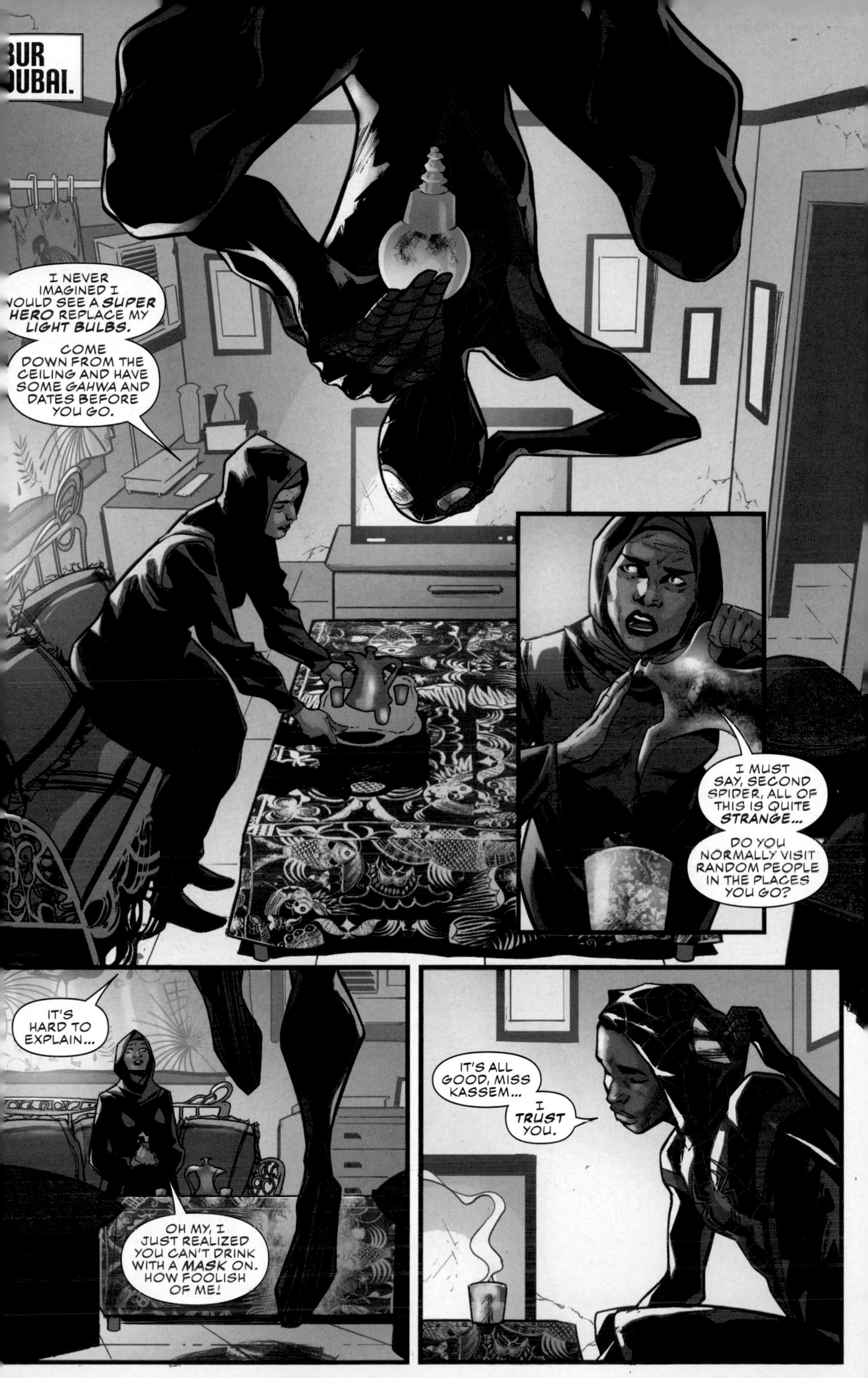
BUR
DUBAI.
I NEVER IMAGINED I WOULD SEE A SUPER HERO REPLACE MY LIGHT BULBS.
COME DOWN FROM THE CEILING AND HAVE SOME GAHWA AND DATES BEFORE YOU GO.
I MUST SAY, SECOND SPIDER, ALL OF THIS IS QUITE STRANGE...
DO YOU NORMALLY VISIT RANDOM PEOPLE IN THE PLACES YOU GO?
IT'S HARD TO EXPLAIN...
OH MY, I JUST REALIZED YOU CAN'T DRINK WITH A MASK ON. HOW FOOLISH OF ME!
IT'S ALL GOOD, MISS KASSEM...
I TRUST YOU.

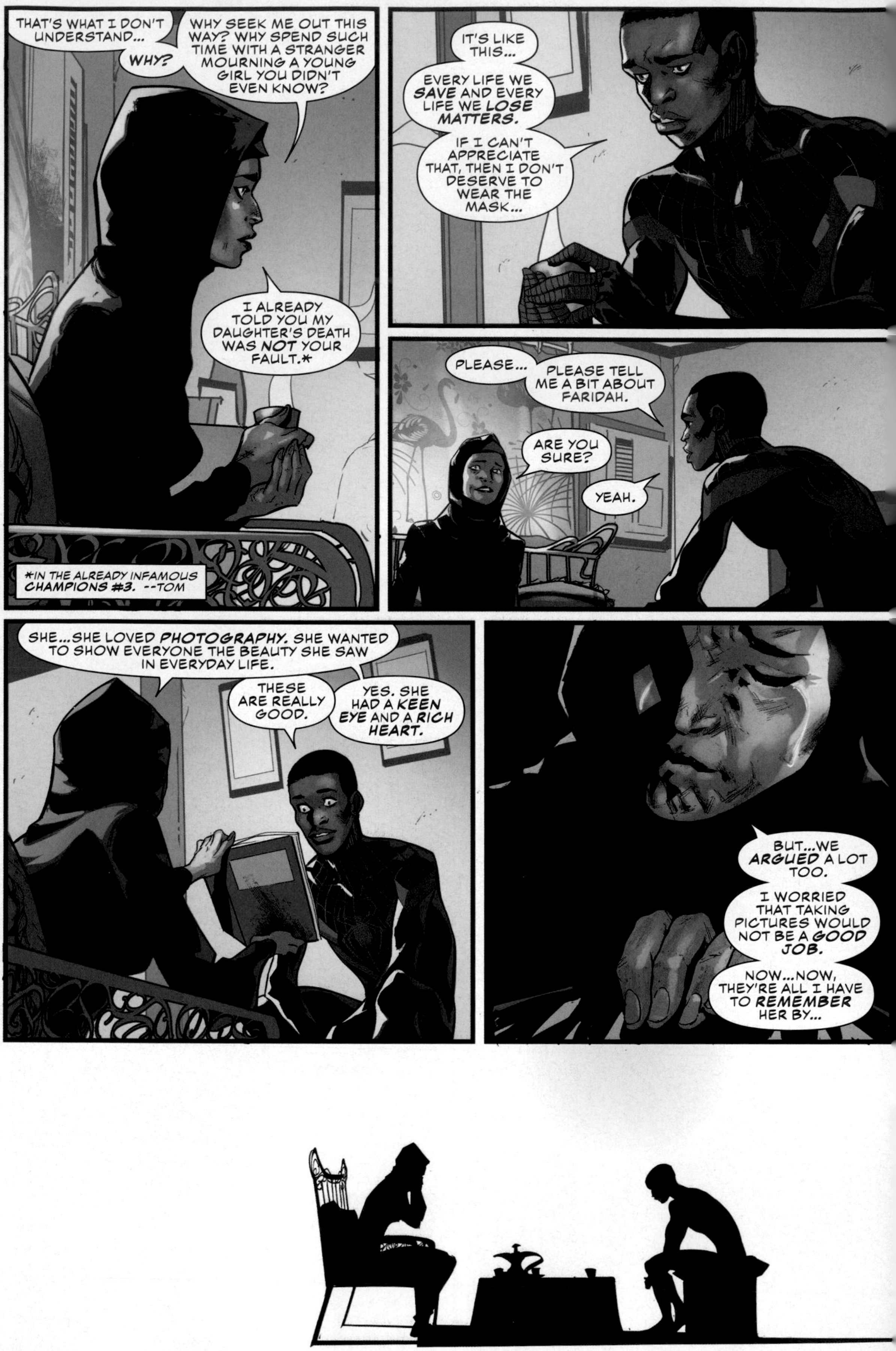
THAT'S WHAT I DON'T UNDERSTAND... WHY?
WHY SEEK ME OUT THIS WAY? WHY SPEND SUCH TIME WITH A STRANGER MOURNING A YOUNG GIRL YOU DIDN'T EVEN KNOW?
I ALREADY TOLD YOU MY DAUGHTER'S DEATH WAS NOT YOUR FAULT.*
*IN THE ALREADY INFAMOUS CHAMPIONS #3. --TOM
IT'S LIKE THIS...
EVERY LIFE WE SAVE AND EVERY LIFE WE LOSE MATTERS.
IF I CAN'T APPRECIATE THAT, THEN I DON'T DESERVE TO WEAR THE MASK...
PLEASE...
PLEASE TELL ME A BIT ABOUT FARIDAH.
ARE YOU SURE?
YEAH.
SHE...SHE LOVED PHOTOGRAPHY. SHE WANTED TO SHOW EVERYONE THE BEAUTY SHE SAW IN EVERYDAY LIFE.
THESE ARE REALLY GOOD.
YES. SHE HAD A KEEN EYE AND A RICH HEART.
BUT...WE ARGUED A LOT TOO.
I WORRIED THAT TAKING PICTURES WOULD NOT BE A GOOD JOB.
NOW...NOW, THEY'RE ALL I HAVE TO REMEMBER HER BY...

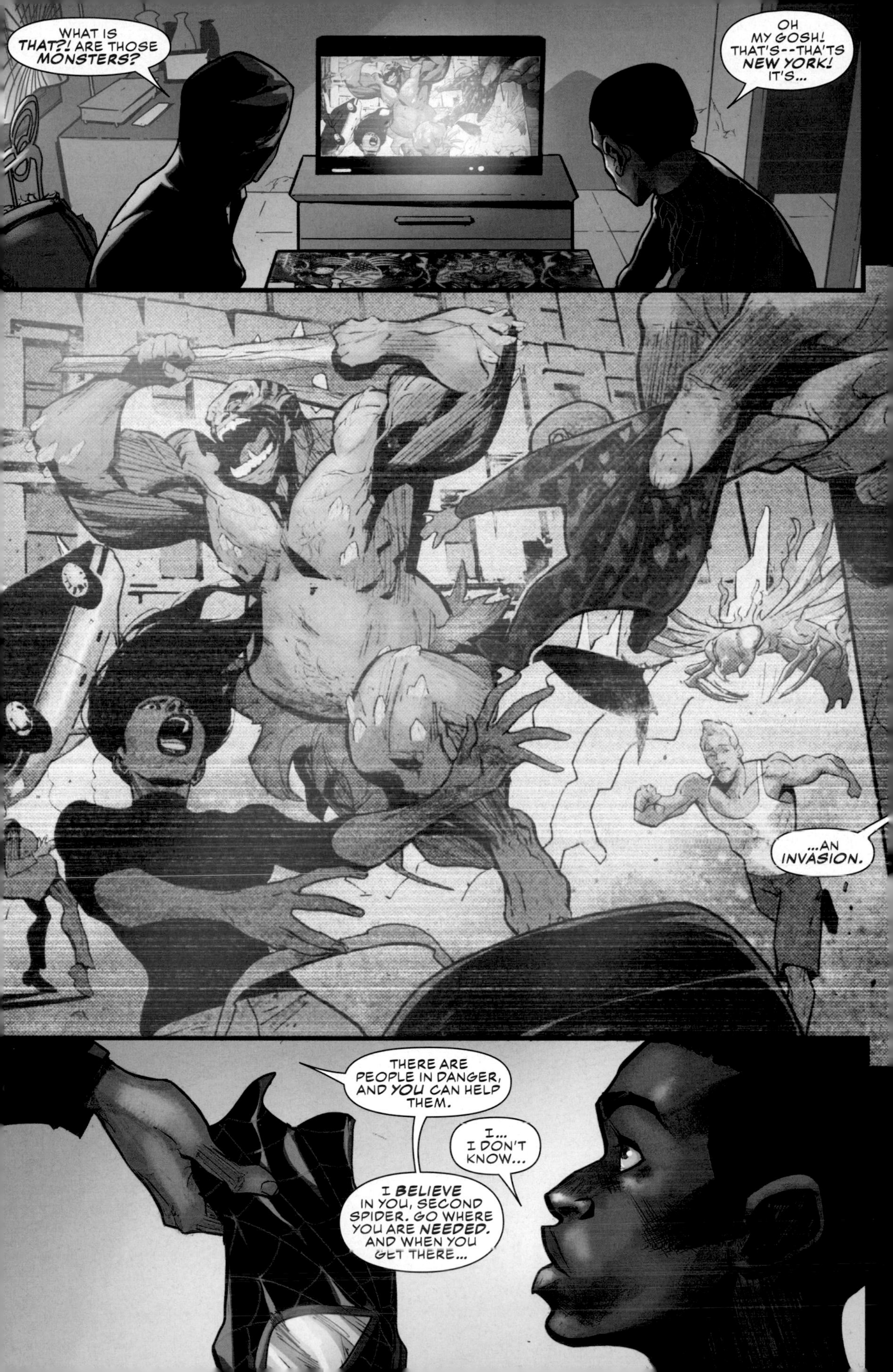
WHAT IS THAT?! ARE THOSE MONSTERS?
OH MY GOSH! THAT'S--THAT'S NEW YORK! IT'S...
...AN INVASION.
THERE ARE PEOPLE IN DANGER, AND YOU CAN HELP THEM.
I... I DON'T KNOW...
I BELIEVE IN YOU, SECOND SPIDER. GO WHERE YOU ARE NEEDED. AND WHEN YOU GET THERE...

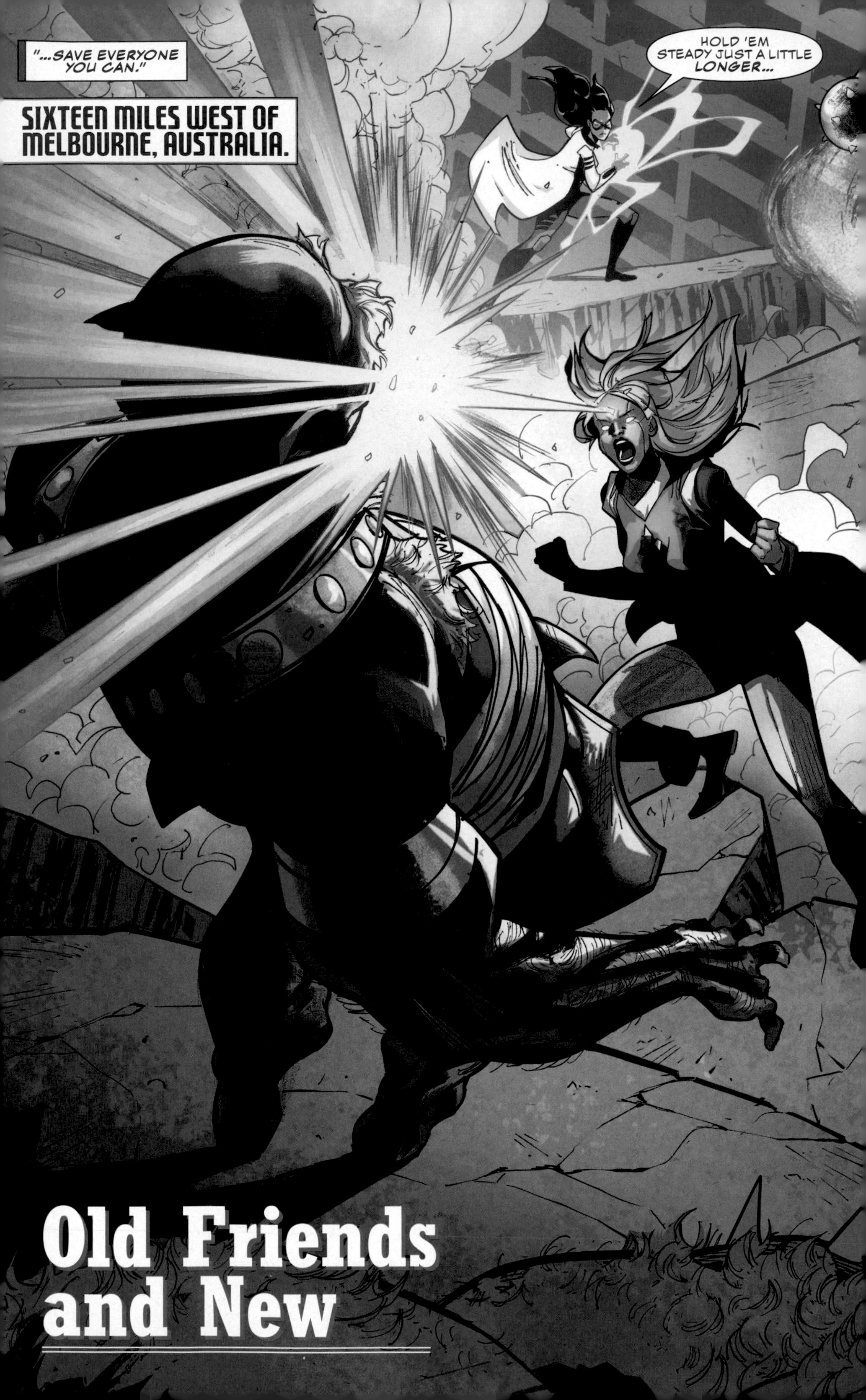

"...SAVE EVERYONE YOU CAN."
SIXTEEN MILES WEST OF MELBOURNE, AUSTRALIA.
HOLD 'EM STEADY JUST A LITTLE LONGER...
Old Friends and New

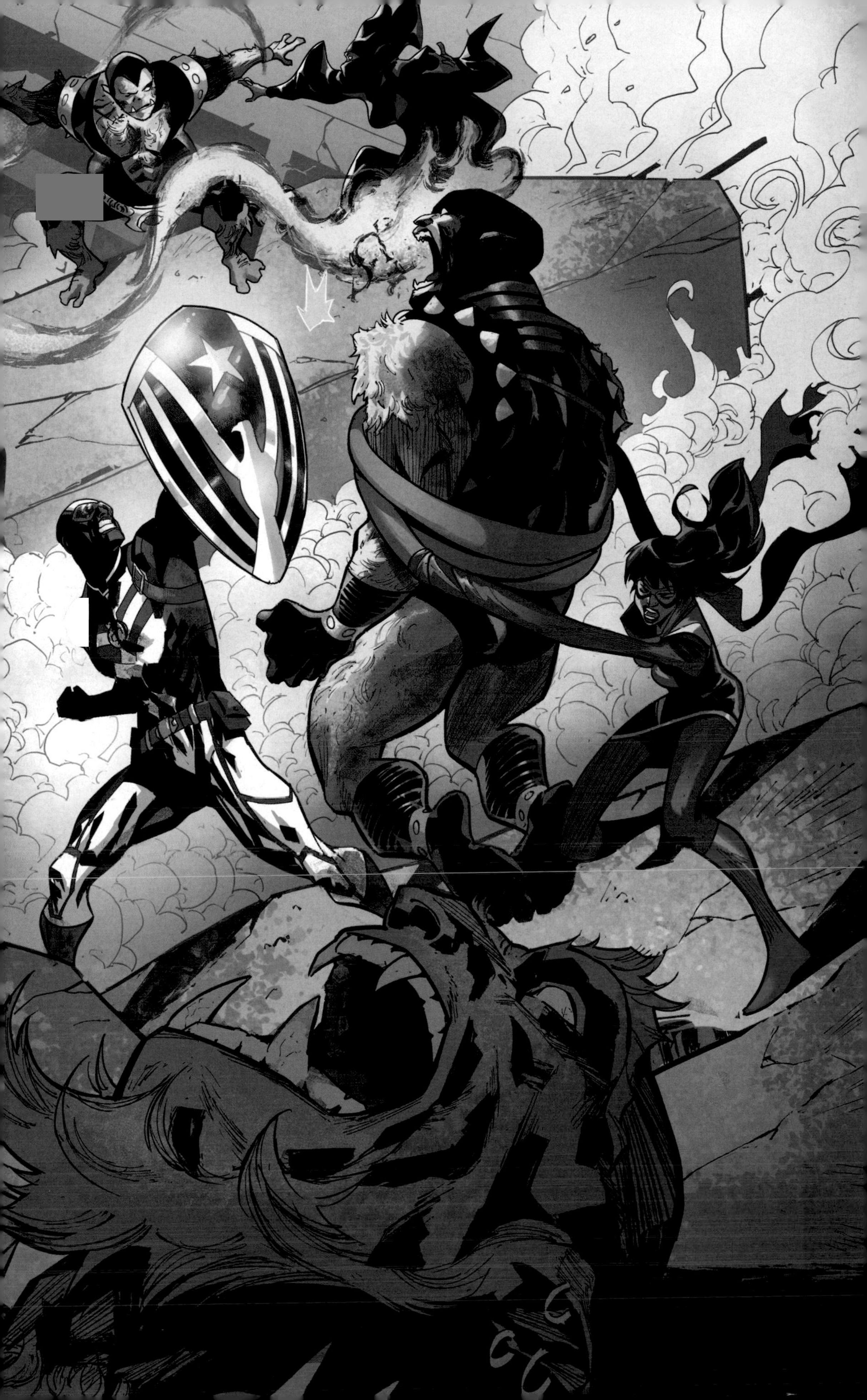

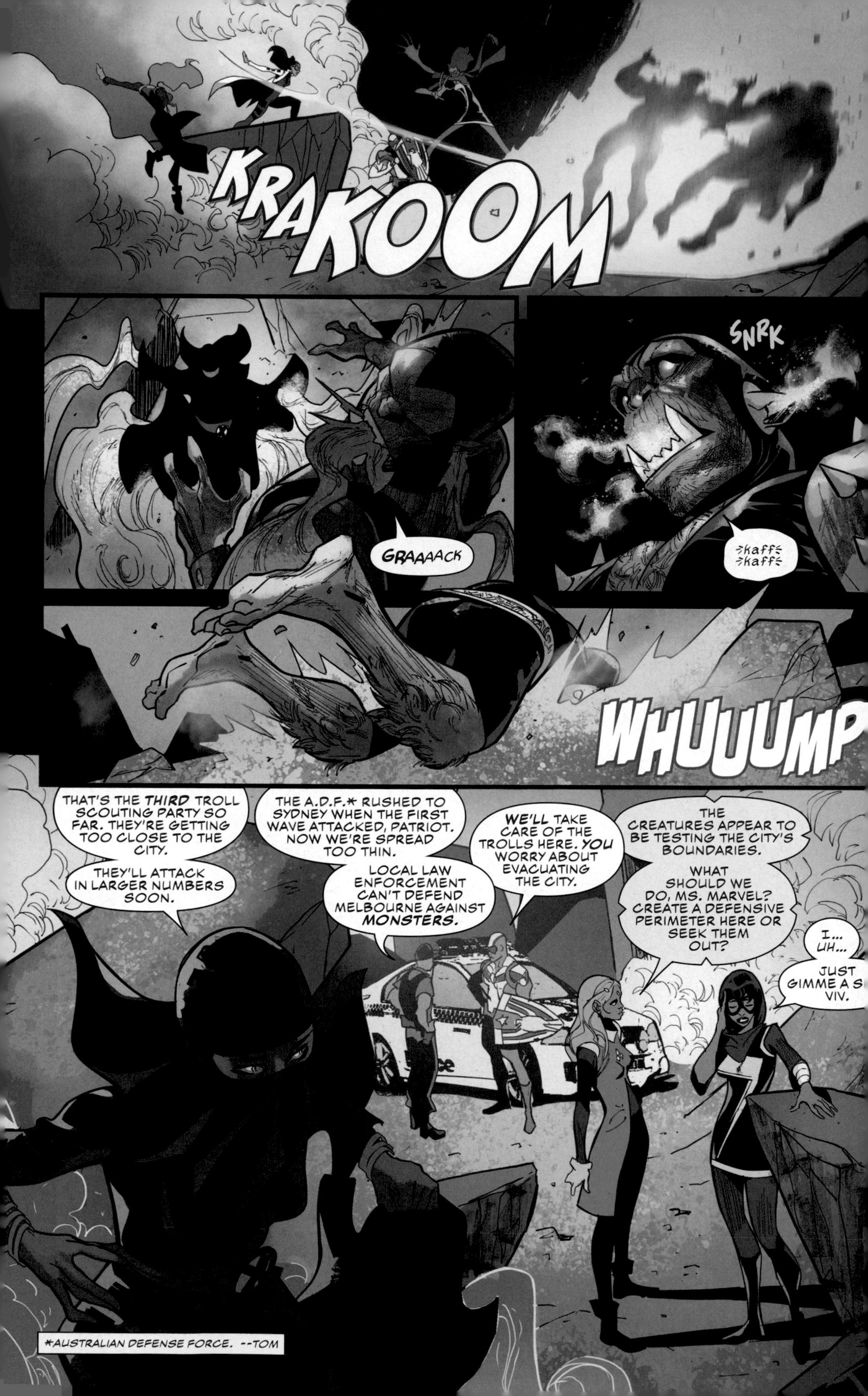
KRAKOOM
GRAAAACK
SNRK
kaff kaff
WHUUUMP
THAT'S THE THIRD TROLL SCOUTING PARTY SO FAR. THEY'RE GETTING TOO CLOSE TO THE CITY.
THEY'LL ATTACK IN LARGER NUMBERS SOON.
THE A.D.F.* RUSHED TO SYDNEY WHEN THE FIRST WAVE ATTACKED, PATRIOT. NOW WE'RE SPREAD TOO THIN.
LOCAL LAW ENFORCEMENT CAN'T DEFEND MELBOURNE AGAINST MONSTERS.
WE'LL TAKE CARE OF THE TROLLS HERE. YOU WORRY ABOUT EVACUATING THE CITY.
THE CREATURES APPEAR TO BE TESTING THE CITY'S BOUNDARIES.
WHAT SHOULD WE DO, MS. MARVEL? CREATE A DEFENSIVE PERIMETER HERE OR SEEK THEM OUT?
I... UH...
JUST GIMME A S
VIV.
*AUSTRALIAN DEFENSE FORCE. --TOM

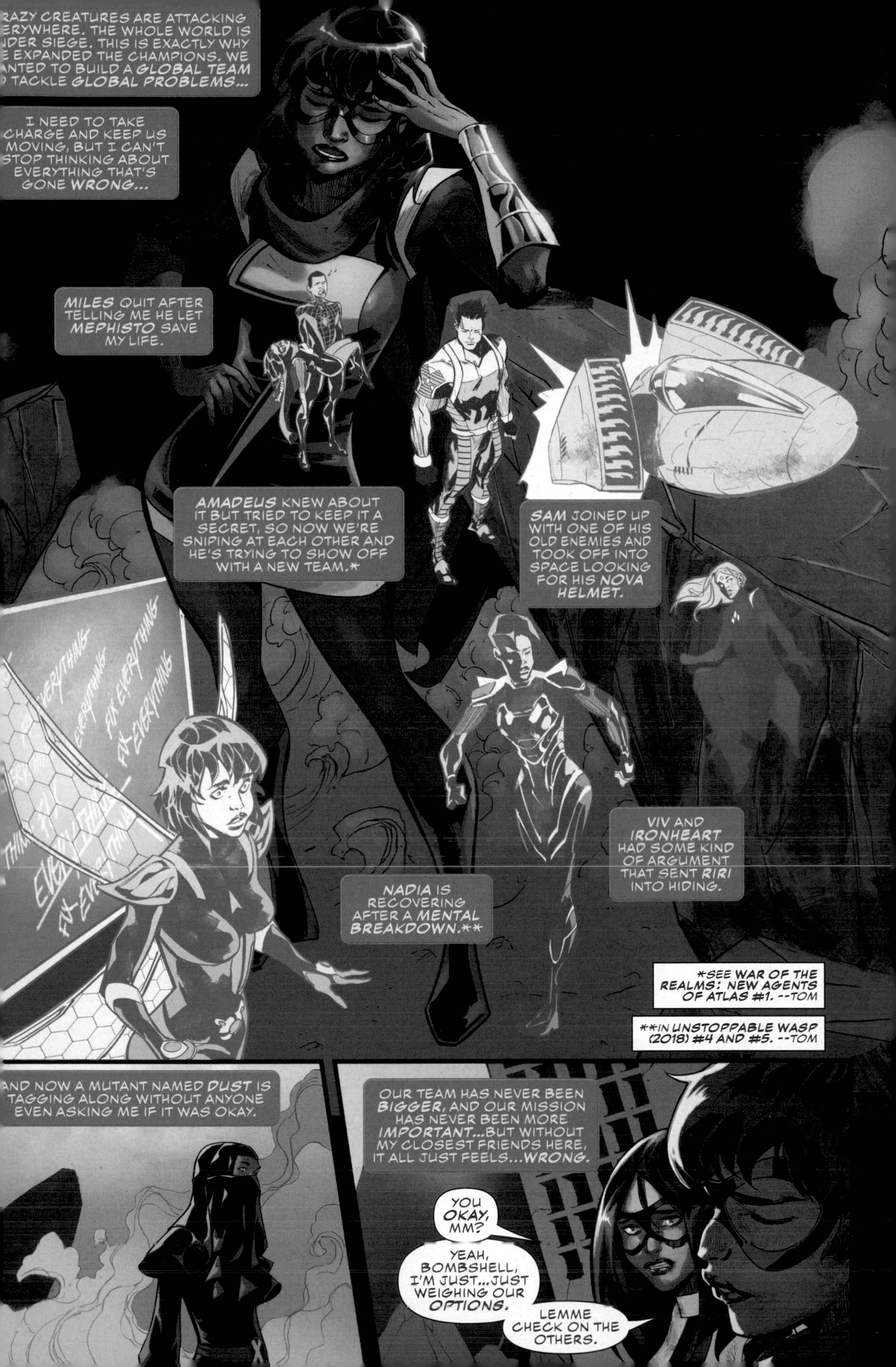

RAZY CREATURES ARE ATTACKING ERYWHERE. THE WHOLE WORLD IS NDER SIEGE. THIS IS EXACTLY WHY E EXPANDED THE CHAMPIONS. WE ANTED TO BUILD A GLOBAL TEAM O TACKLE GLOBAL PROBLEMS...
I NEED TO TAKE CHARGE AND KEEP US MOVING, BUT I CAN'T STOP THINKING ABOUT EVERYTHING THAT'S GONE WRONG...
MILES QUIT AFTER TELLING ME HE LET MEPHISTO SAVE MY LIFE.
AMADEUS KNEW ABOUT IT BUT TRIED TO KEEP IT A SECRET, SO NOW WE'RE SNIPING AT EACH OTHER AND HE'S TRYING TO SHOW OFF WITH A NEW TEAM.*
SAM JOINED UP WITH ONE OF HIS OLD ENEMIES AND TOOK OFF INTO SPACE LOOKING FOR HIS NOVA HELMET.
VIV AND IRONHEART HAD SOME KIND OF ARGUMENT THAT SENT RIRI INTO HIDING.
NADIA IS RECOVERING AFTER A MENTAL BREAKDOWN.**
*SEE WAR OF THE REALMS: NEW AGENTS OF ATLAS #1. --TOM
**IN UNSTOPPABLE WASP (2018) #4 AND #5. --TOM
AND NOW A MUTANT NAMED DUST IS TAGGING ALONG WITHOUT ANYONE EVEN ASKING ME IF IT WAS OKAY.
OUR TEAM HAS NEVER BEEN BIGGER, AND OUR MISSION HAS NEVER BEEN MORE IMPORTANT...BUT WITHOUT MY CLOSEST FRIENDS HERE, IT ALL JUST FEELS...WRONG.
YOU OKAY, MM?
YEAH, BOMBSHELL, I'M JUST...JUST WEIGHING OUR OPTIONS.
LEMME CHECK ON THE OTHERS.

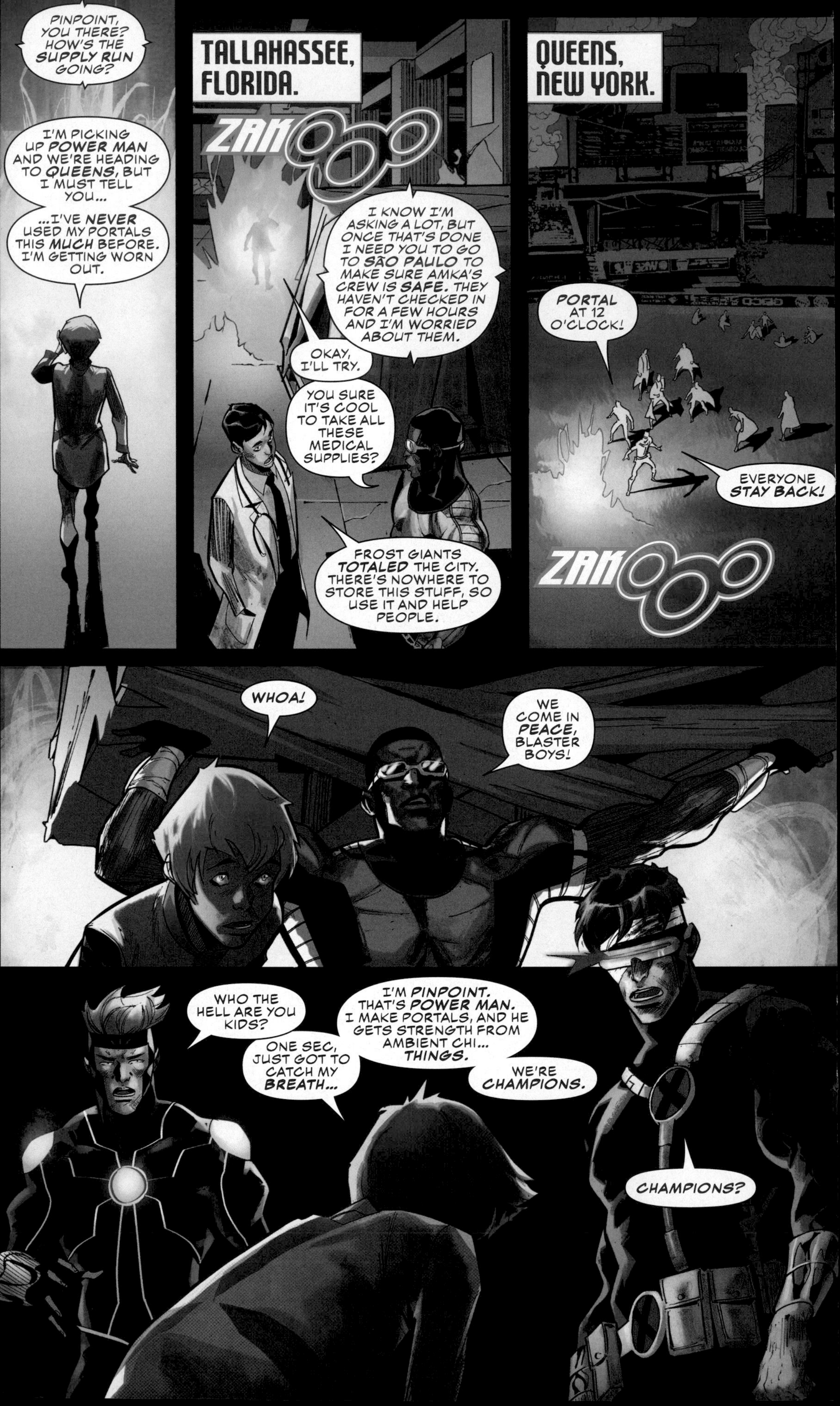
PINPOINT, YOU THERE? HOW'S THE SUPPLY RUN GOING?
I'M PICKING UP POWER MAN AND WE'RE HEADING TO QUEENS, BUT I MUST TELL YOU...
...I'VE NEVER USED MY PORTALS THIS MUCH BEFORE. I'M GETTING WORN OUT.
TALLAHASSEE, FLORIDA.
ZAK
I KNOW I'M ASKING A LOT, BUT ONCE THAT'S DONE I NEED YOU TO GO TO SÃO PAULO TO MAKE SURE AMKA'S CREW IS SAFE. THEY HAVEN'T CHECKED IN FOR A FEW HOURS AND I'M WORRIED ABOUT THEM.
OKAY, I'LL TRY.
YOU SURE IT'S COOL TO TAKE ALL THESE MEDICAL SUPPLIES?
FROST GIANTS TOTALED THE CITY. THERE'S NOWHERE TO STORE THIS STUFF, SO USE IT AND HELP PEOPLE.
QUEENS, NEW YORK.
PORTAL AT 12 O'CLOCK!
EVERYONE STAY BACK!
ZAK
WHOA!
WE COME IN PEACE, BLASTER BOYS!
WHO THE HELL ARE YOU KIDS?
ONE SEC, JUST GOT TO CATCH MY BREATH...
I'M PINPOINT. THAT'S POWER MAN. I MAKE PORTALS, AND HE GETS STRENGTH FROM AMBIENT CHI... THINGS.
WE'RE CHAMPIONS.
CHAMPIONS?

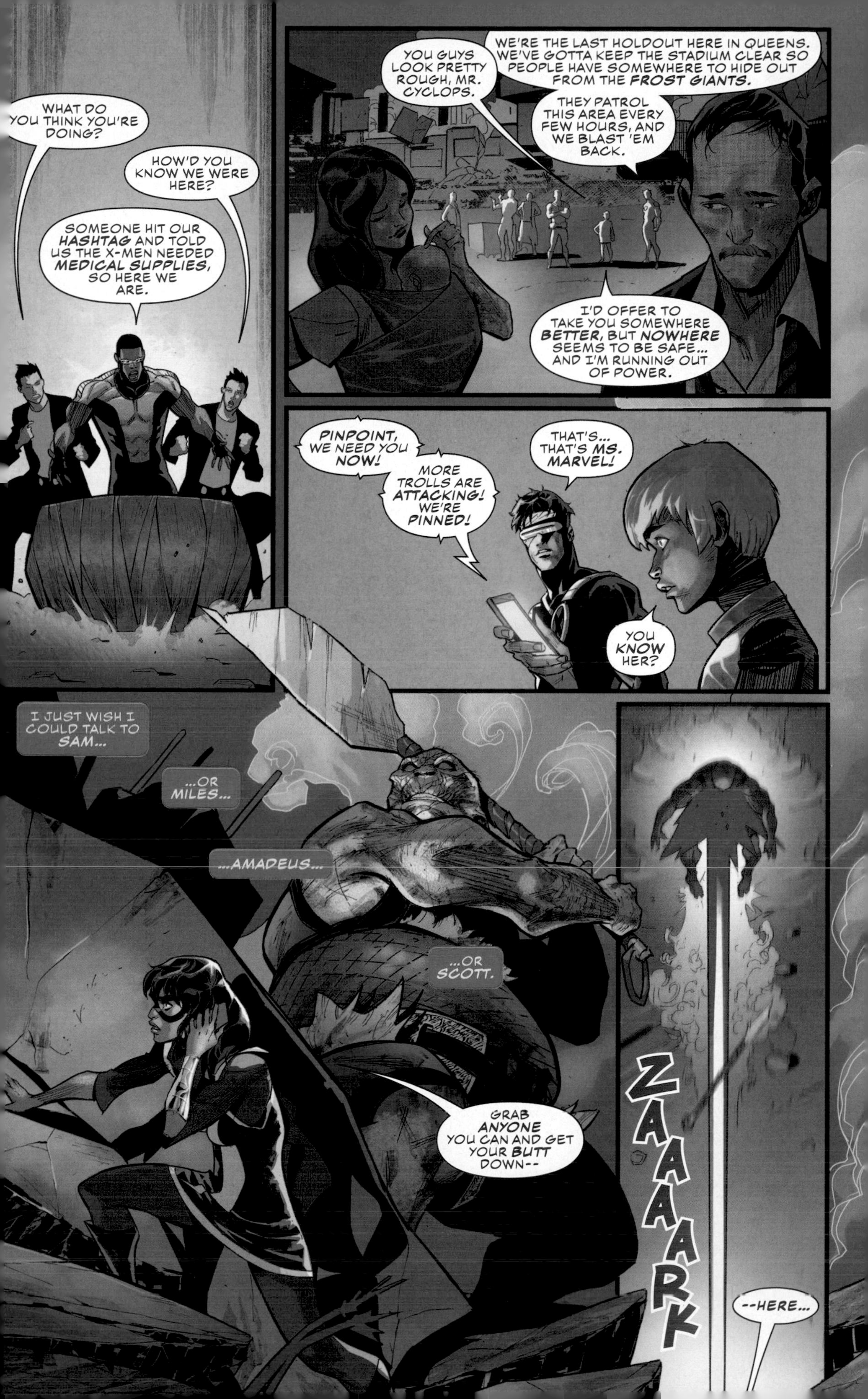

WHAT DO YOU THINK YOU'RE DOING?
HOW'D YOU KNOW WE WERE HERE?
SOMEONE HIT OUR HASHTAG AND TOLD US THE X-MEN NEEDED MEDICAL SUPPLIES, SO HERE WE ARE.
YOU GUYS LOOK PRETTY ROUGH, MR. CYCLOPS.
WE'RE THE LAST HOLDOUT HERE IN QUEENS. WE'VE GOTTA KEEP THE STADIUM CLEAR SO PEOPLE HAVE SOMEWHERE TO HIDE OUT FROM THE FROST GIANTS.
THEY PATROL THIS AREA EVERY FEW HOURS, AND WE BLAST 'EM BACK.
I'D OFFER TO TAKE YOU SOMEWHERE BETTER, BUT NOWHERE SEEMS TO BE SAFE... AND I'M RUNNING OUT OF POWER.
PINPOINT, WE NEED YOU NOW!
MORE TROLLS ARE ATTACKING! WE'RE PINNED!
THAT'S... THAT'S MS. MARVEL!
YOU KNOW HER?
I JUST WISH I COULD TALK TO SAM...
...OR MILES...
...AMADEUS...
...OR SCOTT.
GRAB ANYONE YOU CAN AND GET YOUR BUTT DOWN--
ZAAAARK
--HERE...

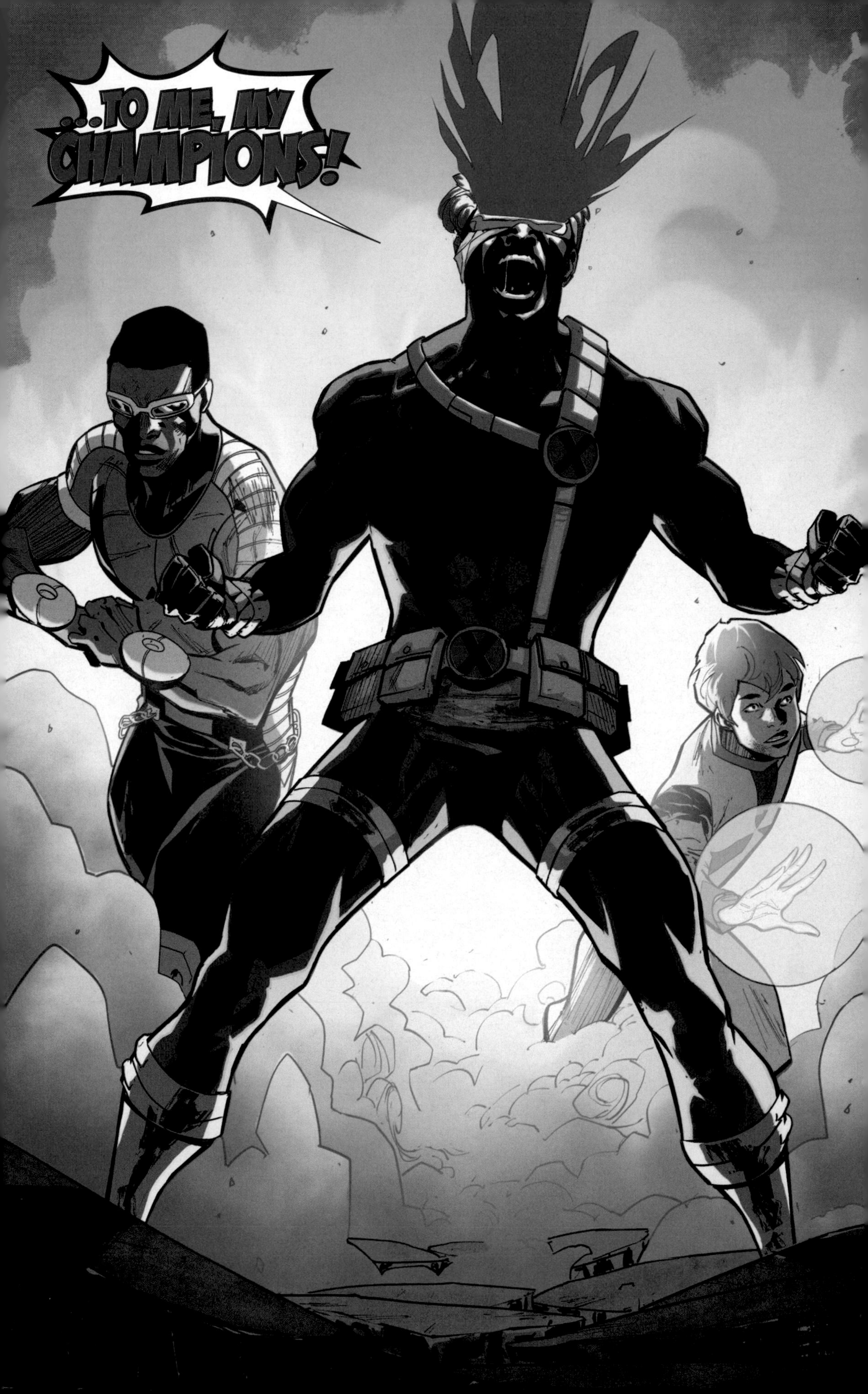
...TO ME, MY CHAMPIONS!

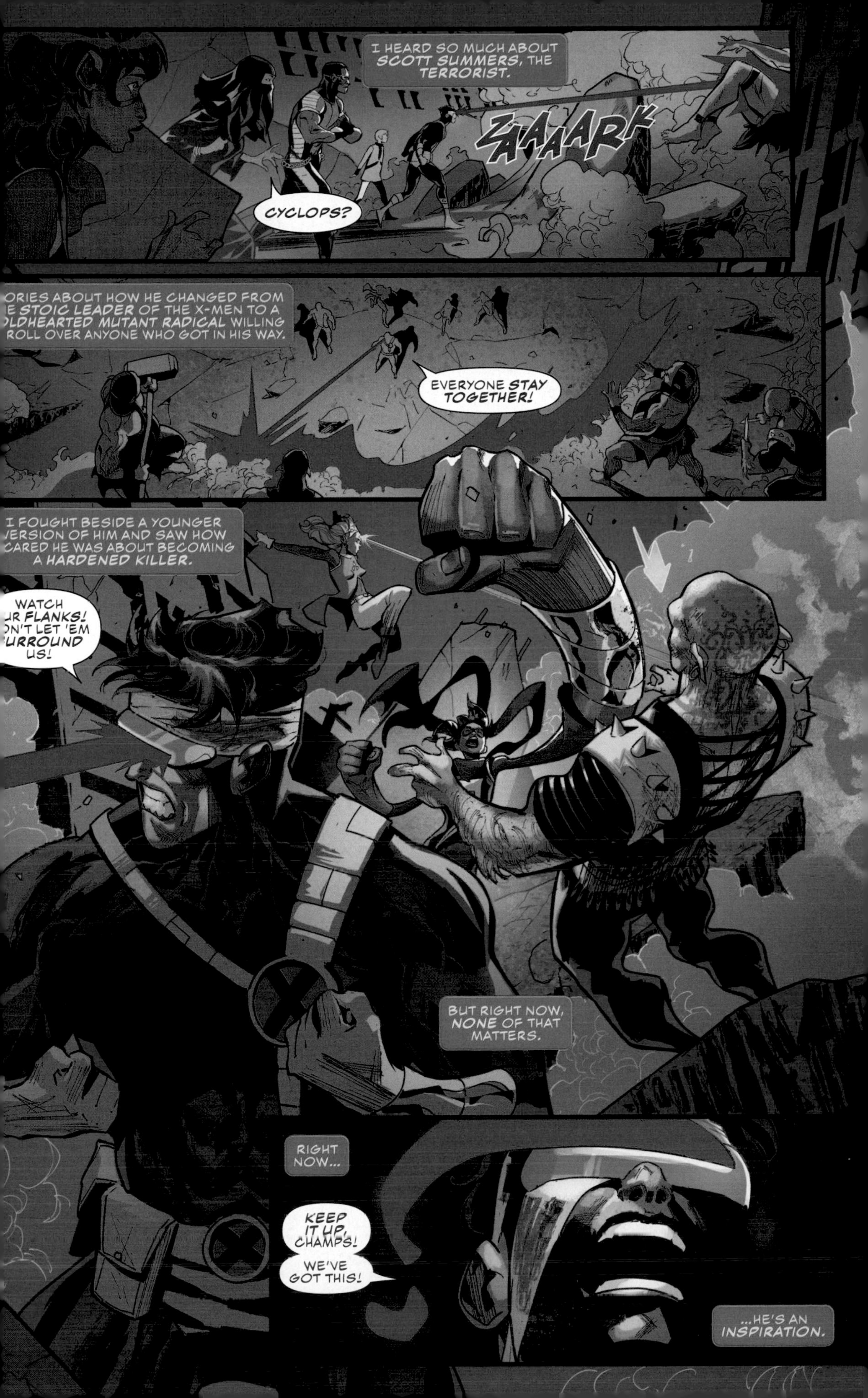
I HEARD SO MUCH ABOUT SCOTT SUMMERS, THE TERRORIST.
CYCLOPS?
ZAAAARK
ORIES ABOUT HOW HE CHANGED FROM E STOIC LEADER OF THE X-MEN TO A OLDHEARTED MUTANT RADICAL WILLING ROLL OVER ANYONE WHO GOT IN HIS WAY.
EVERYONE STAY TOGETHER!
I FOUGHT BESIDE A YOUNGER VERSION OF HIM AND SAW HOW CARED HE WAS ABOUT BECOMING A HARDENED KILLER.
WATCH UR FLANKS! ON'T LET 'EM URROUND US!
BUT RIGHT NOW, NONE OF THAT MATTERS.
RIGHT NOW...
KEEP IT UP, CHAMPS!
WE'VE GOT THIS!
...HE'S AN INSPIRATION.

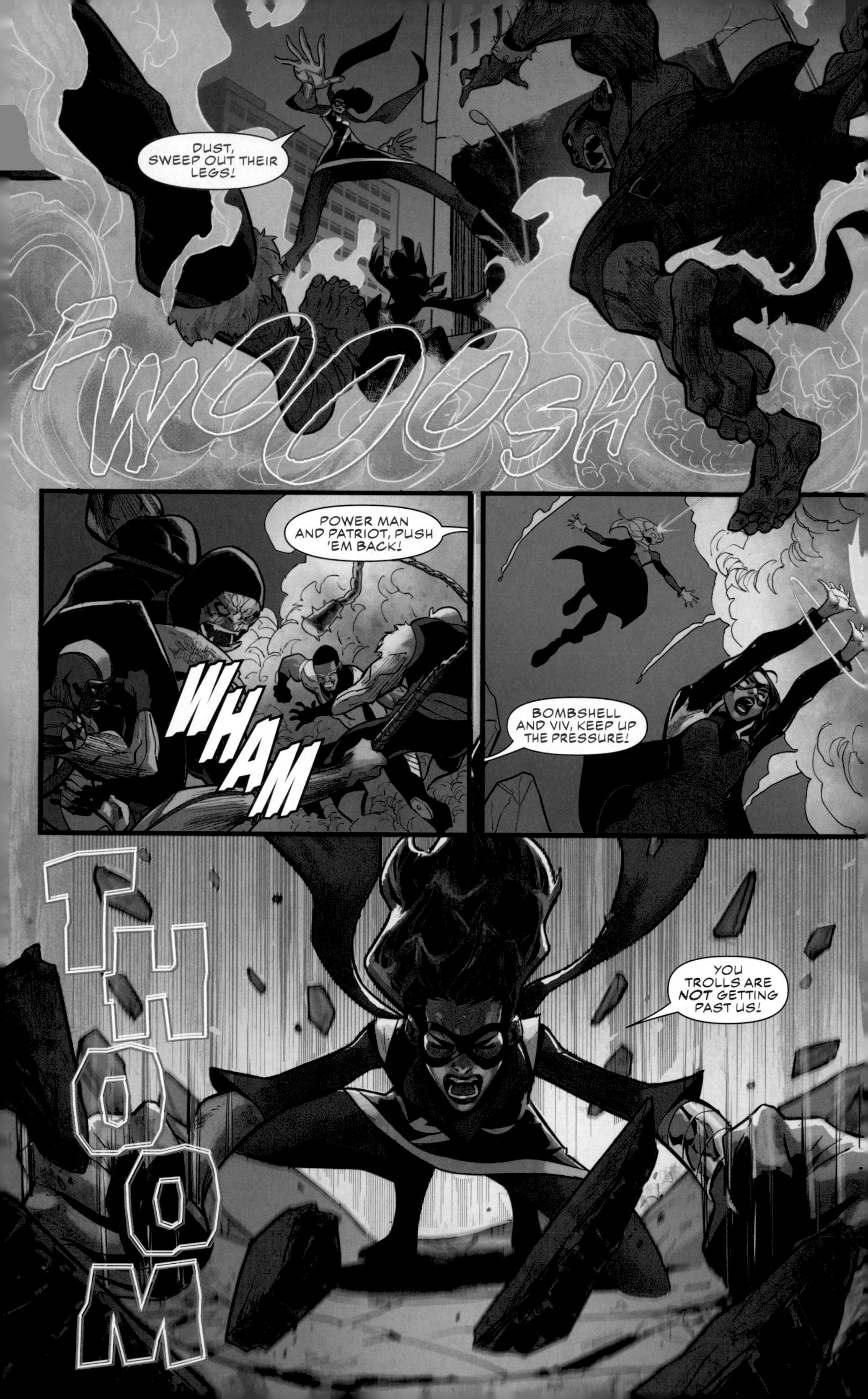
DUST, SWEEP OUT THEIR LEGS!
FWOOOOSH
POWER MAN AND PATRIOT, PUSH 'EM BACK!
WHAM
BOMBSHELL AND VIV, KEEP UP THE PRESSURE!
THOOOM
YOU TROLLS ARE NOT GETTING PAST US!

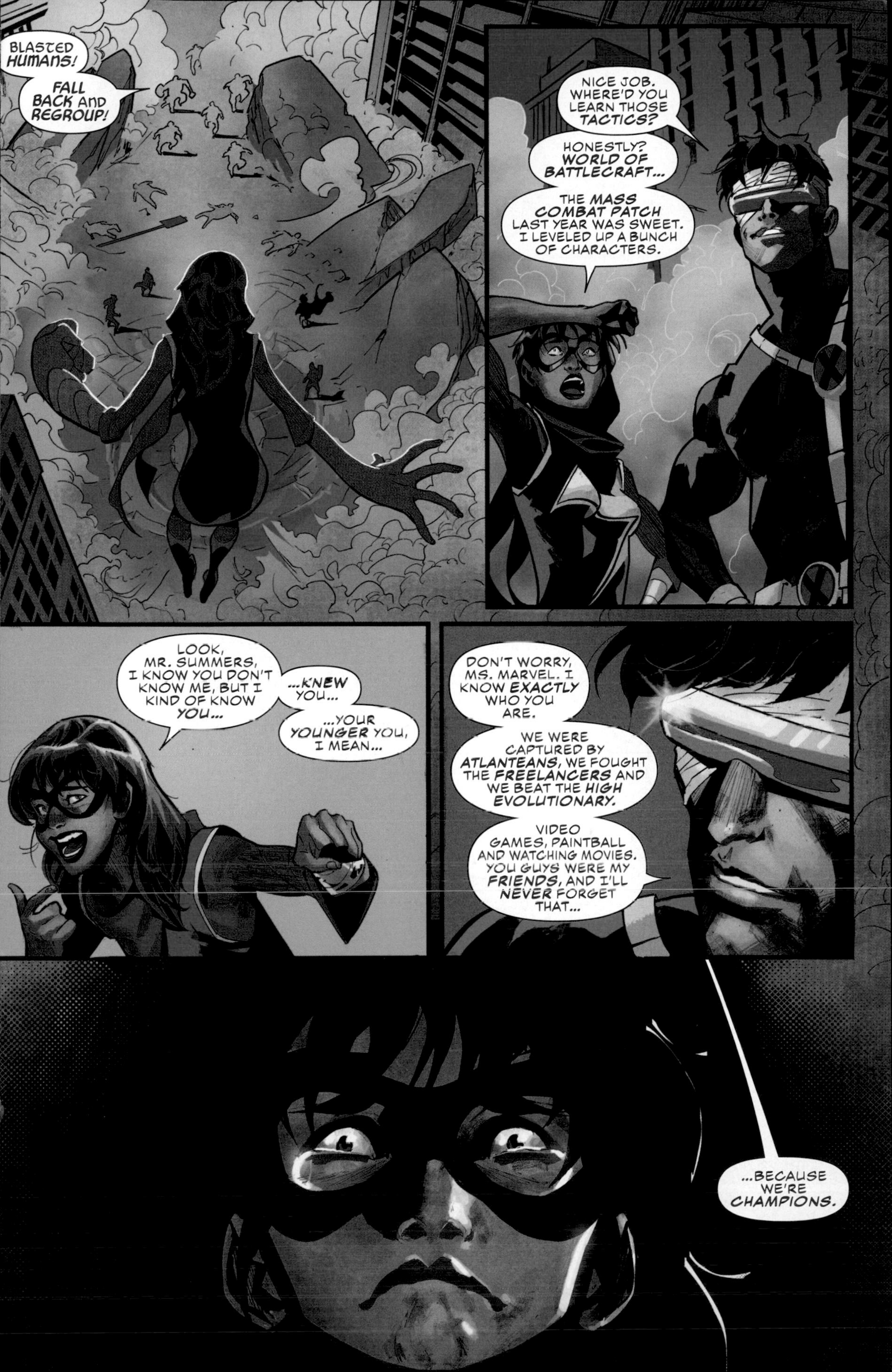

BLASTED HUMANS!
FALL BACK AND REGROUP!
NICE JOB. WHERE'D YOU LEARN THOSE TACTICS?
HONESTLY? WORLD OF BATTLECRAFT...
THE MASS COMBAT PATCH LAST YEAR WAS SWEET. I LEVELED UP A BUNCH OF CHARACTERS.
LOOK, MR. SUMMERS, I KNOW YOU DON'T KNOW ME, BUT I KIND OF KNOW YOU...
...KNEW YOU...
...YOUR YOUNGER YOU, I MEAN...
DON'T WORRY, MS. MARVEL. I KNOW EXACTLY WHO YOU ARE.
WE WERE CAPTURED BY ATLANTEANS, WE FOUGHT THE FREELANCERS AND WE BEAT THE HIGH EVOLUTIONARY.
VIDEO GAMES, PAINTBALL AND WATCHING MOVIES. YOU GUYS WERE MY FRIENDS, AND I'LL NEVER FORGET THAT...
...BECAUSE WE'RE CHAMPIONS.

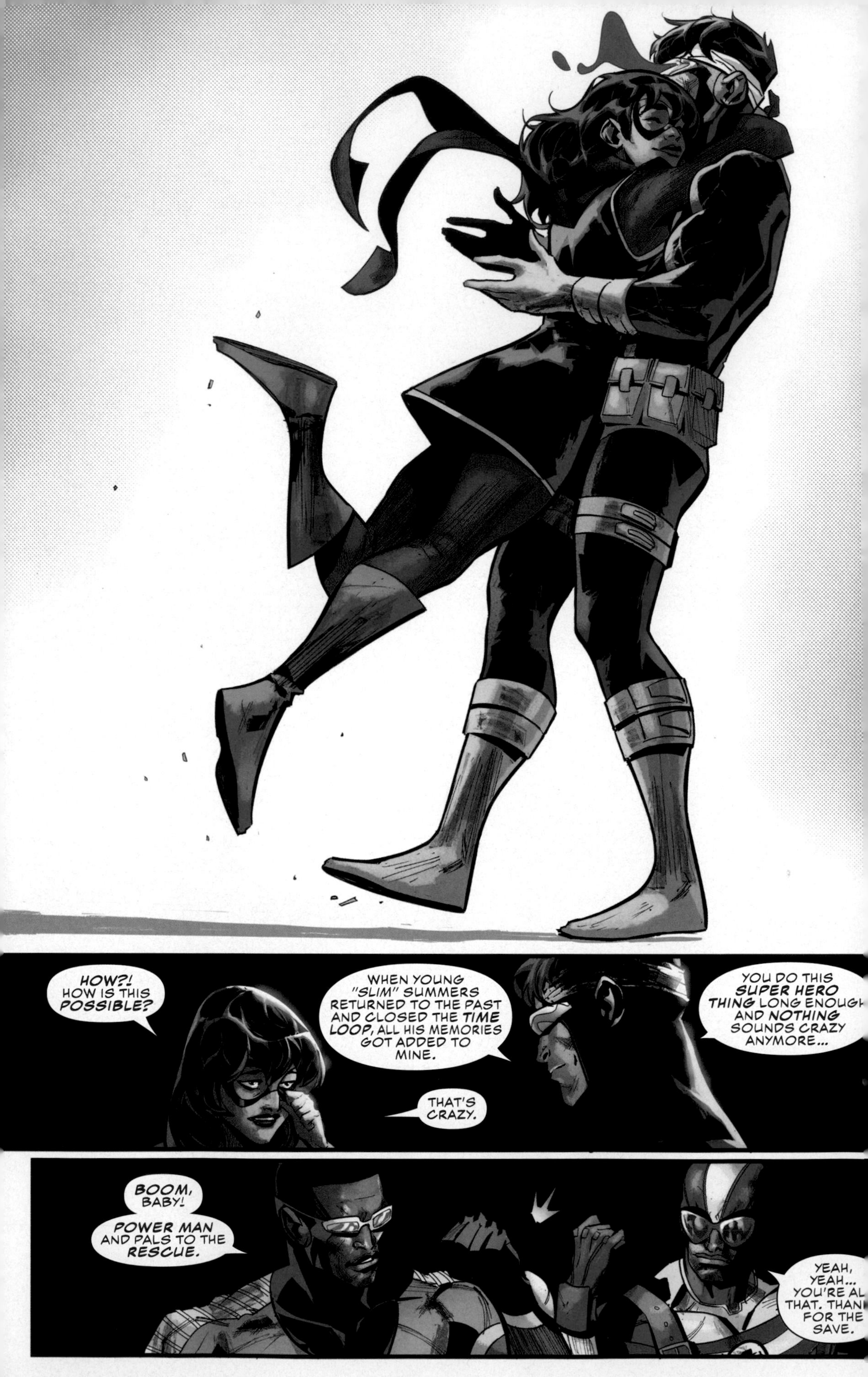
HOW?! HOW IS THIS POSSIBLE?
WHEN YOUNG "SLIM" SUMMERS RETURNED TO THE PAST AND CLOSED THE TIME LOOP, ALL HIS MEMORIES GOT ADDED TO MINE.
THAT'S CRAZY.
YOU DO THIS SUPER HERO THING LONG ENOUG AND NOTHING SOUNDS CRAZY ANYMORE...
BOOM, BABY!
POWER MAN AND PALS TO THE RESCUE.
YEAH, YEAH... YOU'RE AL THAT. THAN FOR THE SAVE.

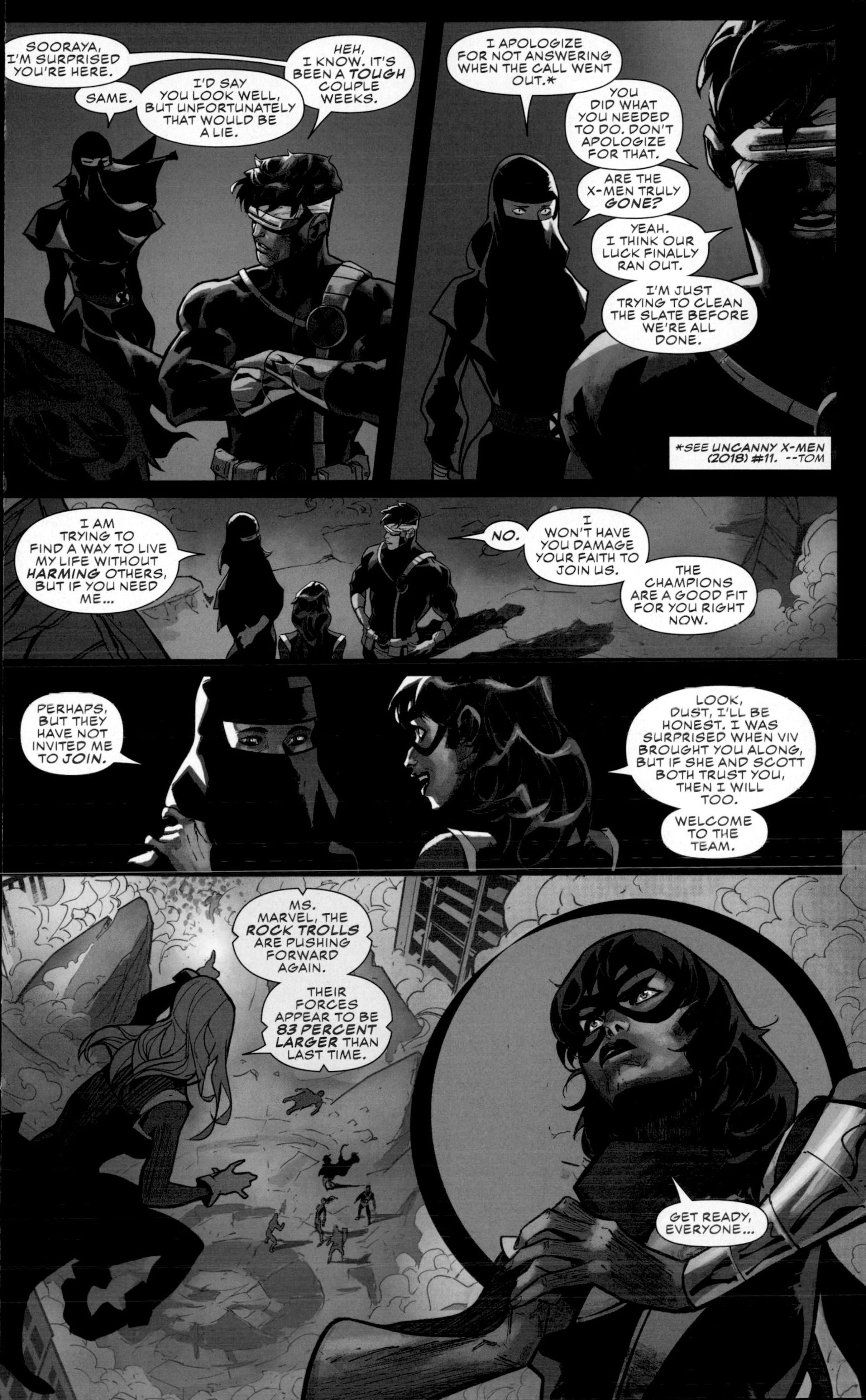
SOORAYA, I'M SURPRISED YOU'RE HERE.
SAME.
I'D SAY YOU LOOK WELL, BUT UNFORTUNATELY THAT WOULD BE A LIE.
HEH, I KNOW. IT'S BEEN A TOUGH COUPLE WEEKS.
I APOLOGIZE FOR NOT ANSWERING WHEN THE CALL WENT OUT.*
YOU DID WHAT YOU NEEDED TO DO. DON'T APOLOGIZE FOR THAT.
ARE THE X-MEN TRULY GONE?
YEAH. I THINK OUR LUCK FINALLY RAN OUT.
I'M JUST TRYING TO CLEAN THE SLATE BEFORE WE'RE ALL DONE.
*SEE UNCANNY X-MEN (2018) #11. --TOM
I AM TRYING TO FIND A WAY TO LIVE MY LIFE WITHOUT HARMING OTHERS, BUT IF YOU NEED ME...
NO.
I WON'T HAVE YOU DAMAGE YOUR FAITH TO JOIN US.
THE CHAMPIONS ARE A GOOD FIT FOR YOU RIGHT NOW.
PERHAPS, BUT THEY HAVE NOT INVITED ME TO JOIN.
LOOK, DUST, I'LL BE HONEST. I WAS SURPRISED WHEN VIV BROUGHT YOU ALONG, BUT IF SHE AND SCOTT BOTH TRUST YOU, THEN I WILL TOO.
WELCOME TO THE TEAM.
MS. MARVEL, THE ROCK TROLLS ARE PUSHING FORWARD AGAIN.
THEIR FORCES APPEAR TO BE 83 PERCENT LARGER THAN LAST TIME.
GET READY, EVERYONE...

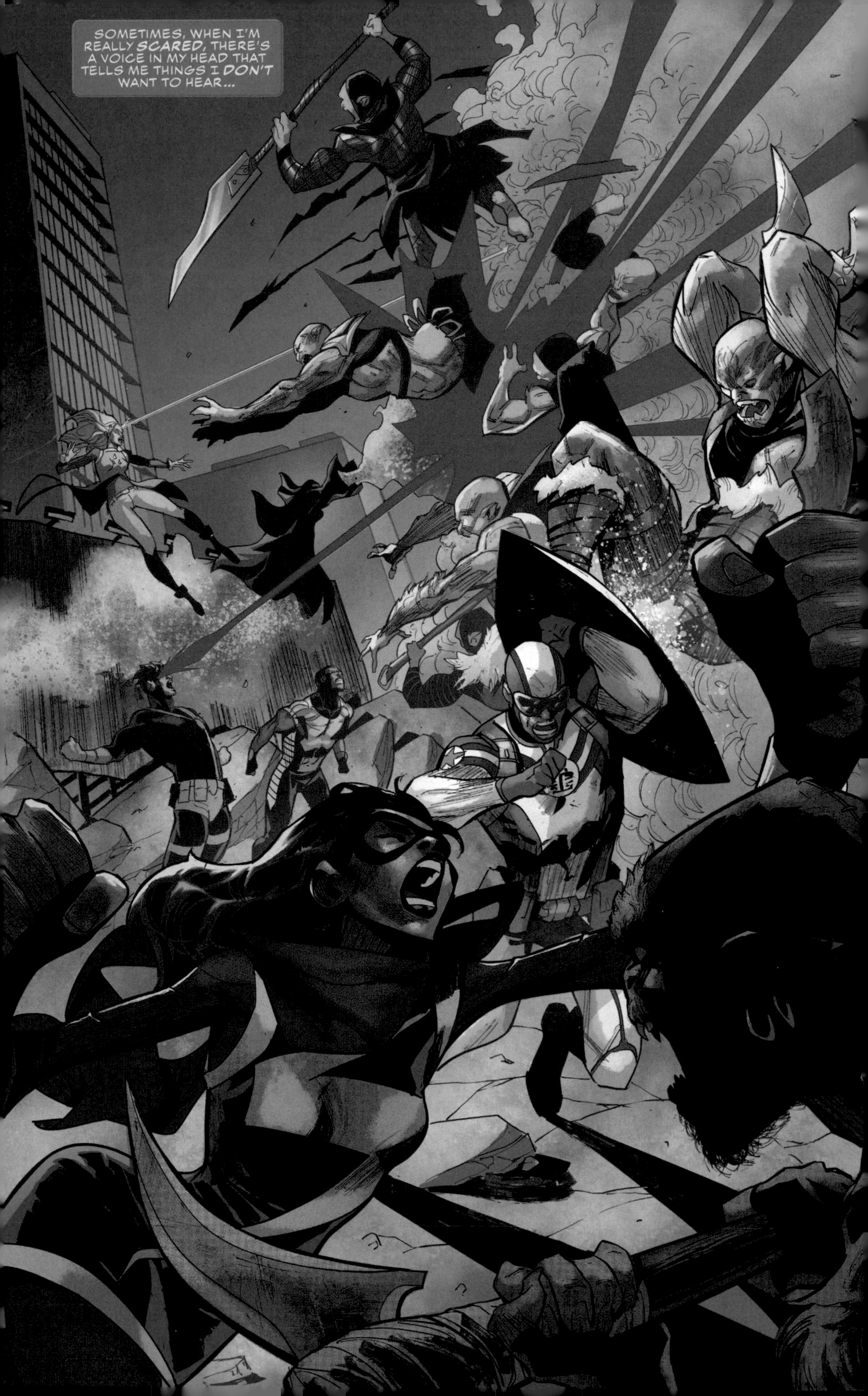
SOMETIMES, WHEN I'M REALLY SCARED, THERE'S A VOICE IN MY HEAD THAT TELLS ME THINGS I DON'T WANT TO HEAR...

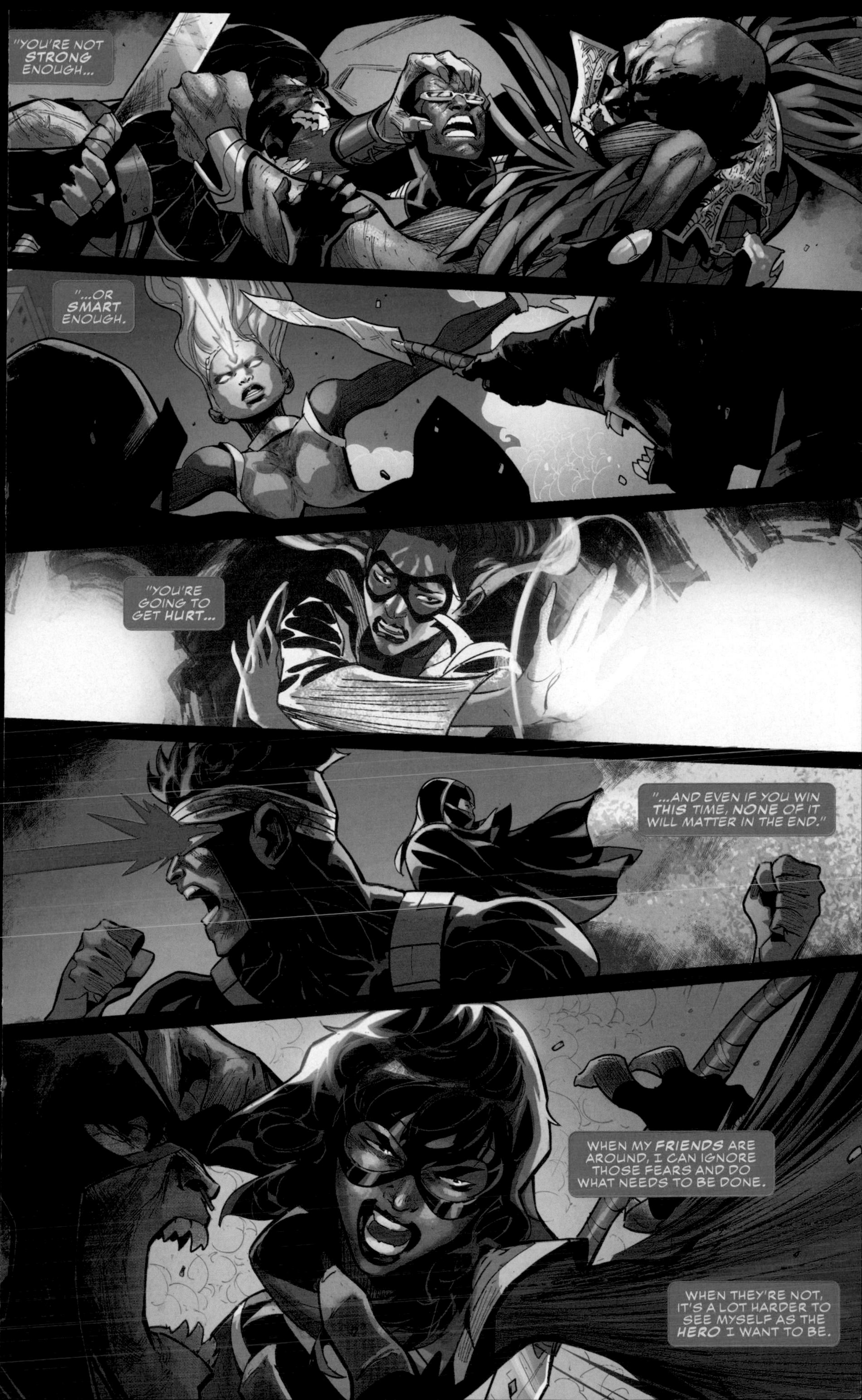
"YOU'RE NOT STRONG ENOUGH...
"...OR SMART ENOUGH.
"YOU'RE GOING TO GET HURT...
"...AND EVEN IF YOU WIN THIS TIME, NONE OF IT WILL MATTER IN THE END."
WHEN MY FRIENDS ARE AROUND, I CAN IGNORE THOSE FEARS AND DO WHAT NEEDS TO BE DONE.
WHEN THEY'RE NOT, IT'S A LOT HARDER TO SEE MYSELF AS THE HERO I WANT TO BE.

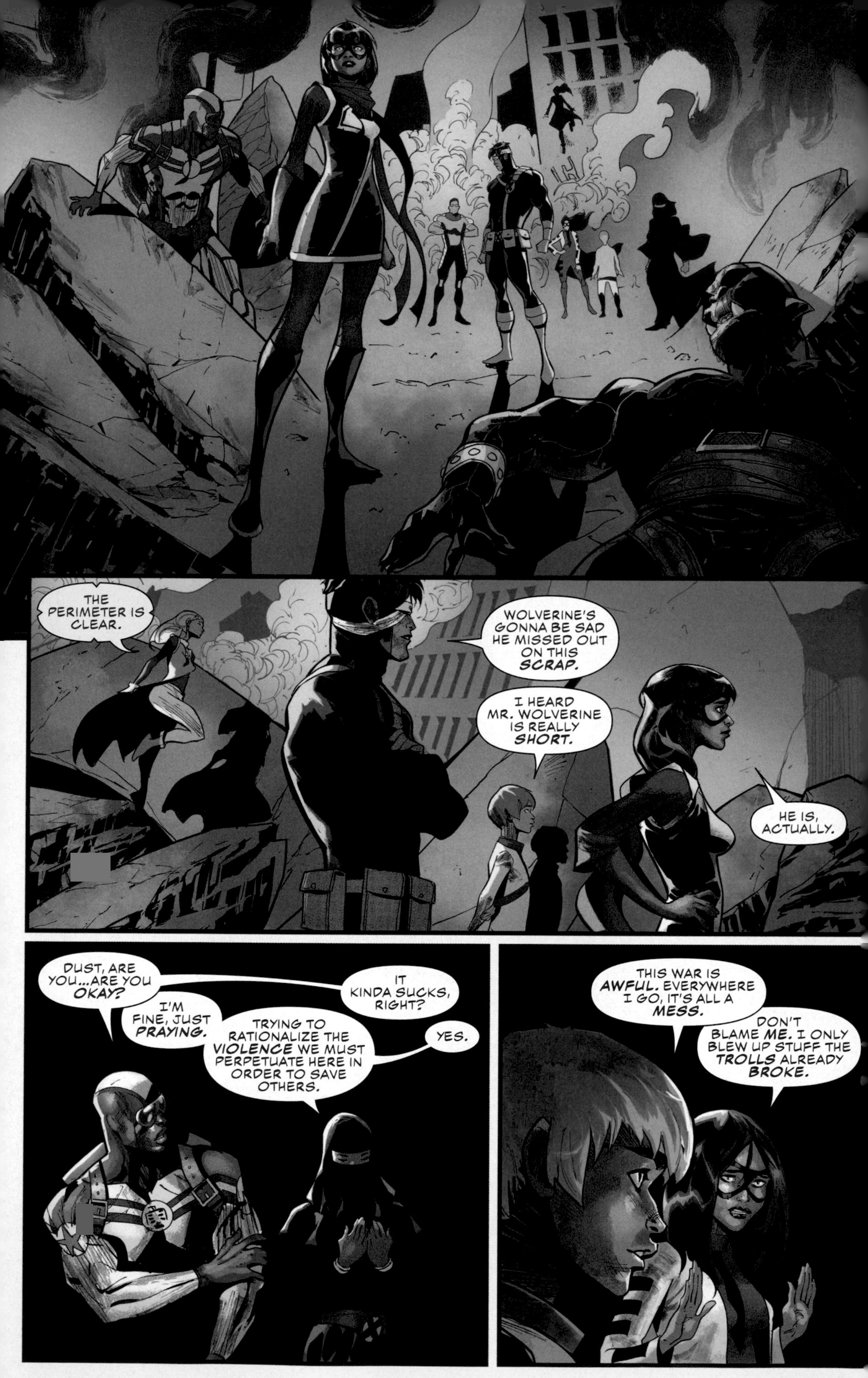
THE PERIMETER IS CLEAR.
WOLVERINE'S GONNA BE SAD HE MISSED OUT ON THIS SCRAP.
I HEARD MR. WOLVERINE IS REALLY SHORT.
HE IS, ACTUALLY.
DUST, ARE YOU...ARE YOU OKAY?
I'M FINE, JUST PRAYING.
TRYING TO RATIONALIZE THE VIOLENCE WE MUST PERPETUATE HERE IN ORDER TO SAVE OTHERS.
IT KINDA SUCKS, RIGHT?
YES.
THIS WAR IS AWFUL. EVERYWHERE I GO, IT'S ALL A MESS.
DON'T BLAME ME. I ONLY BLEW UP STUFF THE TROLLS ALREADY BROKE.

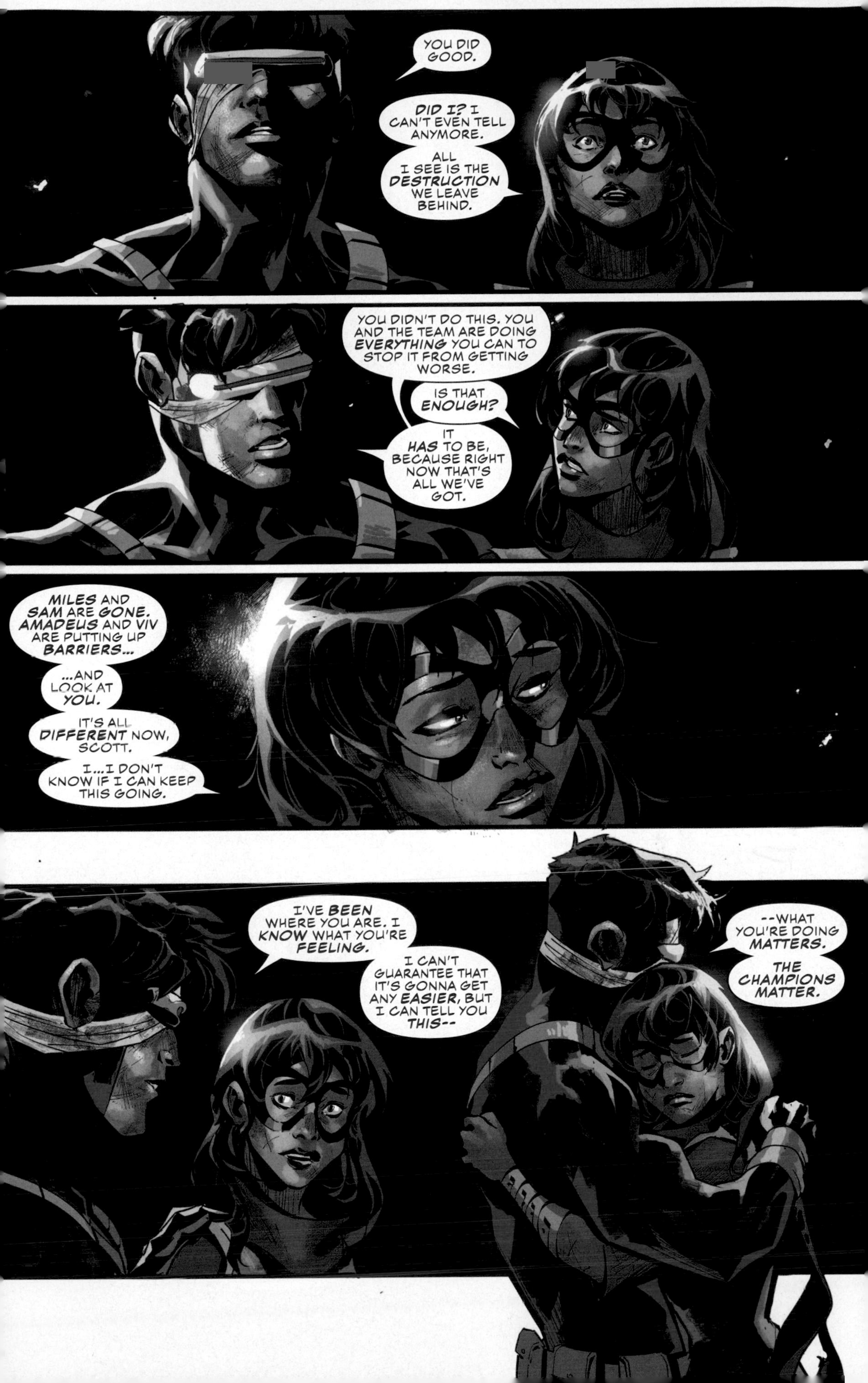
YOU DID GOOD.
DID I? I CAN'T EVEN TELL ANYMORE.
ALL I SEE IS THE DESTRUCTION WE LEAVE BEHIND.
YOU DIDN'T DO THIS. YOU AND THE TEAM ARE DOING EVERYTHING YOU CAN TO STOP IT FROM GETTING WORSE.
IS THAT ENOUGH?
IT HAS TO BE, BECAUSE RIGHT NOW THAT'S ALL WE'VE GOT.
MILES AND SAM ARE GONE. AMADEUS AND VIV ARE PUTTING UP BARRIERS...
...AND LOOK AT YOU.
IT'S ALL DIFFERENT NOW, SCOTT.
I...I DON'T KNOW IF I CAN KEEP THIS GOING.
I'VE BEEN WHERE YOU ARE. I KNOW WHAT YOU'RE FEELING.
I CAN'T GUARANTEE THAT IT'S GONNA GET ANY EASIER, BUT I CAN TELL YOU THIS--
--WHAT YOU'RE DOING MATTERS.
THE CHAMPIONS MATTER.

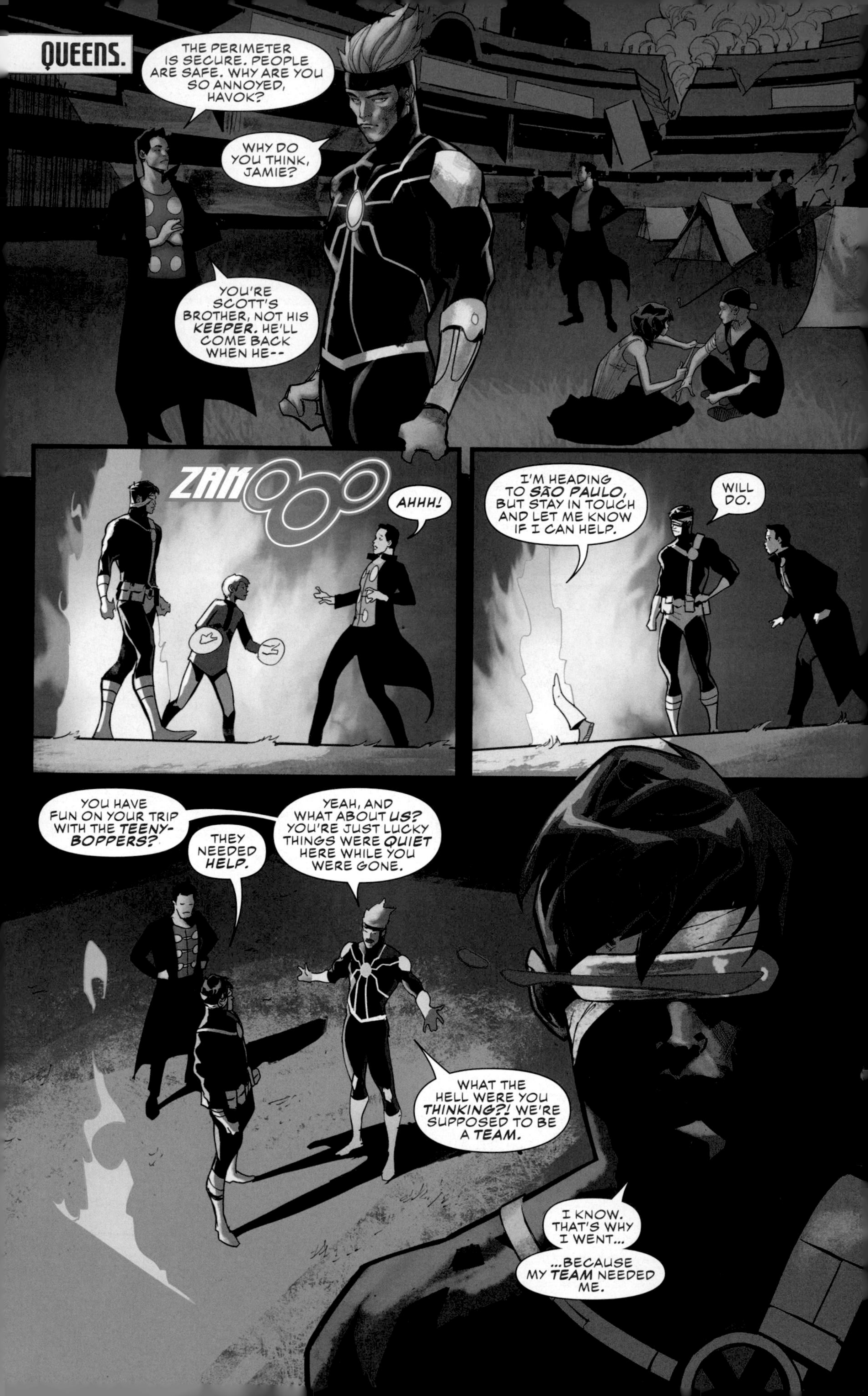
QUEENS.
THE PERIMETER IS SECURE. PEOPLE ARE SAFE. WHY ARE YOU SO ANNOYED, HAVOK?
WHY DO YOU THINK, JAMIE?
YOU'RE SCOTT'S BROTHER, NOT HIS KEEPER. HE'LL COME BACK WHEN HE--
ZAKOOOO
AHHH!
I'M HEADING TO SÃO PAULO, BUT STAY IN TOUCH AND LET ME KNOW IF I CAN HELP.
WILL DO.
YOU HAVE FUN ON YOUR TRIP WITH THE TEENY-BOPPERS?
THEY NEEDED HELP.
YEAH, AND WHAT ABOUT US? YOU'RE JUST LUCKY THINGS WERE QUIET HERE WHILE YOU WERE GONE.
WHAT THE HELL WERE YOU THINKING?! WE'RE SUPPOSED TO BE A TEAM.
I KNOW. THAT'S WHY I WENT...
...BECAUSE MY TEAM NEEDED ME.

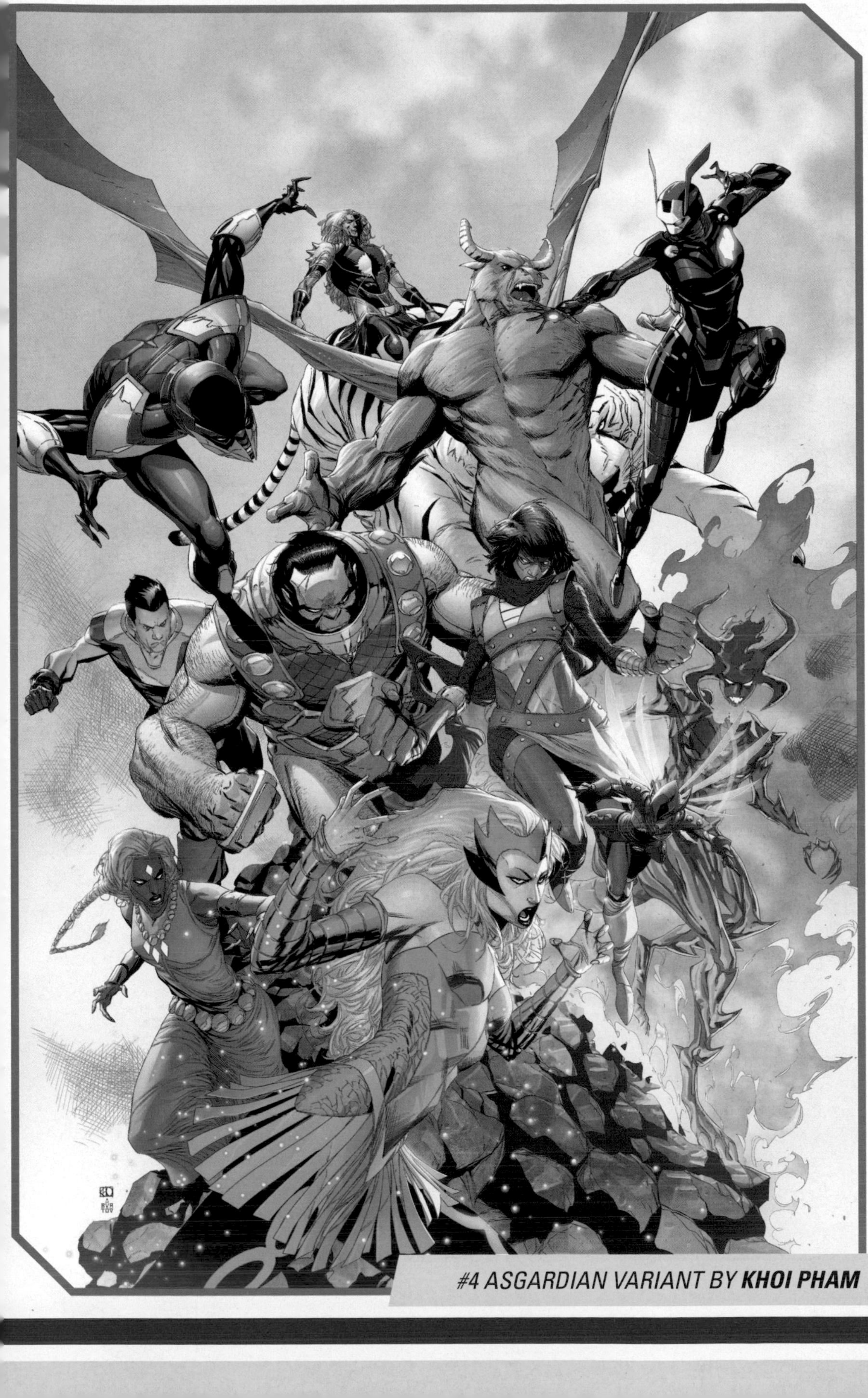

#4 ASGARDIAN VARIANT BY **KHOI PHAM**

6

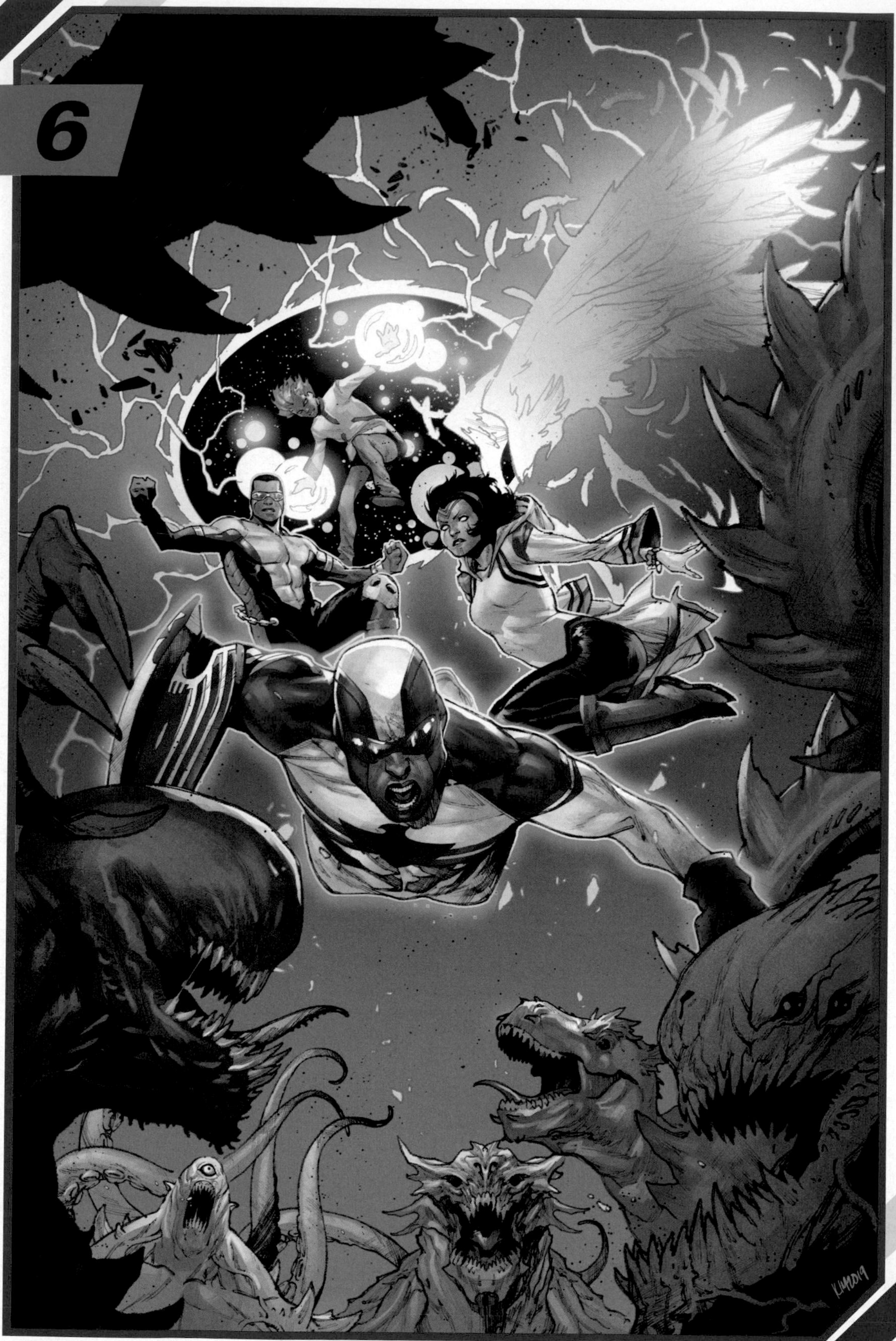

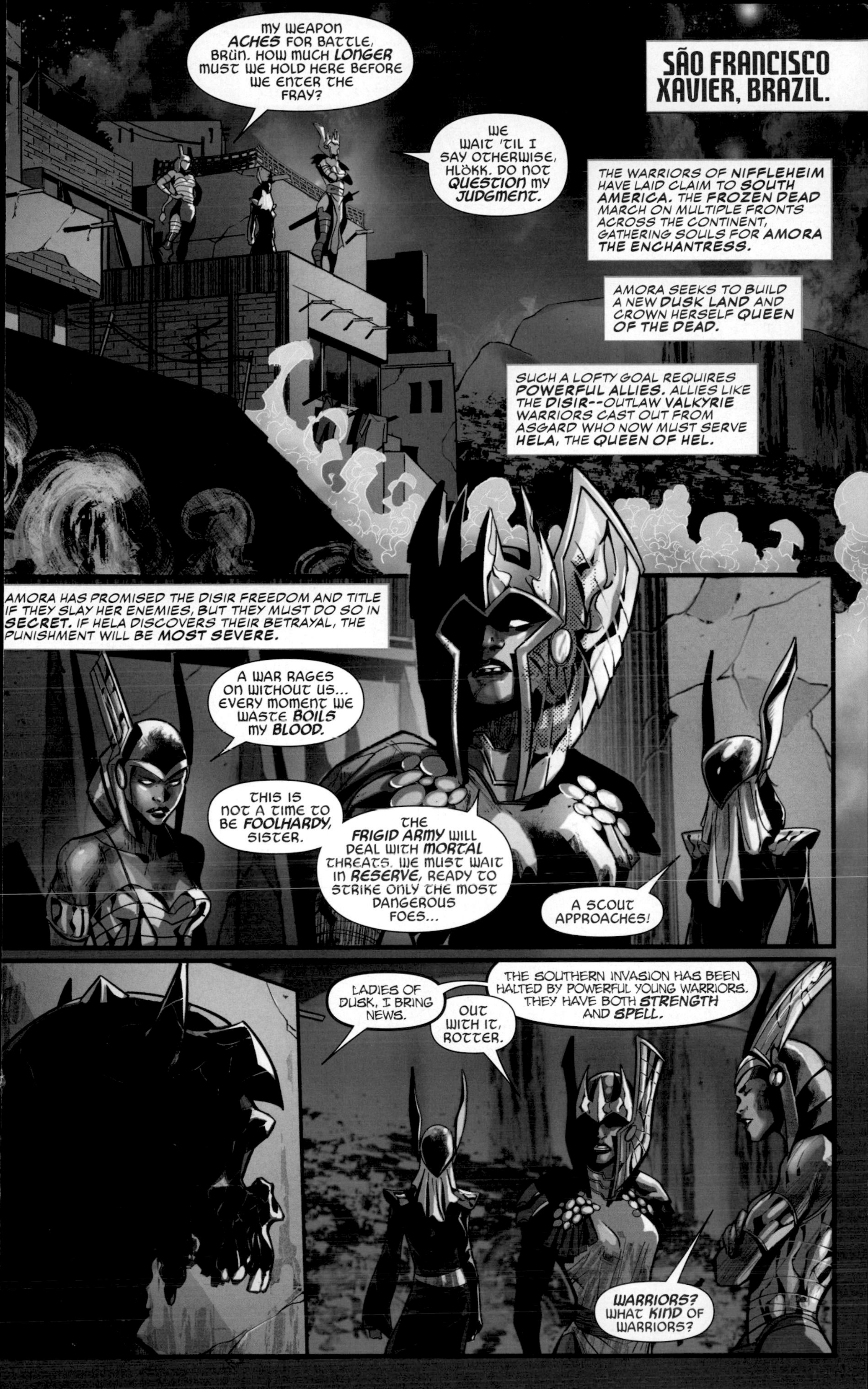
SÃO FRANCISCO XAVIER, BRAZIL.
MY WEAPON ACHES FOR BATTLE, BRÜN. HOW MUCH LONGER MUST WE HOLD HERE BEFORE WE ENTER THE FRAY?
WE WAIT 'TIL I SAY OTHERWISE, HLÖKK. DO NOT QUESTION MY JUDGMENT.
THE WARRIORS OF NIFFLEHEIM HAVE LAID CLAIM TO SOUTH AMERICA. THE FROZEN DEAD MARCH ON MULTIPLE FRONTS ACROSS THE CONTINENT, GATHERING SOULS FOR AMORA THE ENCHANTRESS.
AMORA SEEKS TO BUILD A NEW DUSK LAND AND CROWN HERSELF QUEEN OF THE DEAD.
SUCH A LOFTY GOAL REQUIRES POWERFUL ALLIES. ALLIES LIKE THE DISIR--OUTLAW VALKYRIE WARRIORS CAST OUT FROM ASGARD WHO NOW MUST SERVE HELA, THE QUEEN OF HEL.
AMORA HAS PROMISED THE DISIR FREEDOM AND TITLE IF THEY SLAY HER ENEMIES, BUT THEY MUST DO SO IN SECRET. IF HELA DISCOVERS THEIR BETRAYAL, THE PUNISHMENT WILL BE MOST SEVERE.
A WAR RAGES ON WITHOUT US... EVERY MOMENT WE WASTE BOILS MY BLOOD.
THIS IS NOT A TIME TO BE FOOLHARDY, SISTER.
THE FRIGID ARMY WILL DEAL WITH MORTAL THREATS. WE MUST WAIT IN RESERVE, READY TO STRIKE ONLY THE MOST DANGEROUS FOES...
A SCOUT APPROACHES!
LADIES OF DUSK, I BRING NEWS.
OUT WITH IT, ROTTER.
THE SOUTHERN INVASION HAS BEEN HALTED BY POWERFUL YOUNG WARRIORS. THEY HAVE BOTH STRENGTH AND SPELL.
WARRIORS? WHAT KIND OF WARRIORS?

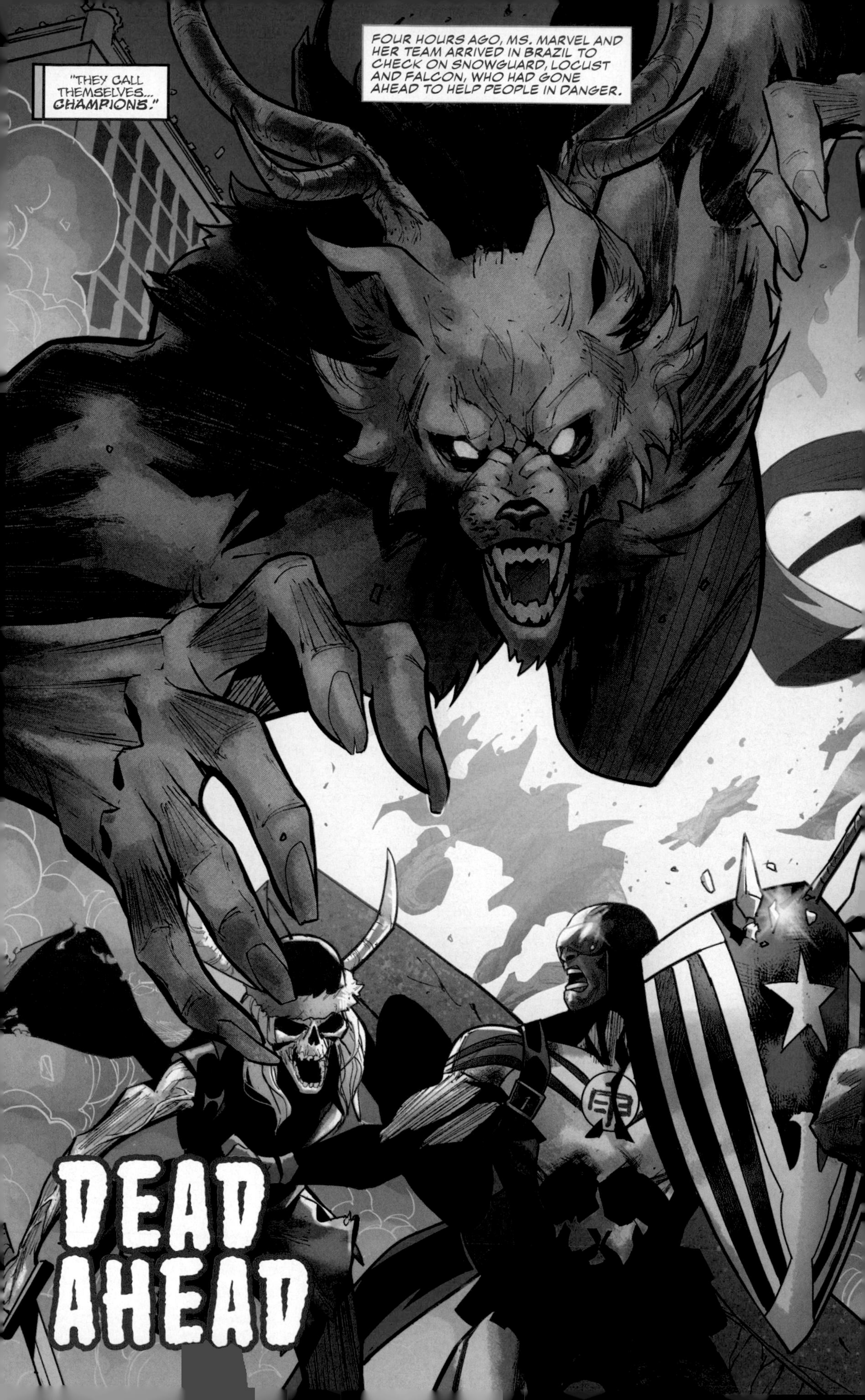
"THEY CALL THEMSELVES... CHAMPIONS."
FOUR HOURS AGO, MS. MARVEL AND HER TEAM ARRIVED IN BRAZIL TO CHECK ON SNOWGUARD, LOCUST AND FALCON, WHO HAD GONE AHEAD TO HELP PEOPLE IN DANGER.
DEAD AHEAD

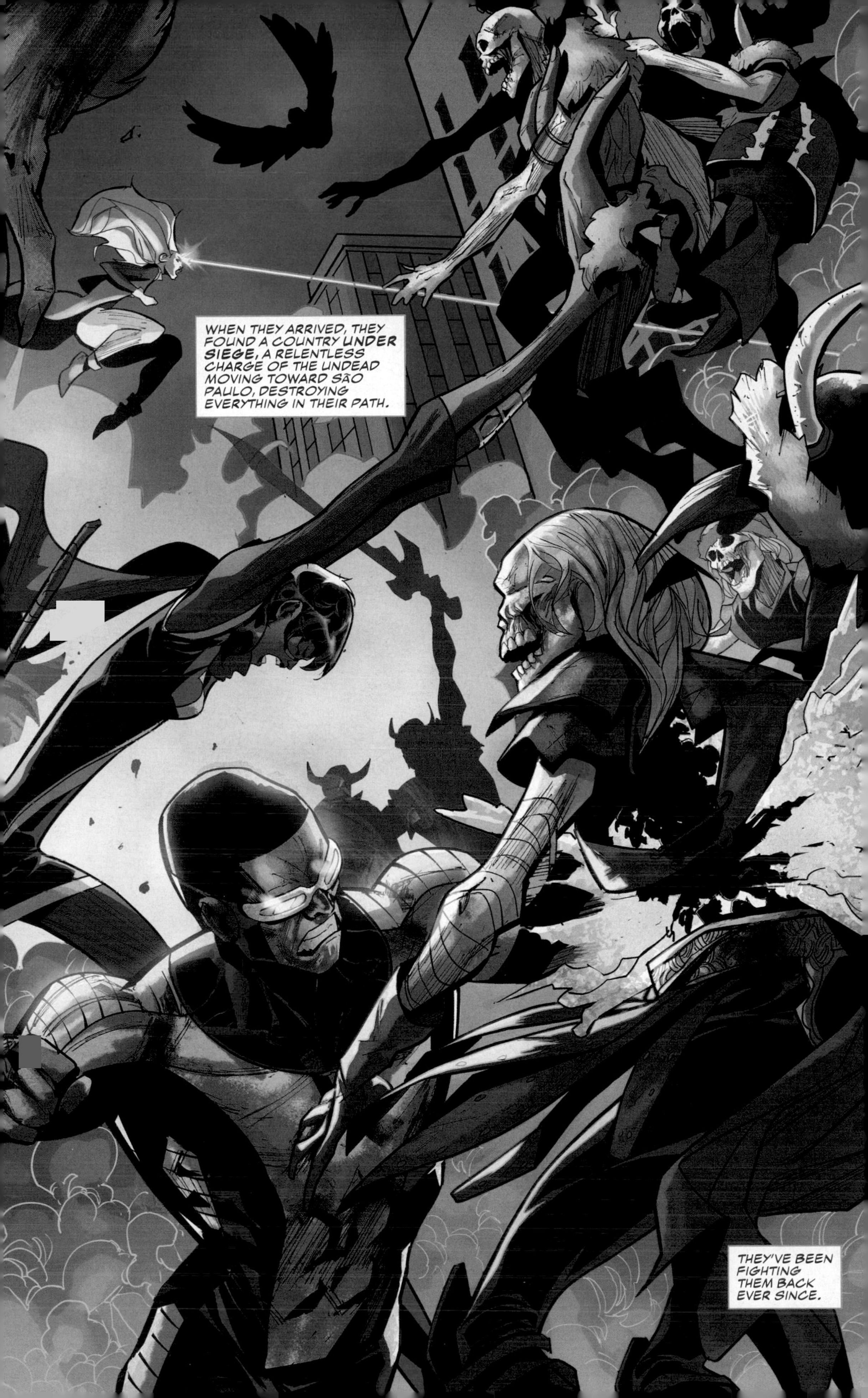
WHEN THEY ARRIVED, THEY FOUND A COUNTRY UNDER SIEGE, A RELENTLESS CHARGE OF THE UNDEAD MOVING TOWARD SÃO PAULO, DESTROYING EVERYTHING IN THEIR PATH.
THEY'VE BEEN FIGHTING THEM BACK EVER SINCE.

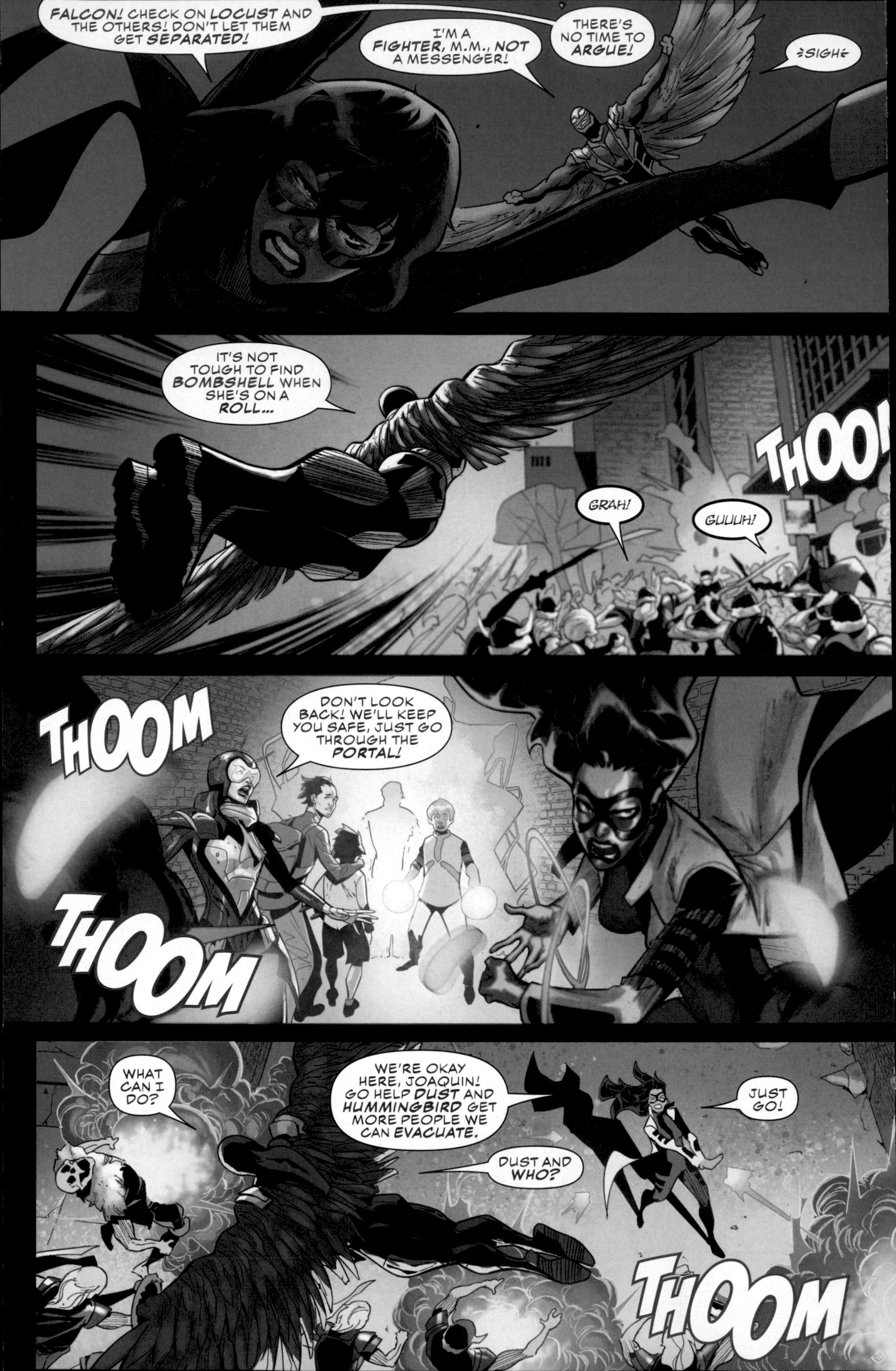
FALCON! CHECK ON LOCUST AND THE OTHERS! DON'T LET THEM GET SEPARATED!
I'M A FIGHTER, M.M., NOT A MESSENGER!
THERE'S NO TIME TO ARGUE!
SIGH
IT'S NOT TOUGH TO FIND BOMBSHELL WHEN SHE'S ON A ROLL...
GRAH!
GUUUH!
DON'T LOOK BACK! WE'LL KEEP YOU SAFE, JUST GO THROUGH THE PORTAL!
THOOM
THOOM
WHAT CAN I DO?
WE'RE OKAY HERE, JOAQUIN! GO HELP DUST AND HUMMINGBIRD GET MORE PEOPLE WE CAN EVACUATE.
JUST GO!
DUST AND WHO?
THOOM

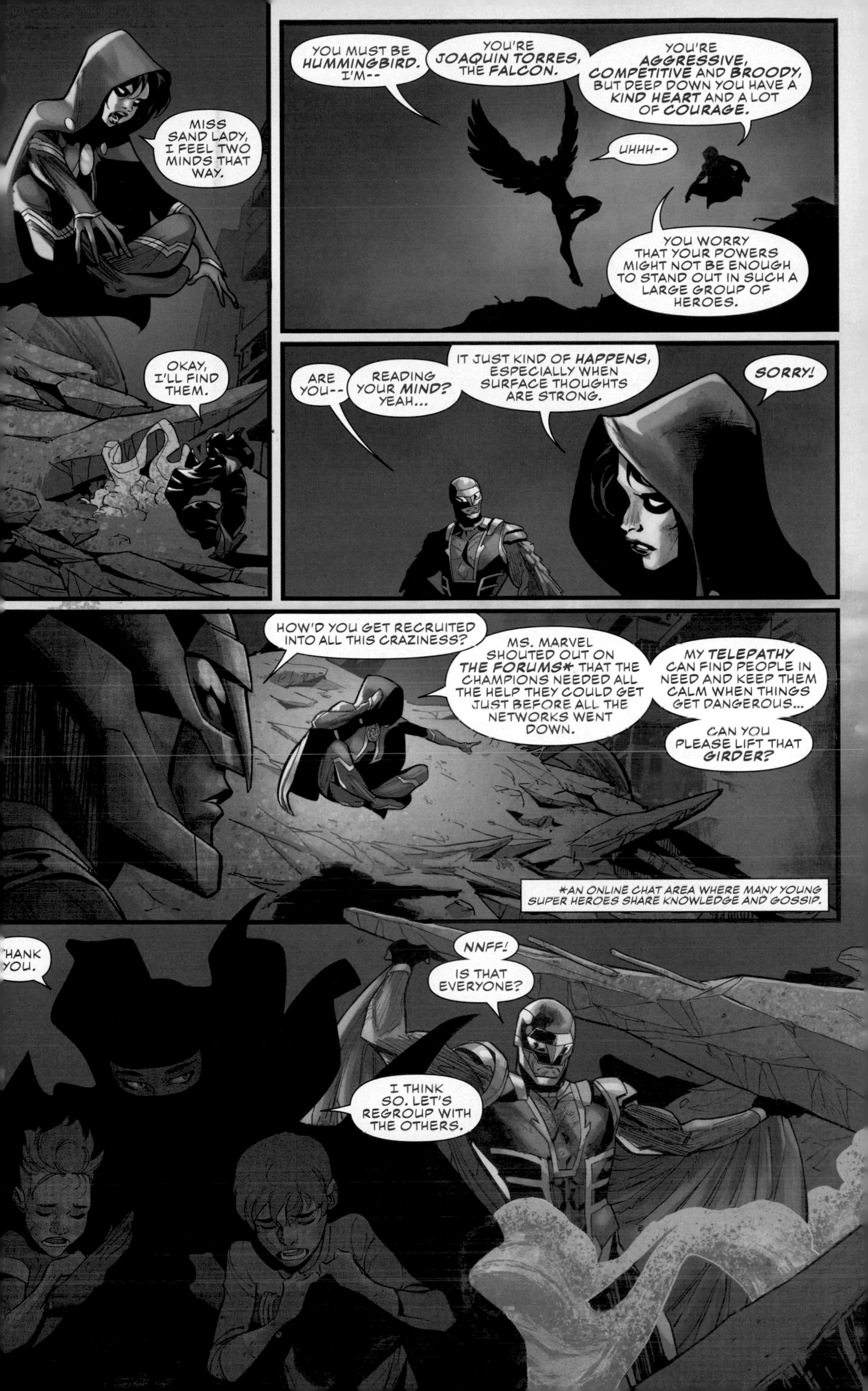
MISS SAND LADY, I FEEL TWO MINDS THAT WAY.
OKAY, I'LL FIND THEM.
YOU MUST BE HUMMINGBIRD. I'M--
YOU'RE JOAQUIN TORRES, THE FALCON.
YOU'RE AGGRESSIVE, COMPETITIVE AND BROODY, BUT DEEP DOWN YOU HAVE A KIND HEART AND A LOT OF COURAGE.
UHHH--
YOU WORRY THAT YOUR POWERS MIGHT NOT BE ENOUGH TO STAND OUT IN SUCH A LARGE GROUP OF HEROES.
ARE YOU--
READING YOUR MIND? YEAH...
IT JUST KIND OF HAPPENS, ESPECIALLY WHEN SURFACE THOUGHTS ARE STRONG.
SORRY!
HOW'D YOU GET RECRUITED INTO ALL THIS CRAZINESS?
MS. MARVEL SHOUTED OUT ON THE FORUMS* THAT THE CHAMPIONS NEEDED ALL THE HELP THEY COULD GET JUST BEFORE ALL THE NETWORKS WENT DOWN.
MY TELEPATHY CAN FIND PEOPLE IN NEED AND KEEP THEM CALM WHEN THINGS GET DANGEROUS...
CAN YOU PLEASE LIFT THAT GIRDER?
*AN ONLINE CHAT AREA WHERE MANY YOUNG SUPER HEROES SHARE KNOWLEDGE AND GOSSIP.
THANK YOU.
NNFF!
IS THAT EVERYONE?
I THINK SO. LET'S REGROUP WITH THE OTHERS.

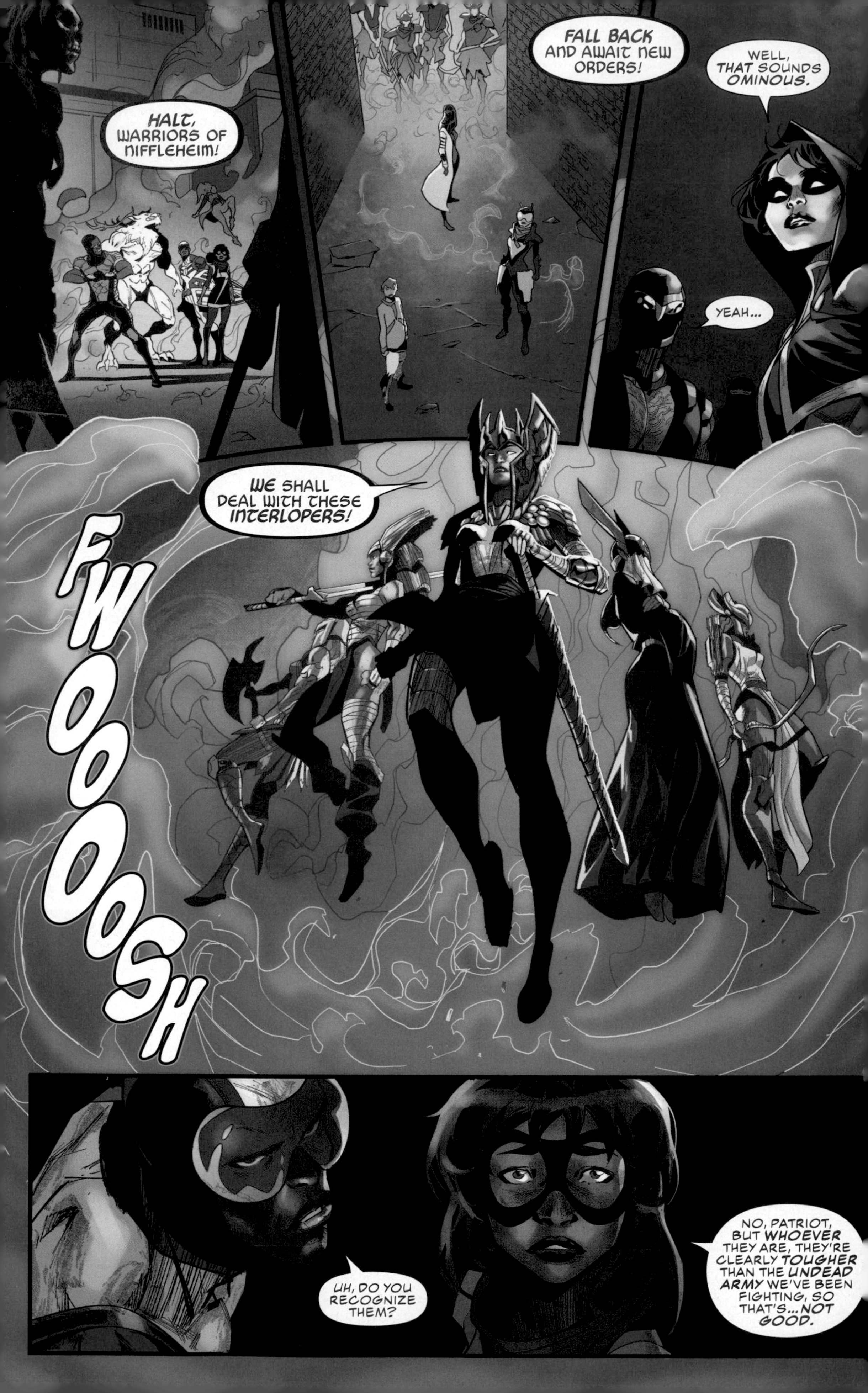

HALT, WARRIORS OF NIFFLEHEIM!
FALL BACK AND AWAIT NEW ORDERS!
WELL, THAT SOUNDS OMINOUS.
YEAH...
WE SHALL DEAL WITH THESE INTERLOPERS!
FWOOOOSH
UH, DO YOU RECOGNIZE THEM?
NO, PATRIOT, BUT WHOEVER THEY ARE, THEY'RE CLEARLY TOUGHER THAN THE UNDEAD ARMY WE'VE BEEN FIGHTING, SO THAT'S... NOT GOOD.

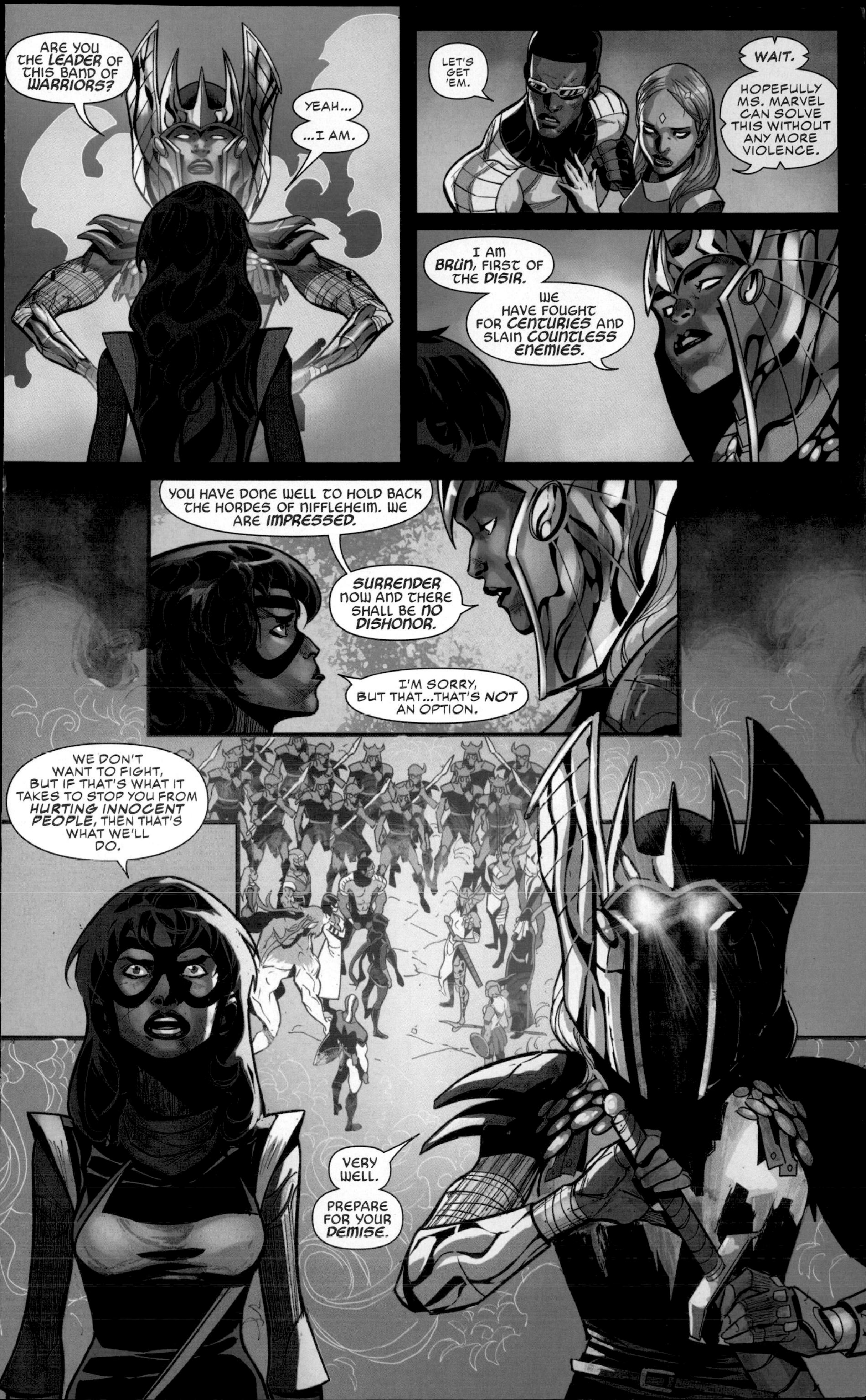
ARE YOU THE LEADER OF THIS BAND OF WARRIORS?
YEAH...
...I AM.
LET'S GET 'EM.
WAIT.
HOPEFULLY MS. MARVEL CAN SOLVE THIS WITHOUT ANY MORE VIOLENCE.
I AM BRÜN, FIRST OF THE DISIR.
WE HAVE FOUGHT FOR CENTURIES AND SLAIN COUNTLESS ENEMIES.
YOU HAVE DONE WELL TO HOLD BACK THE HORDES OF NIFFLEHEIM. WE ARE IMPRESSED.
SURRENDER NOW AND THERE SHALL BE NO DISHONOR.
I'M SORRY, BUT THAT...THAT'S NOT AN OPTION.
WE DON'T WANT TO FIGHT, BUT IF THAT'S WHAT IT TAKES TO STOP YOU FROM HURTING INNOCENT PEOPLE, THEN THAT'S WHAT WE'LL DO.
VERY WELL.
PREPARE FOR YOUR DEMISE.

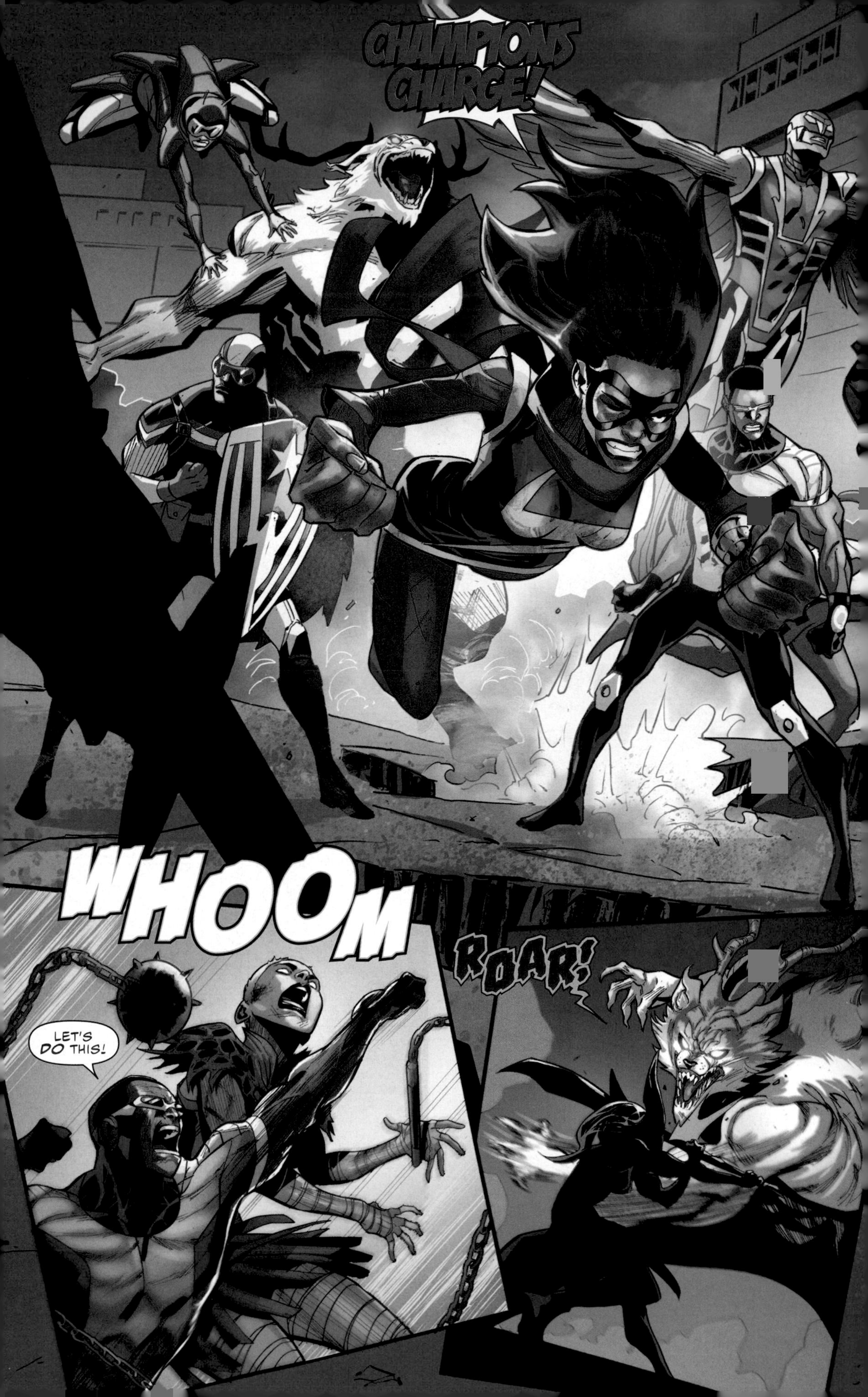
CHAMPIONS CHARGE!
WHOOM
LET'S DO THIS!
ROAR!

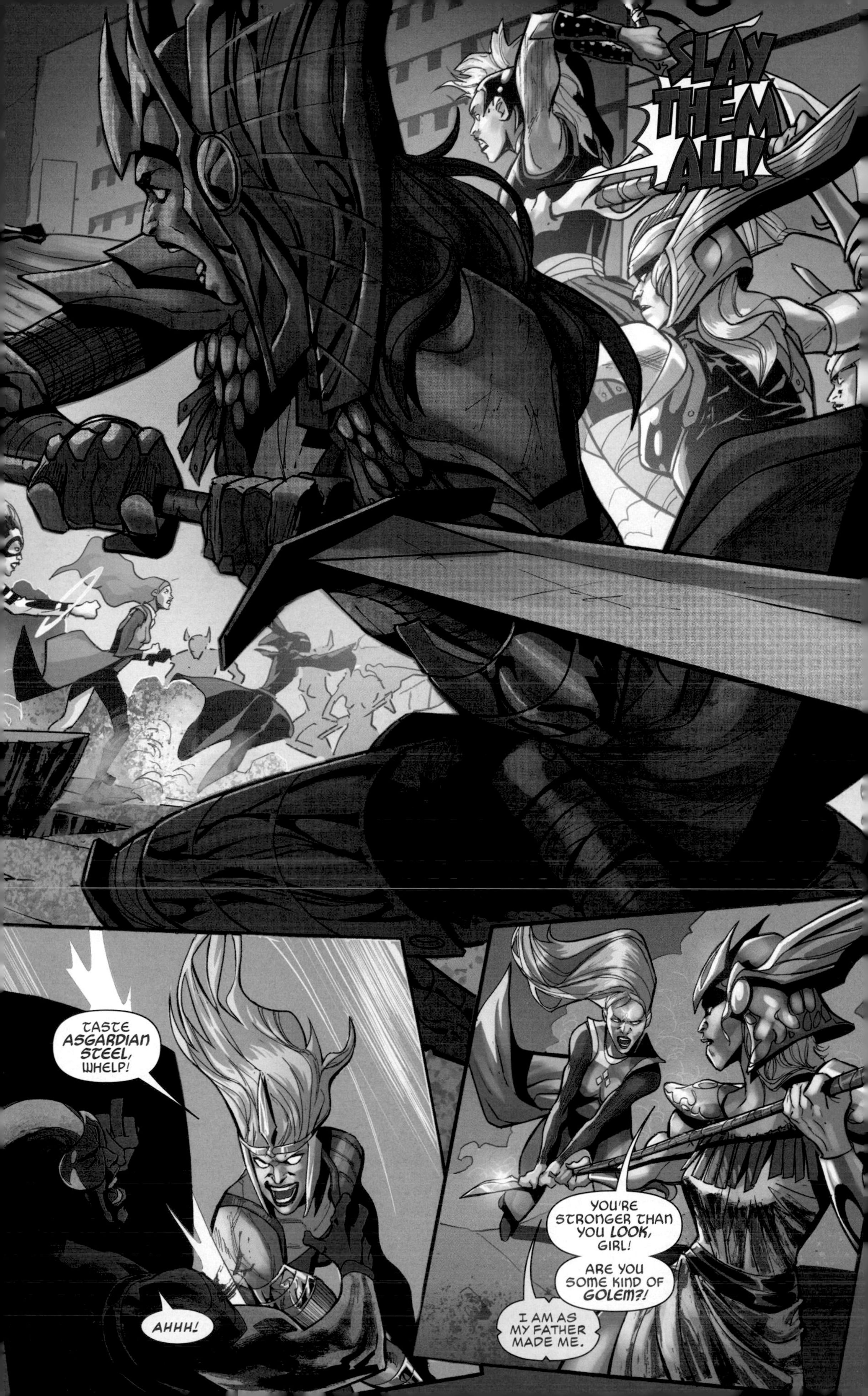
SLAY THEM ALL!
TASTE ASGARDIAN STEEL, WHELP!
AHHH!
YOU'RE STRONGER THAN YOU LOOK, GIRL!
ARE YOU SOME KIND OF GOLEM?!
I AM AS MY FATHER MADE ME.

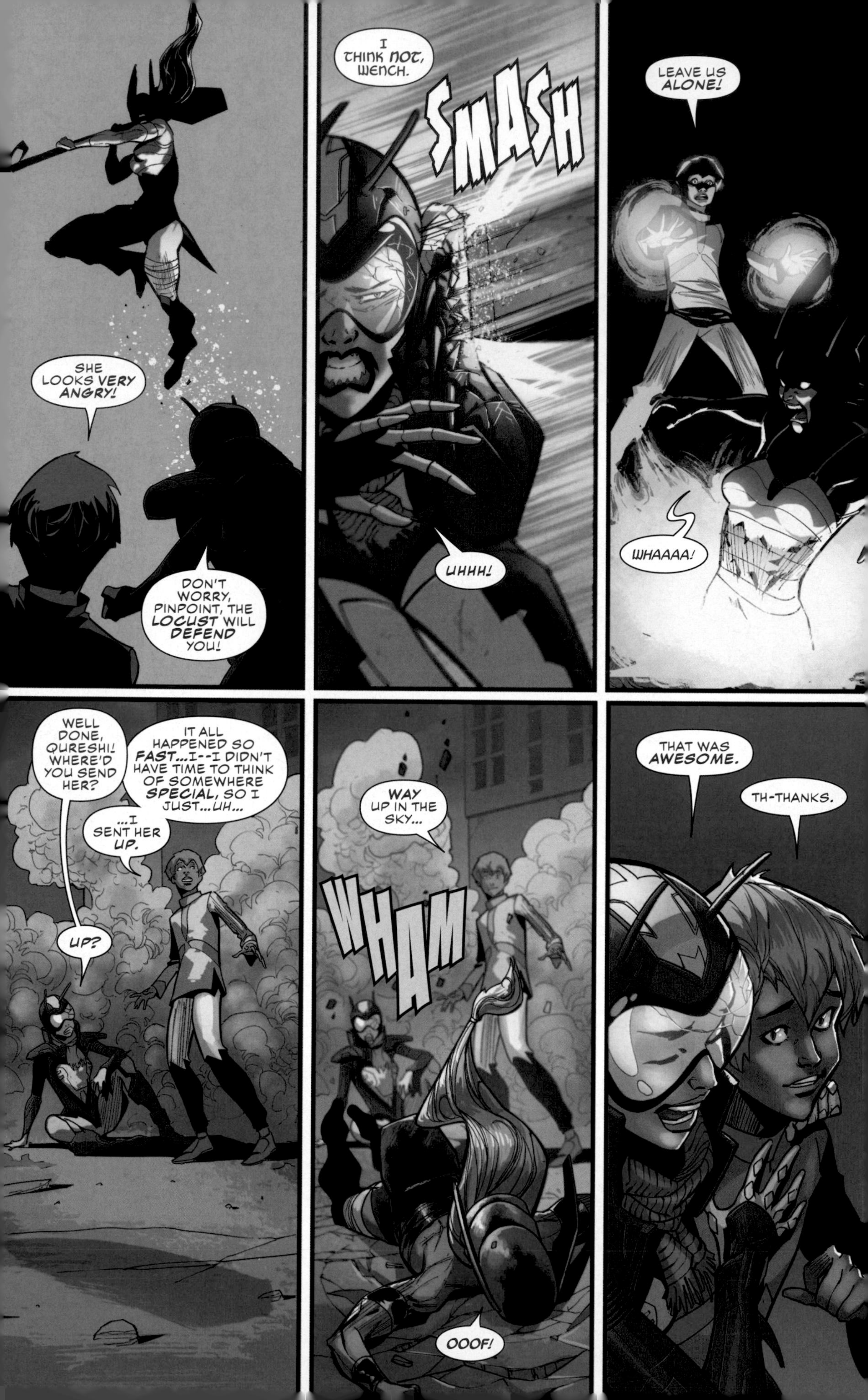
SHE LOOKS VERY ANGRY!
DON'T WORRY, PINPOINT, THE LOCUST WILL DEFEND YOU!
I THINK NOT, WENCH.
SMASH
UHHH!
LEAVE US ALONE!
WHAAAA!
WELL DONE, QURESHI! WHERE'D YOU SEND HER?
IT ALL HAPPENED SO FAST...I--I DIDN'T HAVE TIME TO THINK OF SOMEWHERE SPECIAL, SO I JUST...UH...
...I SENT HER UP.
UP?
WAY UP IN THE SKY...
WHAM
OOOF!
THAT WAS AWESOME.
TH-THANKS.

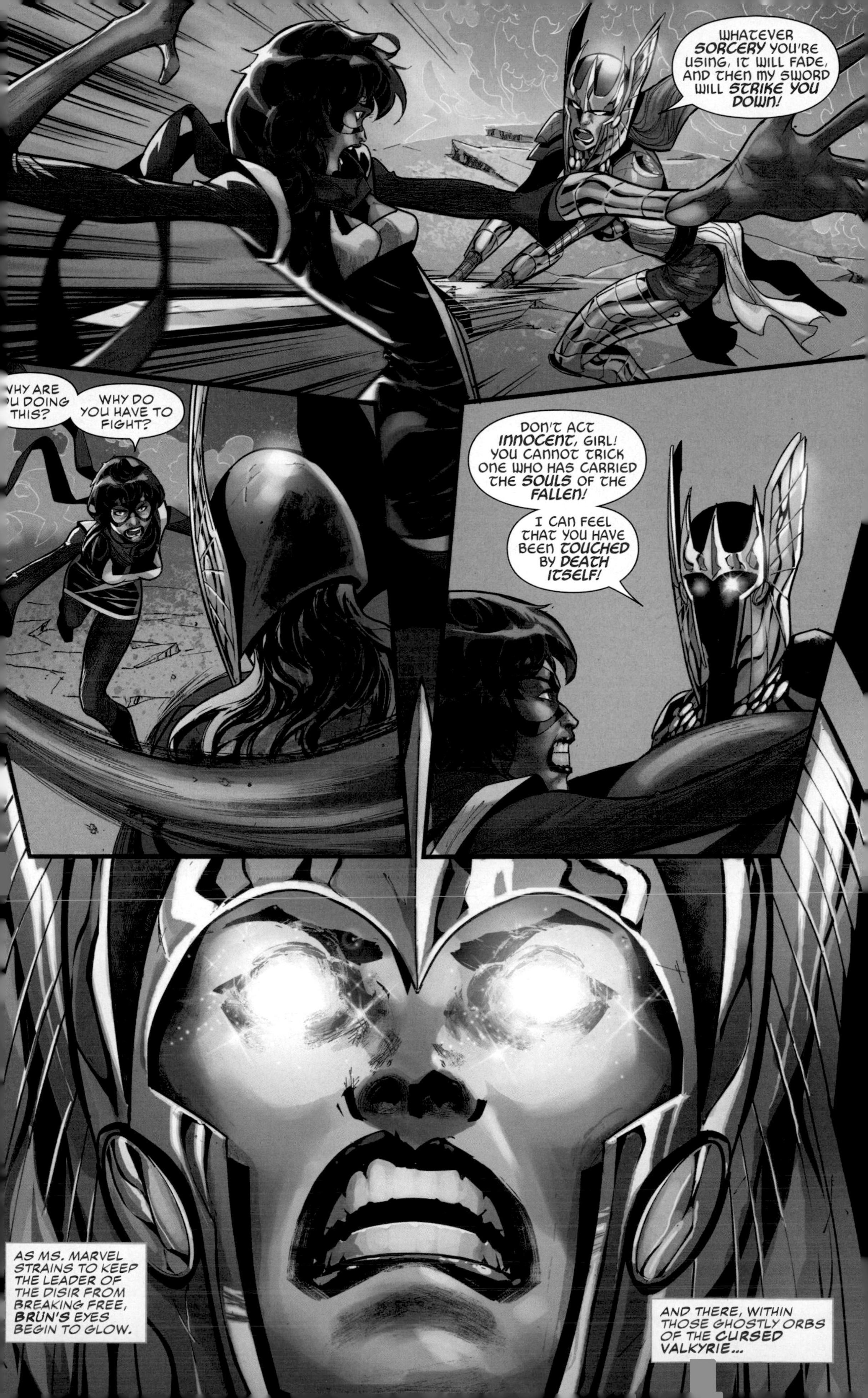
WHATEVER SORCERY YOU'RE USING, IT WILL FADE, AND THEN MY SWORD WILL STRIKE YOU DOWN!
WHY ARE YOU DOING THIS?
WHY DO YOU HAVE TO FIGHT?
DON'T ACT INNOCENT, GIRL! YOU CANNOT TRICK ONE WHO HAS CARRIED THE SOULS OF THE FALLEN!
I CAN FEEL THAT YOU HAVE BEEN TOUCHED BY DEATH ITSELF!
AS MS. MARVEL STRAINS TO KEEP THE LEADER OF THE DISIR FROM BREAKING FREE, BRÜN'S EYES BEGIN TO GLOW.
AND THERE, WITHIN THOSE GHOSTLY ORBS OF THE CURSED VALKYRIE...

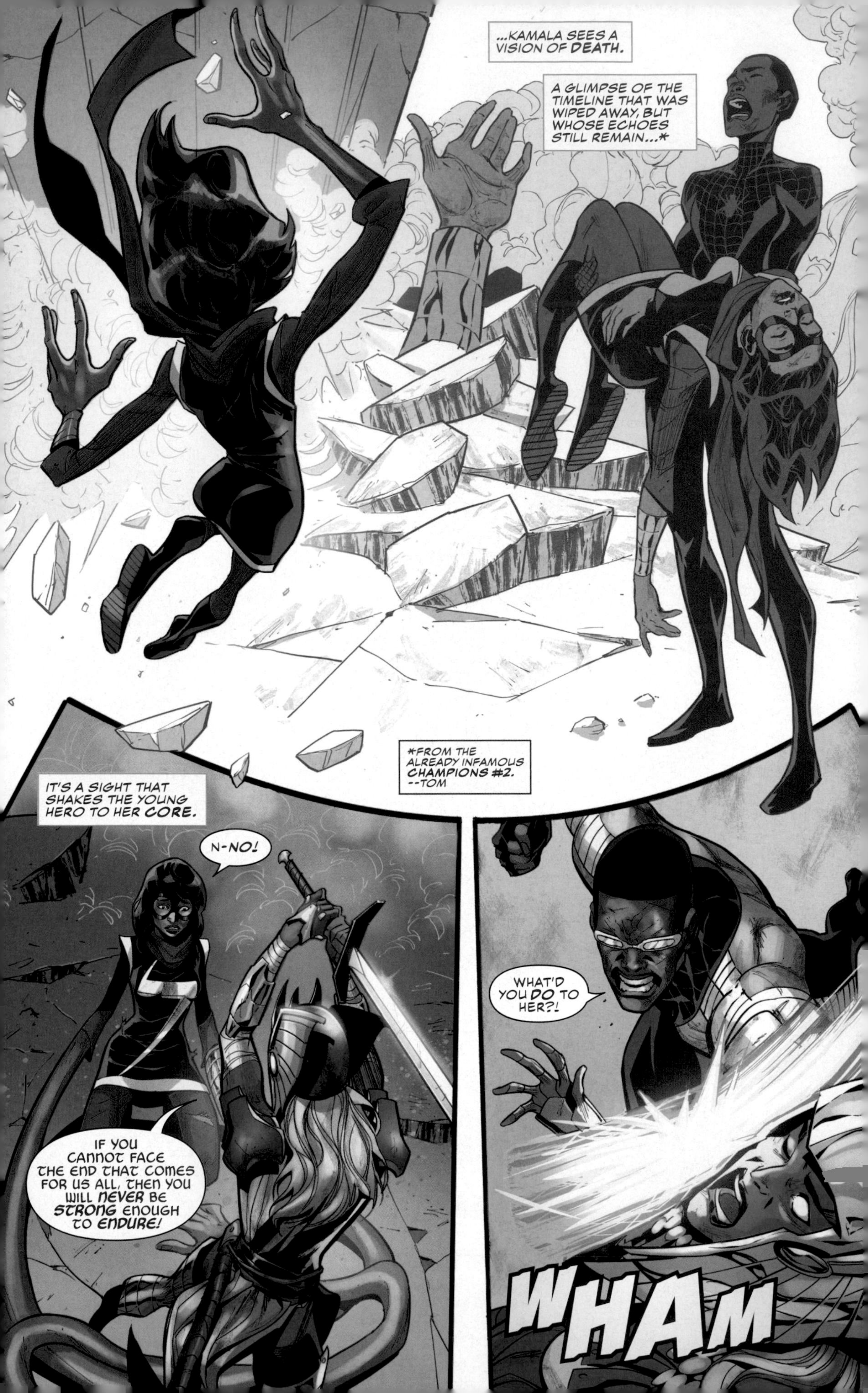
...KAMALA SEES A VISION OF DEATH.
A GLIMPSE OF THE TIMELINE THAT WAS WIPED AWAY, BUT WHOSE ECHOES STILL REMAIN...*
*FROM THE ALREADY INFAMOUS CHAMPIONS #2. --TOM
IT'S A SIGHT THAT SHAKES THE YOUNG HERO TO HER CORE.
N-NO!
IF YOU CANNOT FACE THE END THAT COMES FOR US ALL, THEN YOU WILL NEVER BE STRONG ENOUGH TO ENDURE!
WHAT'D YOU DO TO HER?!
WHAM

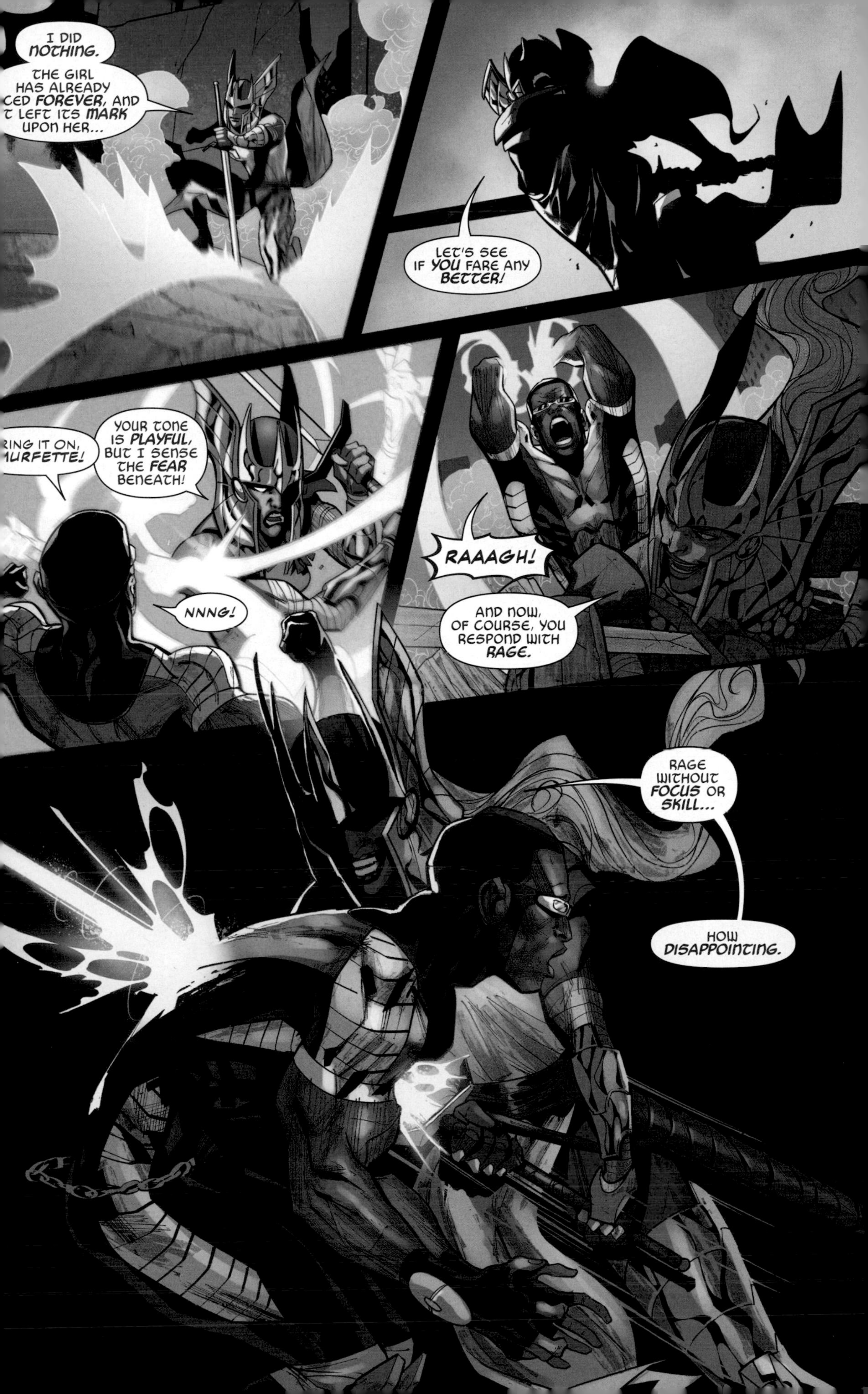
I DID NOTHING.
THE GIRL HAS ALREADY CED FOREVER, AND T LEFT ITS MARK UPON HER...
LET'S SEE IF YOU FARE ANY BETTER!
RING IT ON, MURFETTE!
YOUR TONE IS PLAYFUL, BUT I SENSE THE FEAR BENEATH!
NNNG!
RAAAGH!
AND NOW, OF COURSE, YOU RESPOND WITH RAGE.
RAGE WITHOUT FOCUS OR SKILL...
HOW DISAPPOINTING.

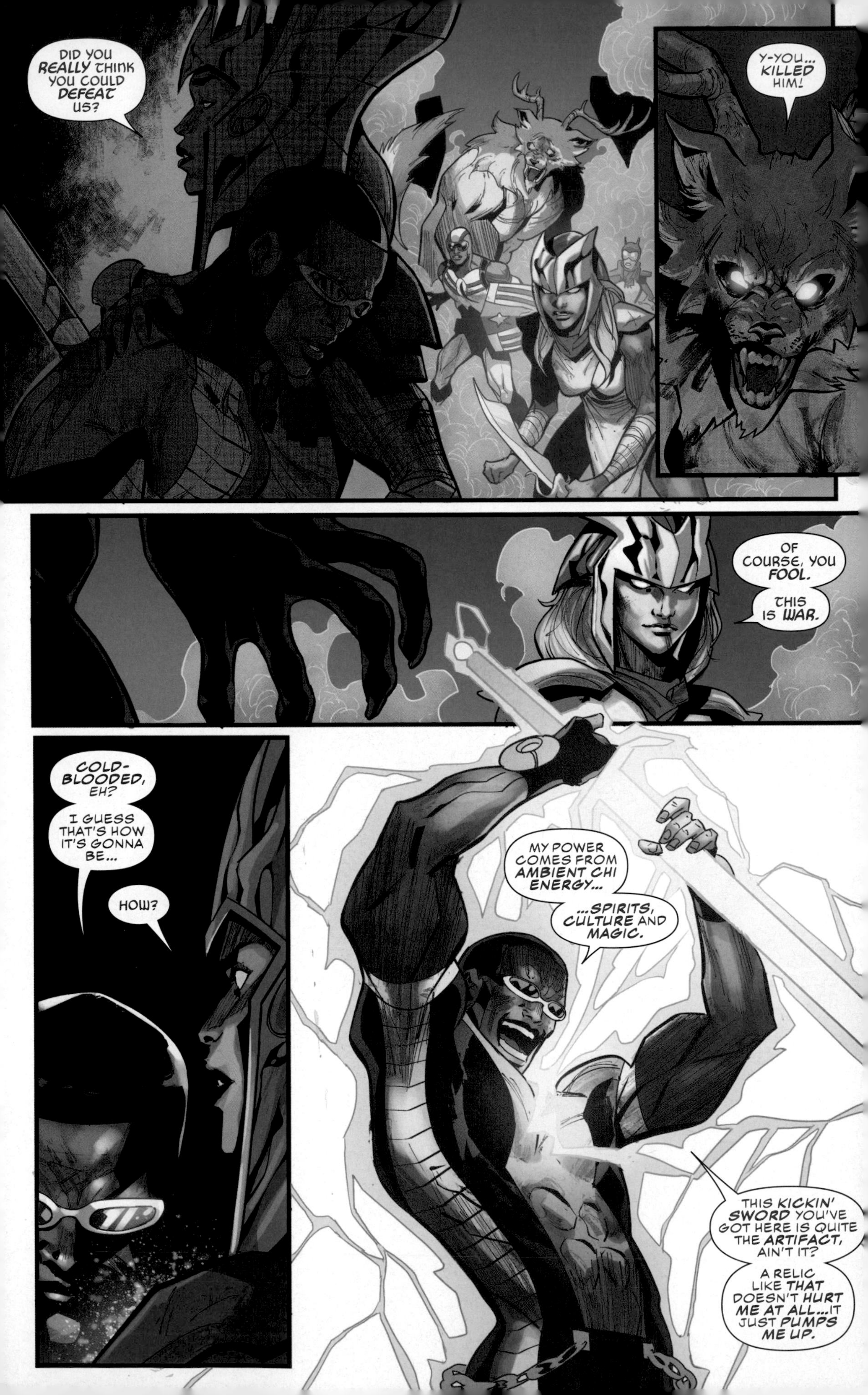
DID YOU REALLY THINK YOU COULD DEFEAT US?
Y-YOU... KILLED HIM!
OF COURSE, YOU FOOL.
THIS IS WAR.
COLD-BLOODED, EH?
I GUESS THAT'S HOW IT'S GONNA BE...
HOW?
MY POWER COMES FROM AMBIENT CHI ENERGY...
...SPIRITS, CULTURE AND MAGIC.
THIS KICKIN' SWORD YOU'VE GOT HERE IS QUITE THE ARTIFACT, AIN'T IT?
A RELIC LIKE THAT DOESN'T HURT ME AT ALL...IT JUST PUMPS ME UP.

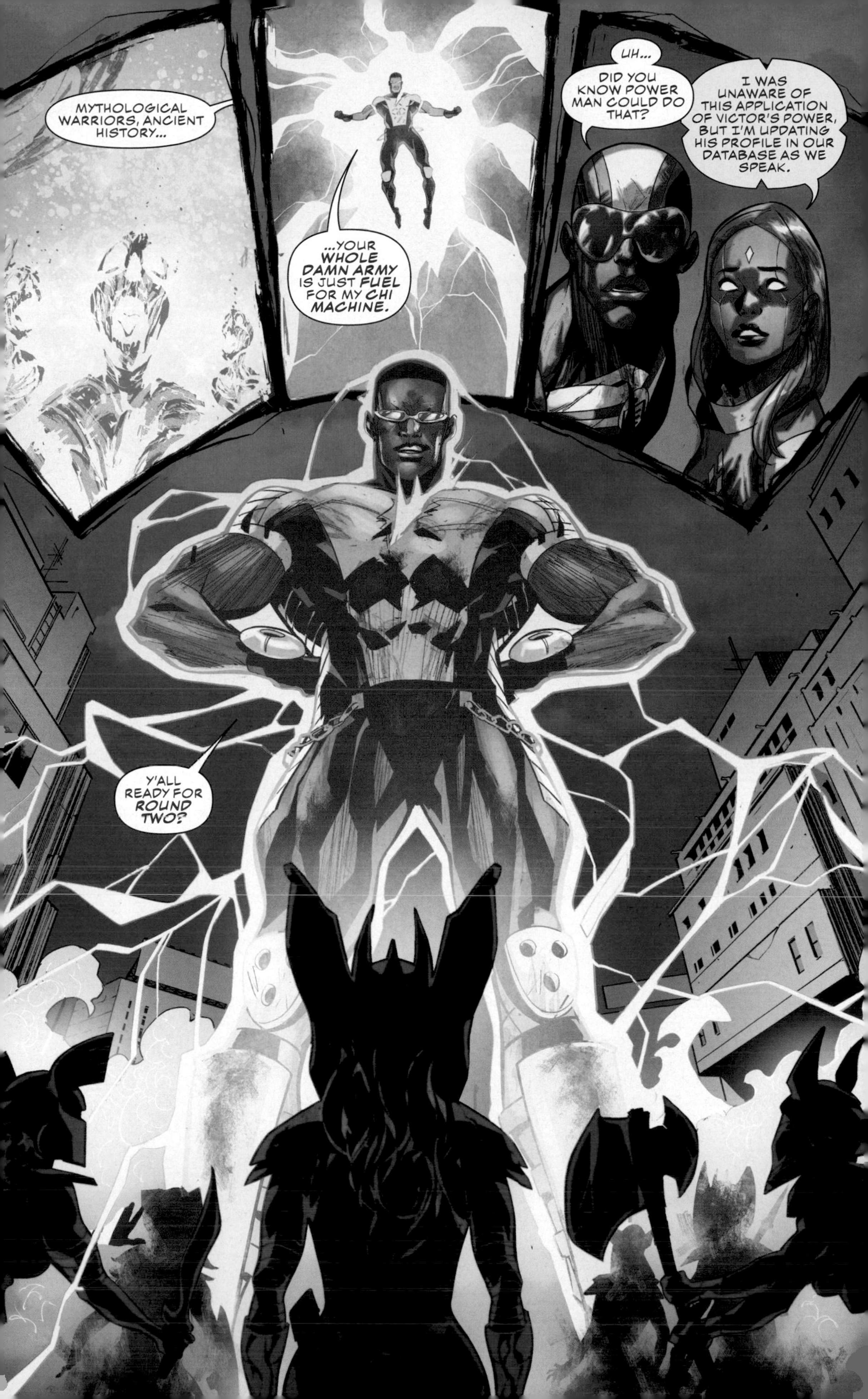
MYTHOLOGICAL WARRIORS, ANCIENT HISTORY...
...YOUR WHOLE DAMN ARMY IS JUST FUEL FOR MY CHI MACHINE.
UH...
DID YOU KNOW POWER MAN COULD DO THAT?
I WAS UNAWARE OF THIS APPLICATION OF VICTOR'S POWER, BUT I'M UPDATING HIS PROFILE IN OUR DATABASE AS WE SPEAK.
Y'ALL READY FOR ROUND TWO?

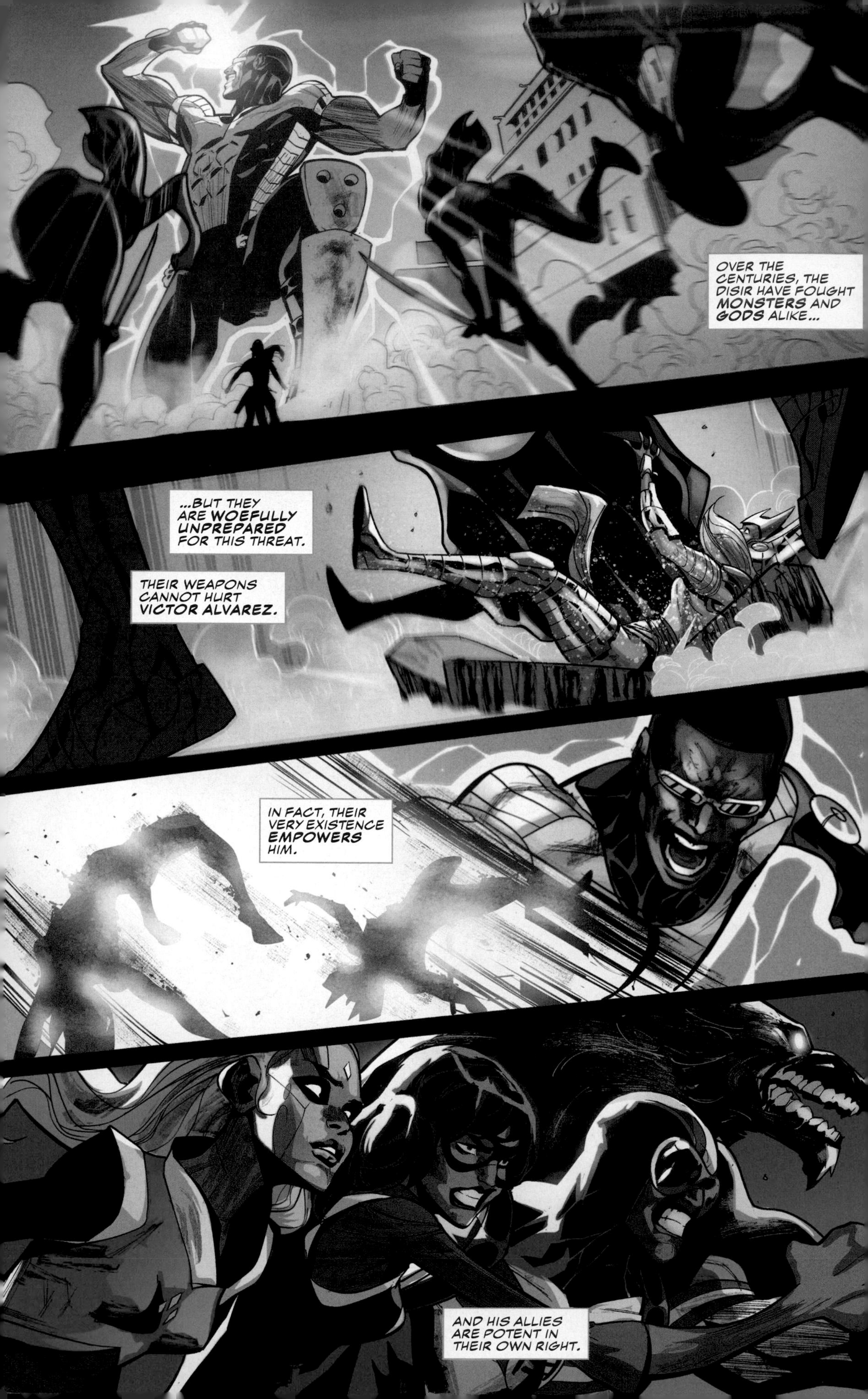
OVER THE CENTURIES, THE DISIR HAVE FOUGHT MONSTERS AND GODS ALIKE...
...BUT THEY ARE WOEFULLY UNPREPARED FOR THIS THREAT.
THEIR WEAPONS CANNOT HURT VICTOR ALVAREZ.
IN FACT, THEIR VERY EXISTENCE EMPOWERS HIM.
AND HIS ALLIES ARE POTENT IN THEIR OWN RIGHT.

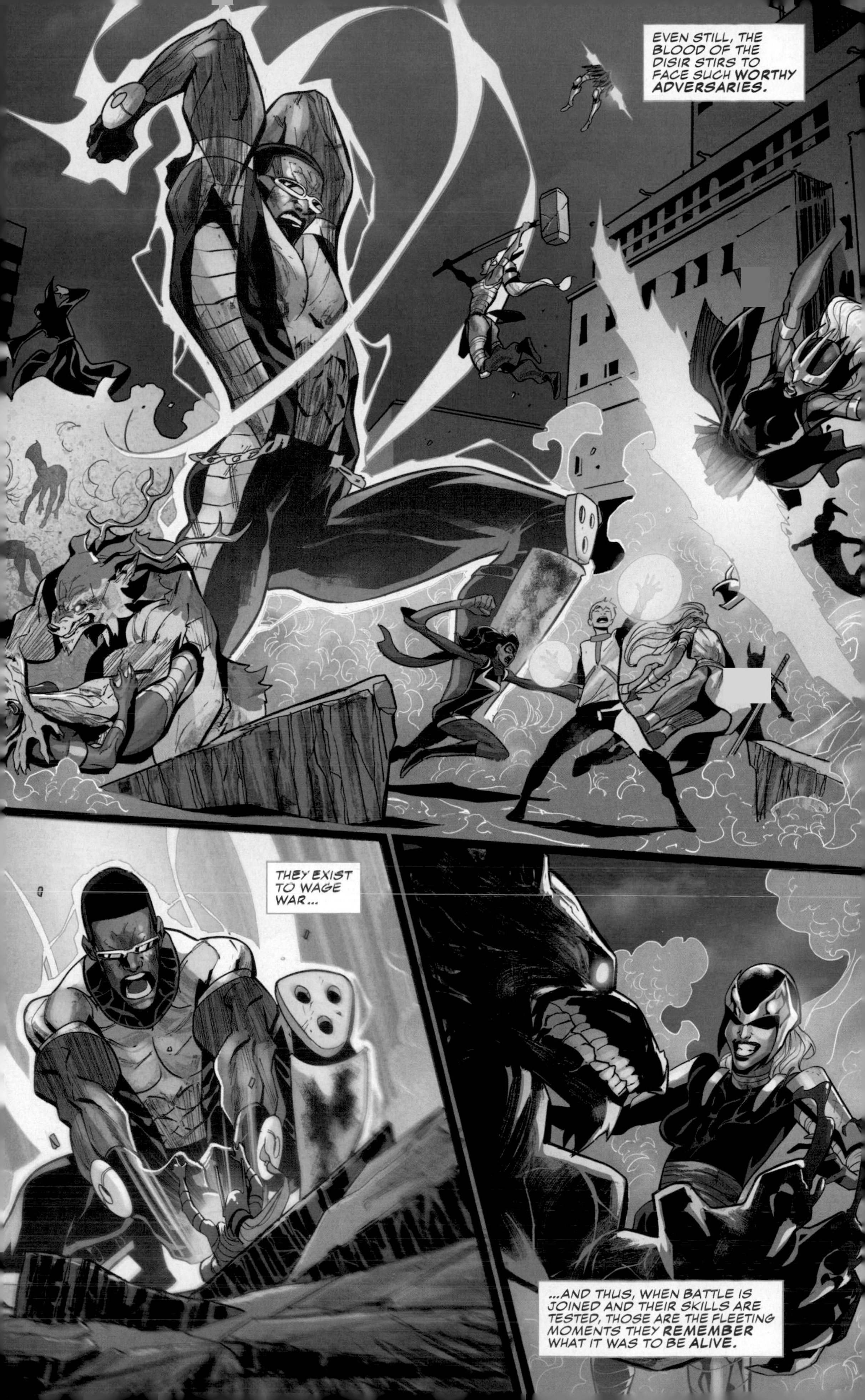
EVEN STILL, THE BLOOD OF THE DISIR STIRS TO FACE SUCH WORTHY ADVERSARIES.
THEY EXIST TO WAGE WAR...
...AND THUS, WHEN BATTLE IS JOINED AND THEIR SKILLS ARE TESTED, THOSE ARE THE FLEETING MOMENTS THEY REMEMBER WHAT IT WAS TO BE ALIVE.

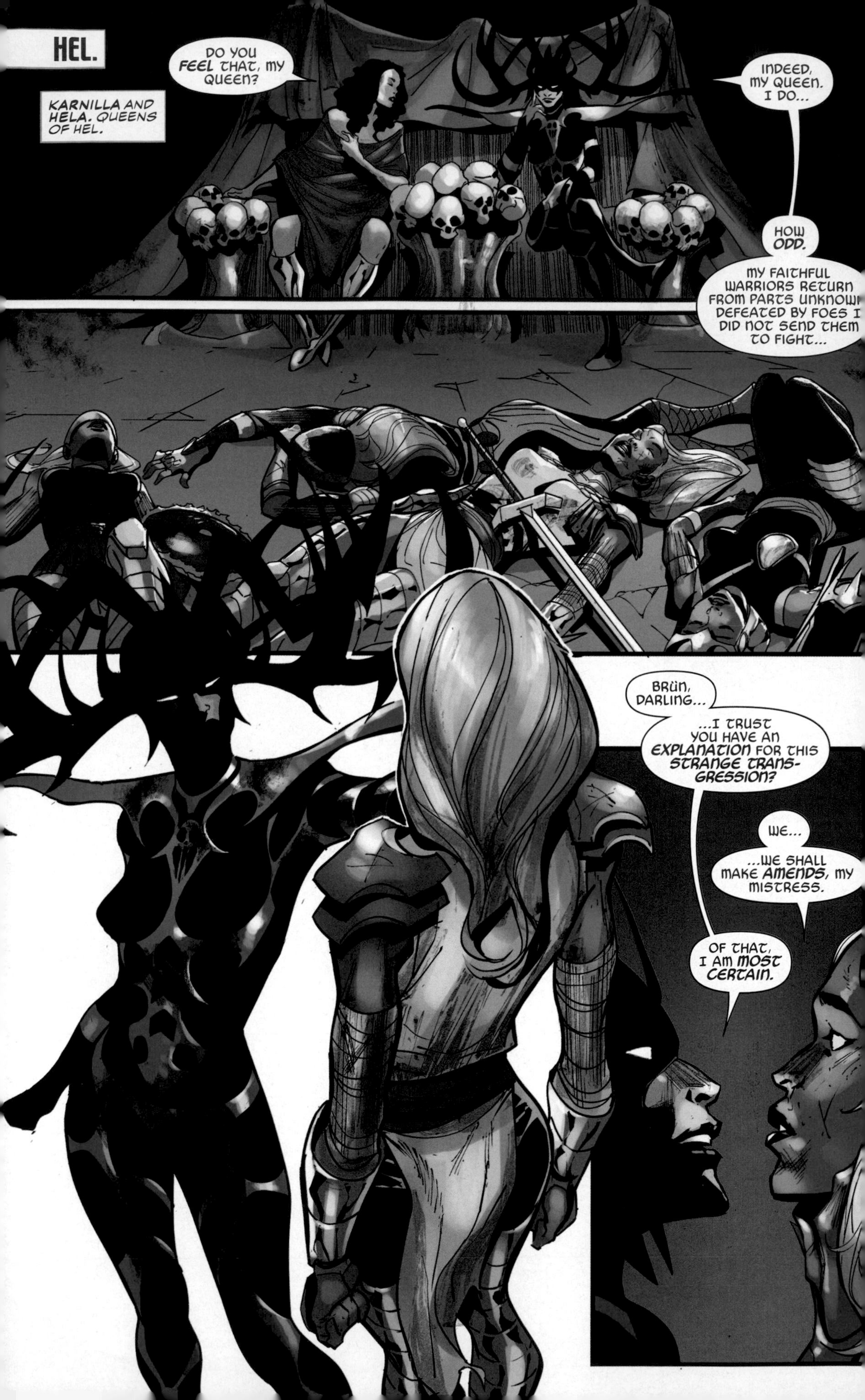
HEL.
KARNILLA AND HELA. QUEENS OF HEL.
DO YOU FEEL THAT, MY QUEEN?
INDEED, MY QUEEN. I DO...
HOW ODD.
MY FAITHFUL WARRIORS RETURN FROM PARTS UNKNOWN DEFEATED BY FOES I DID NOT SEND THEM TO FIGHT...
BRÜN, DARLING...
...I TRUST YOU HAVE AN EXPLANATION FOR THIS STRANGE TRANSGRESSION?
WE...
...WE SHALL MAKE AMENDS, MY MISTRESS.
OF THAT, I AM MOST CERTAIN.

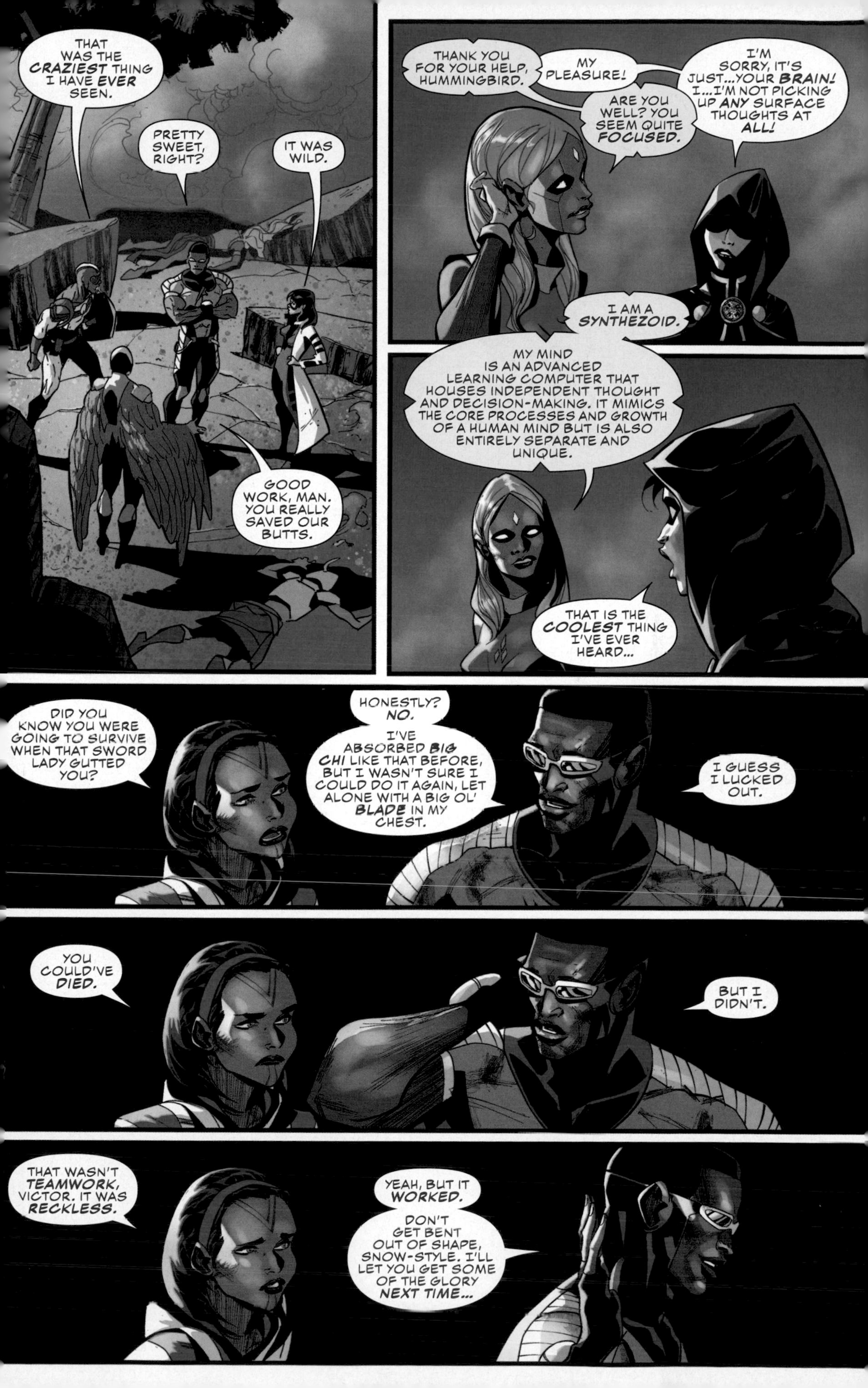
THAT WAS THE CRAZIEST THING I HAVE EVER SEEN.
PRETTY SWEET, RIGHT?
IT WAS WILD.
GOOD WORK, MAN. YOU REALLY SAVED OUR BUTTS.
THANK YOU FOR YOUR HELP, HUMMINGBIRD.
MY PLEASURE!
I'M SORRY, IT'S JUST...YOUR BRAIN! I...I'M NOT PICKING UP ANY SURFACE THOUGHTS AT ALL!
ARE YOU WELL? YOU SEEM QUITE FOCUSED.
I AM A SYNTHEZOID.
MY MIND IS AN ADVANCED LEARNING COMPUTER THAT HOUSES INDEPENDENT THOUGHT AND DECISION-MAKING. IT MIMICS THE CORE PROCESSES AND GROWTH OF A HUMAN MIND BUT IS ALSO ENTIRELY SEPARATE AND UNIQUE.
THAT IS THE COOLEST THING I'VE EVER HEARD...
DID YOU KNOW YOU WERE GOING TO SURVIVE WHEN THAT SWORD LADY GUTTED YOU?
HONESTLY? NO.
I'VE ABSORBED BIG CHI LIKE THAT BEFORE, BUT I WASN'T SURE I COULD DO IT AGAIN, LET ALONE WITH A BIG OL' BLADE IN MY CHEST.
I GUESS I LUCKED OUT.
YOU COULD'VE DIED.
BUT I DIDN'T.
THAT WASN'T TEAMWORK, VICTOR. IT WAS RECKLESS.
YEAH, BUT IT WORKED.
DON'T GET BENT OUT OF SHAPE, SNOW-STYLE. I'LL LET YOU GET SOME OF THE GLORY NEXT TIME...

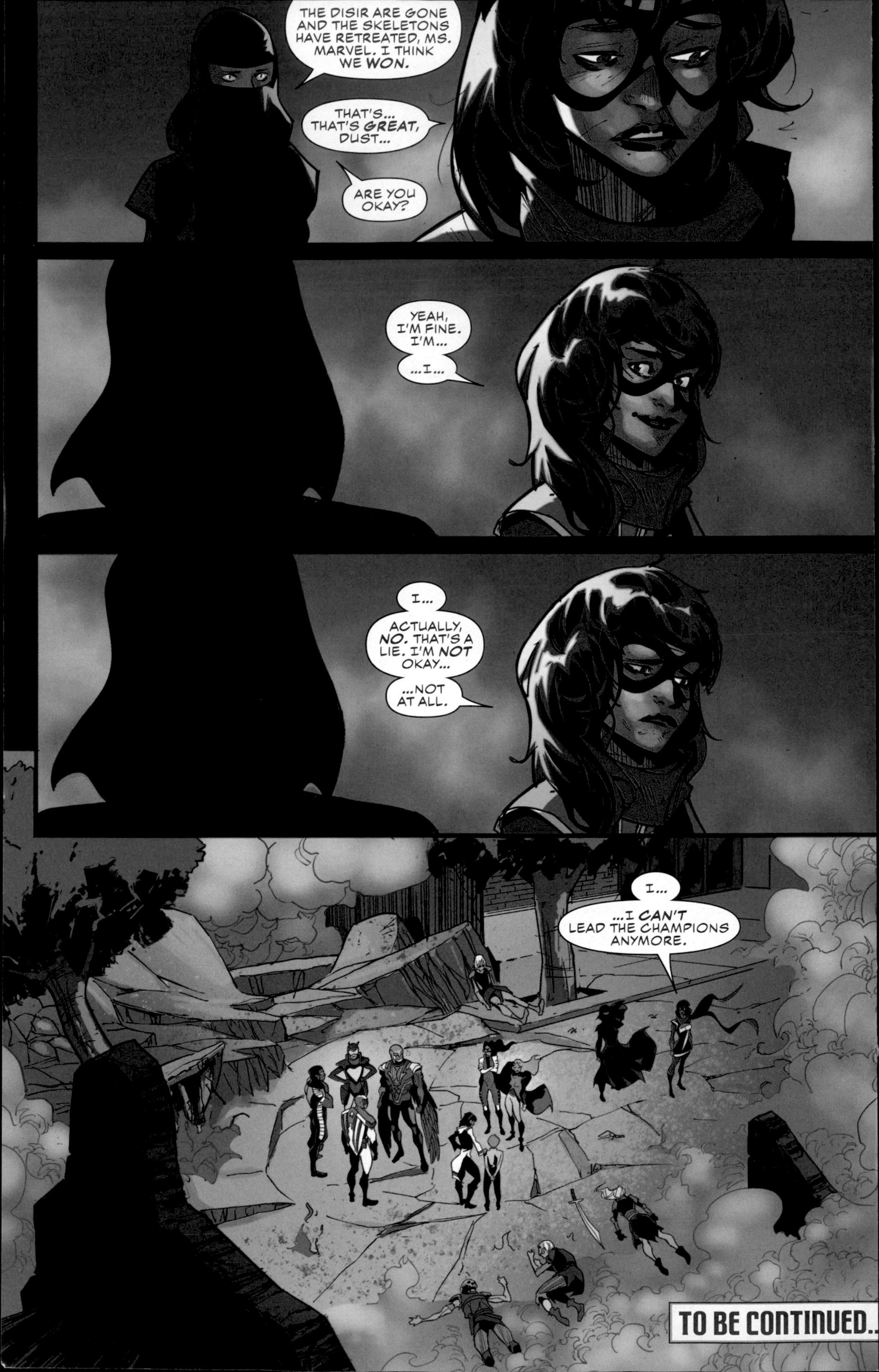
THE DISIR ARE GONE AND THE SKELETONS HAVE RETREATED, MS. MARVEL. I THINK WE WON.
THAT'S... THAT'S GREAT, DUST...
ARE YOU OKAY?
YEAH, I'M FINE. I'M...
...I...
I...
ACTUALLY, NO. THAT'S A LIE. I'M NOT OKAY...
...NOT AT ALL.
I...
...I CAN'T LEAD THE CHAMPIONS ANYMORE.
TO BE CONTINUED...

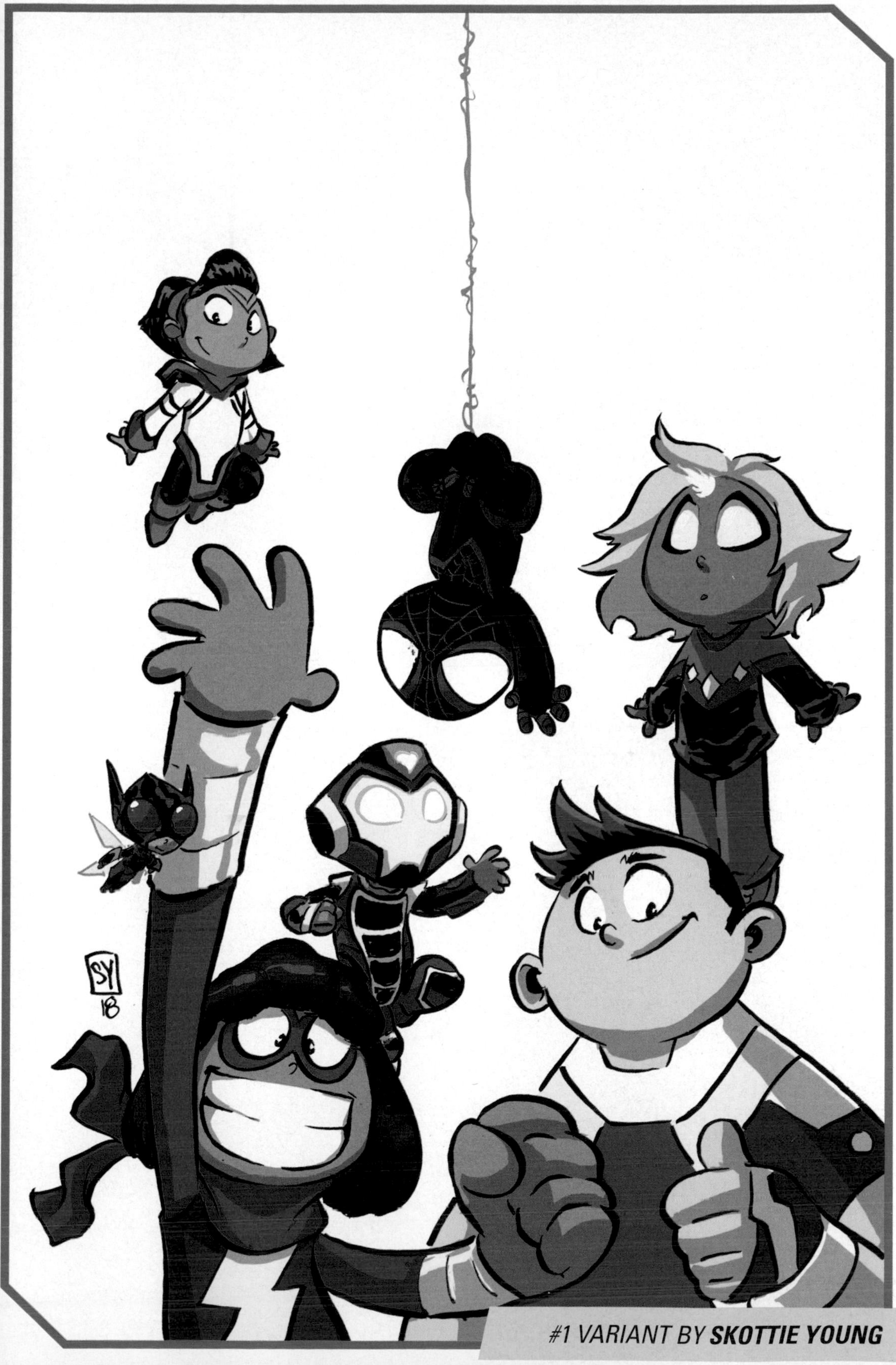

#1 VARIANT BY **SKOTTIE YOUNG**

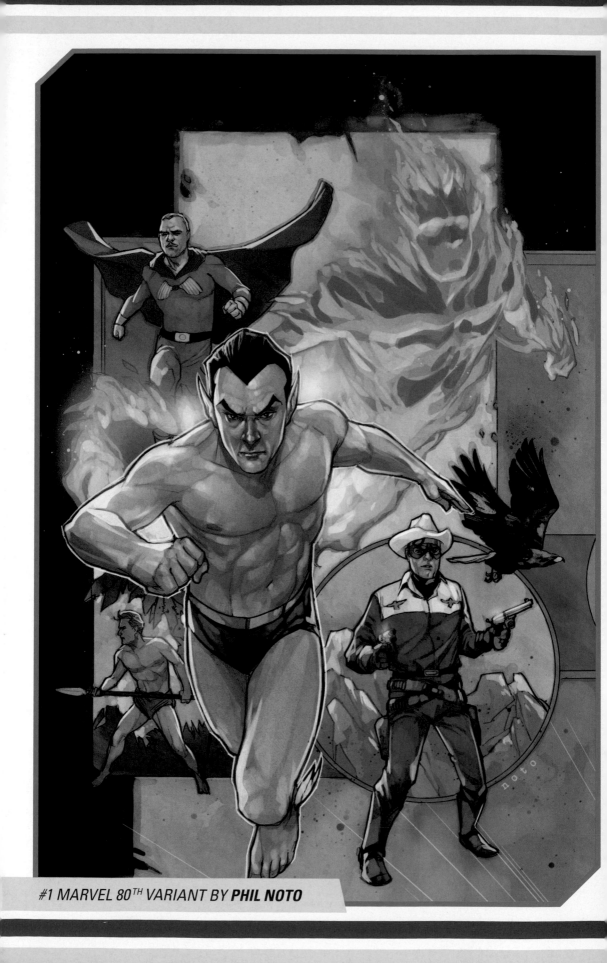

#1 MARVEL 80TH VARIANT BY **PHIL NOTO**

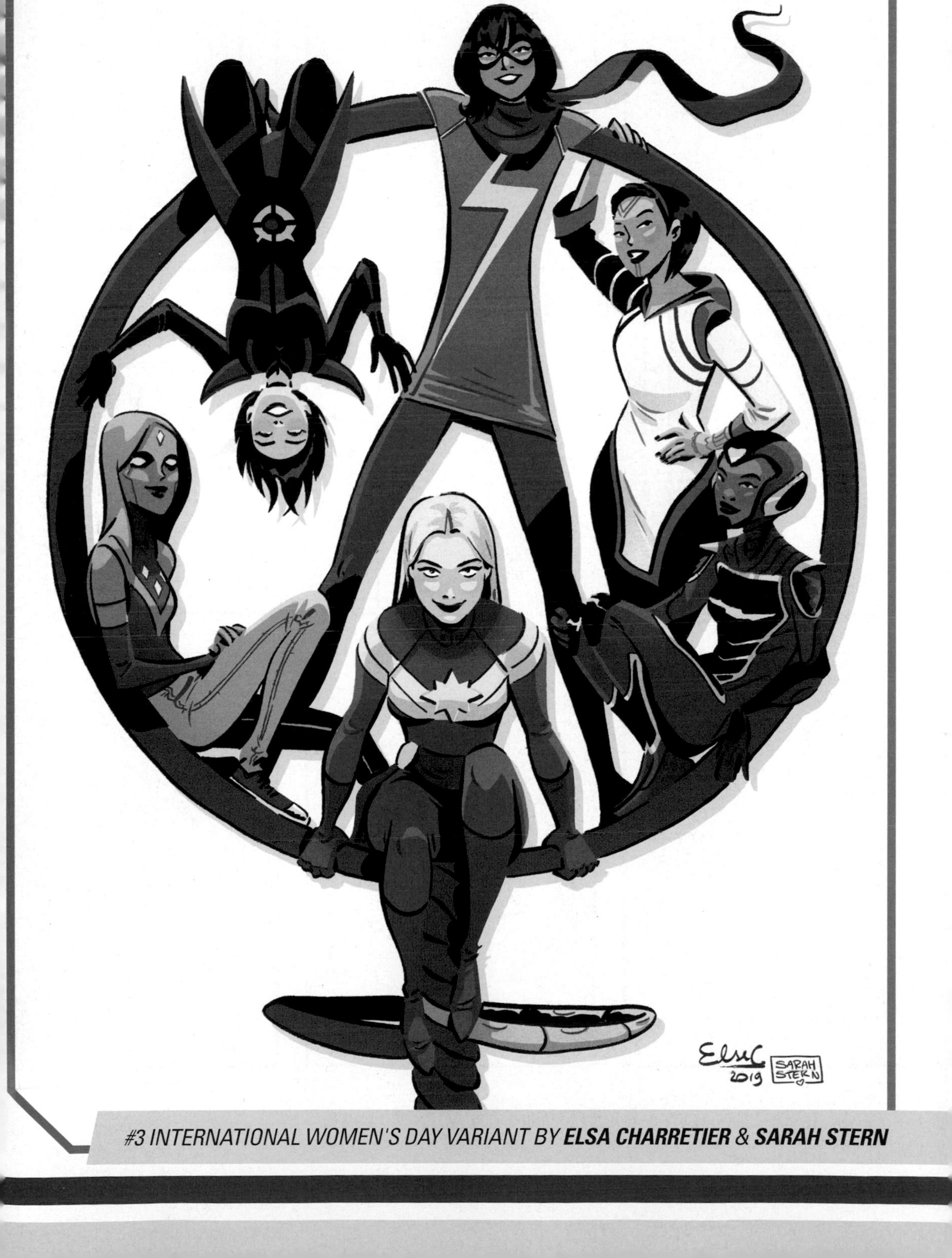
ElsaC
2019
SARAH
STERN

#3 INTERNATIONAL WOMEN'S DAY VARIANT BY **ELSA CHARRETIER** & **SARAH STERN**

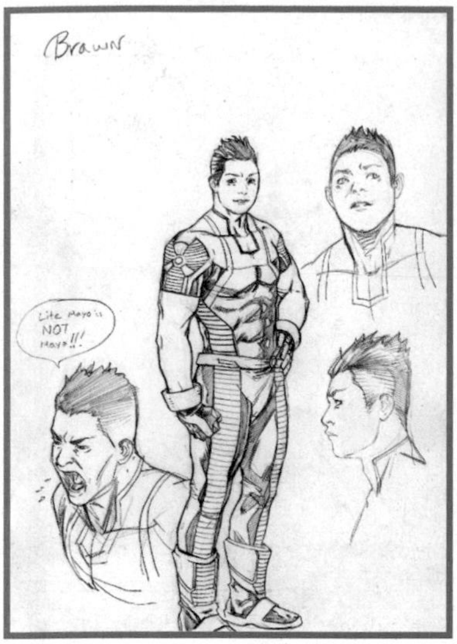
Brawn
Lite Mayo's NOT Mayo!!!

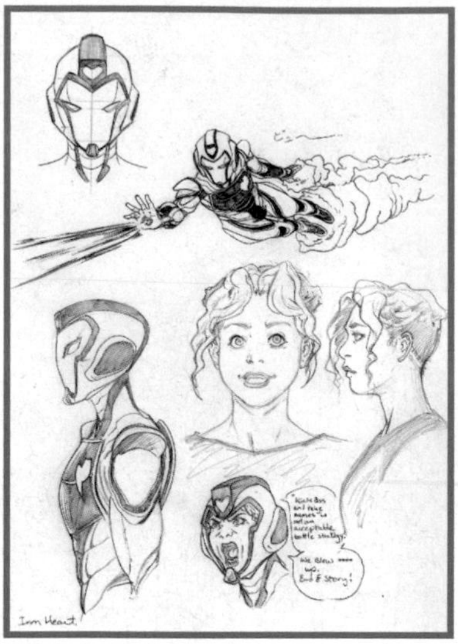
Iron Heart!

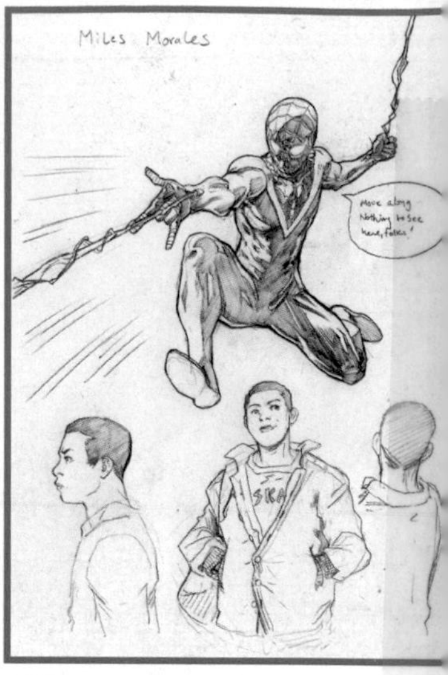
Miles Morales
Move along Nothing to see here, folks!

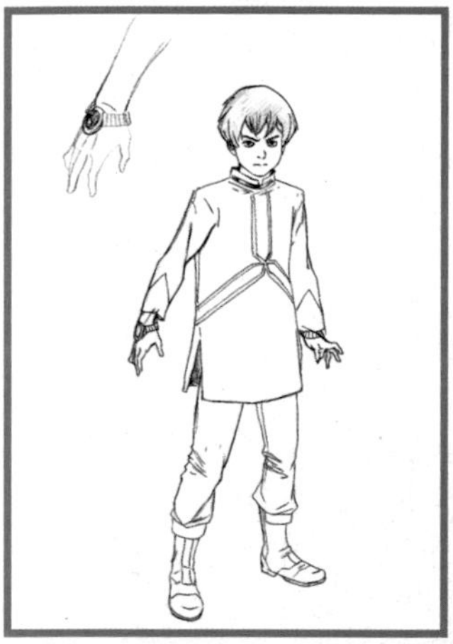

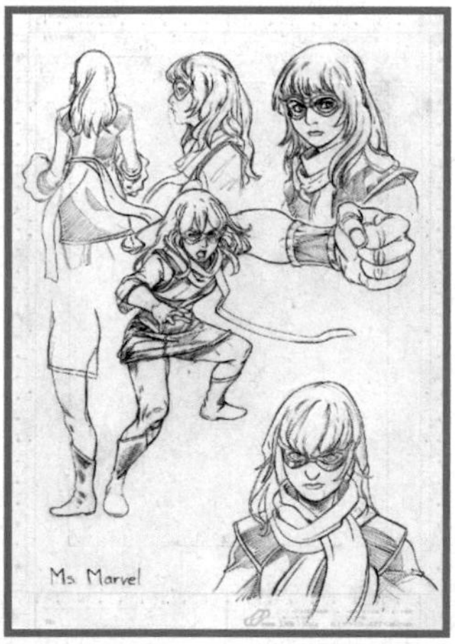
Ms Marvel

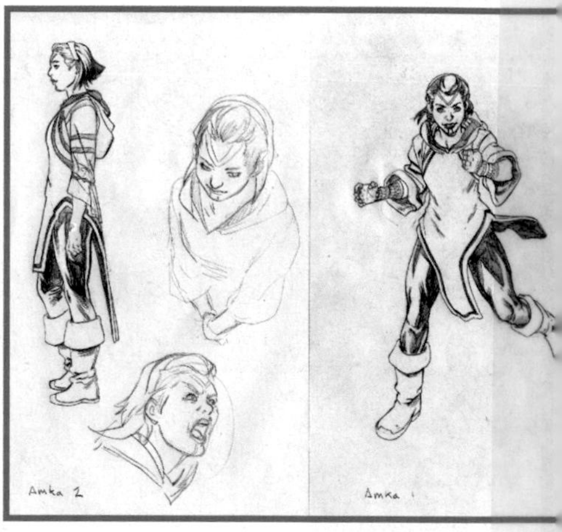
Amka 2
Amka

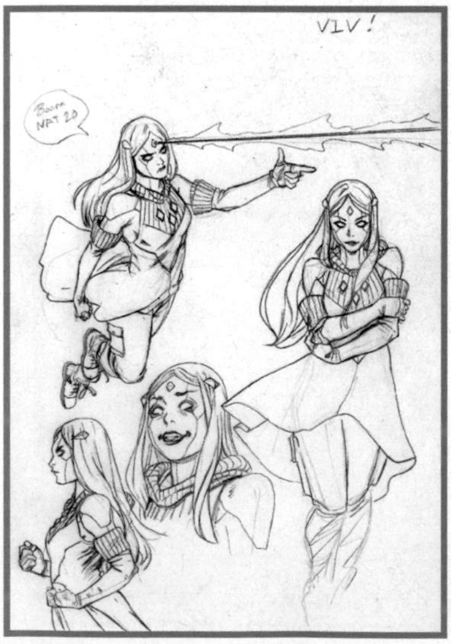
VIV!
Boom NAT 20

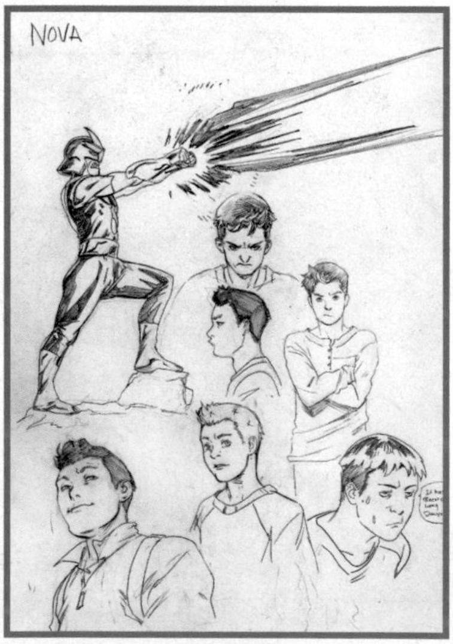
NOVA

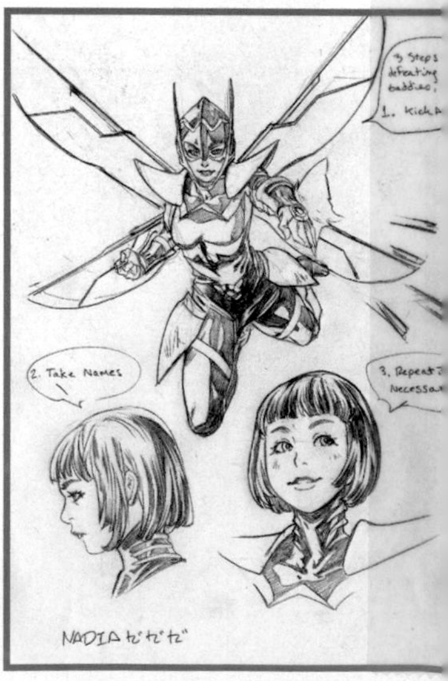
2. Take Names
NADIA

CHARACTER SKETCHES BY **STEVEN CUMMINGS**

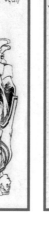